NO LONGER PROPERTY OF
THE SEATTLE PUBLIC LIBRARY

D0949809

BILLY PORTER
UNPROTECTED
A MEMOIR

ABRAMS PRESS, NEW YORK

Copyright © 2021 Billy Porter

Jacket © 2021 Abrams

Published in 2021 by Abrams Press, an imprint of ABRAMS. All rights reserved. No portion of this book may be reproduced, stored in a retrieval system, or transmitted in any form or by any means, mechanical, electronic, photocopying, recording, or otherwise, without written permission from the publisher.

Library of Congress Control Number: 2021934842

ISBN: 978-1-4197-4619-2
eISBN: 978-1-68335-954-8
B&N exclusive edition ISBN: 978-1-4197-6072-3
Signed edition ISBN: 978-1-4197-6074-7

Printed and bound in the United States
10 9 8 7 6 5 4 3 2 1

The names and identifying characteristics of some individuals have been changed, and some dialogue has been re-created.

Abrams books are available at special discounts when purchased in quantity for premiums and promotions as well as fundraising or educational use. Special editions can also be created to specification. For details, contact specialsales@abramsbooks.com or the address below.

Abrams Press® is a registered trademark of Harry N. Abrams, Inc.

ABRAMS The Art of Books
195 Broadway, New York, NY 10007
abramsbooks.com

We won't die secret deaths anymore. The world only spins forward. We will be citizens. The time has come. Bye now. You are fabulous creatures, each and every one. And I bless you: More Life. The Great Work Begins . . .

—PRIOR WALTER, IN *ANGELS IN AMERICA, PART TWO: PERESTROIKA*, BY TONY KUSHNER

PROLOGUE

This is not a coming-out story. It's not a down-low story either. I never could have passed for straight, even if I'd wanted to, and so I never had the dubious luxury of living a lie.

By the time I was five, it was all too clear that something was wrong with me. Everyone knew it, and I knew it too. It was why grown-ups shook their heads and spoke in lowered tones whenever I was in the room. It was why I had to talk to a Nice White Man once a week, in his office in the big building up the street. The man and I played games, and he asked me a lot of questions. Sometimes I knew the answers and sometimes I was confused.

But I wasn't confused about why I was there. The Nice White Man was a doctor. He was working to help fix me. I didn't know the name of my mysterious affliction, but I did know that it had already manifested itself in many unacceptable ways.

For one, I was drawn to all the wrong pastimes. Double Dutch jump rope and hopscotch and jacks were for girls. It was wrong to want an Easy-Bake Oven for Christmas, and therefore Santa was never going to bring me one. I would get a set of drums instead (but the noise would bother Aunt Dorothy and I would seldom be allowed to play them). It was wrong not to care about football, wrong to shun contact sports in general.

1

I was also taken with all the wrong clothing. I brightened at the sight of all the wrong colors, the deep jewel tones and soft pastels. I loved the wrong fabrics too: taffeta and lace and velvet and lamé, material that rustled and swished and swirled with every step. It was wrong to love all the glorious hats on the ladies at church. And the trimmings on those hats! Veils and feathers and flowers and sequins and beads and rhinestones and ribbons and bows. Paul the Apostle had decreed that women should cover their heads during worship, and Black ladies had turned this directive into an art form.

It was wrong to be mesmerized by Aunt Sharon's shoe closet. To be excited by the rows of slingbacks and stilettos in silver and lilac and violet and mauve. To run my fingertips along their leather and satin and crocodile sides. It was especially wrong to slip on my very favorite pair—the candy-apple red pumps with the highest heels—and sashay back and forth before the full-length mirror, overcome by the splendor of them on my very own feet. It was why I was no longer allowed in her room.

Though I could not have articulated it back then, not even to myself, my fixation on fashion went deeper than mere aesthetics. I sensed that clothing was a potent signifier—that its import went beyond its visual appeal. Later I would come to understand that the finery donned by Black churchgoers was a powerful form of resistance. Many of them were employed during the week as domestic servants, or security guards, or custodians, and were required to wear uniforms meant to reinforce their status as less-than. To dress impeccably and regally on the Lord's day, then, was to insist on their own dignity and worth in a world that sought to systematically strip them of both. It was a way to assert that they were God's children too, and in His house, they would adorn themselves in a manner befitting the glory of the Lord!

I didn't have the words for any of this at the time, just a child's aware-ness that people carried themselves differently in different clothing, that fashion could effect a profound transformation, on the outside and inside both. The dazzling pageantry of Sunday worship filled me with delight, and I longed to be a part of it—but even in this, my desires were all wrong, for while I adored rockin' a three-piece, reversible Easter or Christmas suit situation, I also longed to dress like the ladies, from spike heel to majestic crown.

But I'm getting ahead of myself. To render a childhood in which I was continually urged to seek the Bible's guidance in all matters, let us do as that Good Book does, and start *in the beginning.*

CHAPTER ONE

The luminous soul at the center of my genesis story is Cloerinda Jean Johnson Porter-Ford. My beautiful mother, who loved me into life, held on to that love through every trial and tribulation over the next several decades, and underwent her own tumultuous journey alongside my own. In my half century of life, I've never encountered another with a fraction of her faith, grace, courage, or endurance. If—as Christian tradition would have it—earthly suffering is a preparation for heaven, then my mother has earned the rank of archangel in the hereafter. But each morning she pulls herself back up and into this world, pressing on with nothing but gratitude in her heart. She has been my lifelong model of fortitude and faith. Every day I thank God for the gift of being her son.

My mother was born with a degenerative neurological condition that, to this day, no doctor or specialist has been able to name. Today we would call the cause of this condition medical malpractice, but in 1946, lawsuits were nothing more than a distant dream for Black folks. We couldn't even sit at the same lunch counter as white people, so how were we gonna sue someone white for damages? Within the next two decades, the civil rights movement would stoke our hope, tantalize us with the promise of equality, but it would also show how ruthlessly brutal white society would be in response to that prospect. Beatings with billy clubs, vicious dogs straining to attack, fire hoses that could send a bitch hydroplaning up in these streets like a rag doll, and the systemic imprisonment and assassination of our leaders: These instances of white brutality would shock the world, but they would not shock us, for we never had any illusions about the way things were. This country was built on the backs of my ancestors, the enslaved, remember, so delusions of justice being served on behalf of my mother had been harbored by no one.

When my grandmother Martha Johnson went into labor, she was rushed to a hospital where there was no doctor on call to deliver her baby. In those days, medical professionals administered tocolytic therapy to mothers in premature labor, drugs that would delay delivery for up to forty-eight hours, allowing doctors to administer steroid hormones that could speed up the development of the baby's lungs. The staff in charge of my grandmother's care decided to pursue this course of action. There was just one problem: My mother's arrival was not premature in the slightest. My mother was ready right on time, like she is in real life to this day. Suppressing my grandmother's contractions and locking her baby back into her uterus made no more sense than stuffing a butterfly back into its chrysalis.

The doctor arrived soon after these drugs had taken their intended effect. He consulted the notes on my grandmother's chart with an air of annoyed impatience, rebuked the staff for needlessly complicating and prolonging her labor, and then, with a few brusque and brutal motions, he yanked the baby from her constricted womb. The damage was extensive and irreparable.

A vast range of conditions are associated with birth trauma of this nature. Seventy-six years after the fact, we will likely never know the precise response of my mother's body to the disastrous mismanagement of her passage into this world. Today, the steady deterioration of her nervous system has left her extremities immobile. She can't wash, eat, or relieve herself without assistance. She relies on the kindness of the exquisite staff of the Actors Fund nursing home in Englewood, New Jersey.

But it wasn't always this way. Though my mother was visibly different even as a child, with a compromised gait and bodily tremors, she once had much more mobility than she does now. Learning to walk was harder for her than for other children, but she managed it. She could hardly hold a pen and her handwriting looked like chicken scratch, but there was nothing wrong with her mind. Unfortunately, in the '40s, educators were less discerning than they are now, and all disabled children tended to be treated the same way: as outcasts, freaks relegated to windowless basement classrooms, out of sight of mainstream society. My mother was no exception. Throughout her elementary school years, she was grouped and shamed with children who had severe cognitive impairments.

"I'm not stupid, just handicapped," was her plaintive refrain, and it remains so even now.

My mother grew up in Lawrenceville in Pittsburgh in a modest three-story home—the Big House, if you will—under the punitive rule of her aunt Dorothy. My grandmother had relinquished her child-rearing responsibilities to her sister for reasons that remained a mystery throughout my childhood. But in the Big House, Aunt Dot's word was law, and she laid it down with a hickory switch and an acid tongue.

Dorothy seemed to resent my mother's very presence. It was as if she had wronged Aunt Dot simply by being born, like she owed her money or some shit. My mother's younger twin sisters, Karen and Sharon, were allowed to take part in social activities—birthday parties, sleepovers, whole afternoons in the park with friends—while my mother was treated like some Black Cinderella, or, as she likes to say, *Black-erella*, before the ball, constantly put to work and seldom allowed out of the house. *You cain't do nothin' anyways, and won't ever be able to do nothin', so why bother,* was the message she received from Aunt Dot and very often everybody else. The world had given up on her before she even began.

Salvation seemed to materialize in the form of William Ellis Porter. He was a handsome, dark-chocolate babe with almond eyes and a sparkling personality. He was gregarious and sociable, an extrovert, a church boy with a job, who checked all the necessary boxes. Most importantly, when he met my mother, he seemed to see past her disability. He was the first man who showed her any romantic interest, and everybody on the planet wants to simply just be seen. My mother was smitten, and the rest is history.

Later she would learn that he had married her on a wager. That is, he had bet his best friend that he could seduce the "church cripple." My mother was an easy mark: lonely, naive, a prisoner in her own home who would have done almost anything to get out. It's harder to fathom her fiancé's motives. Maybe he was enticed by the prospect of a woman he could control. I don't think he expected his little game to go as far as the altar, but, as improbable as it seems, he followed through with wedding my mother.

"I left that house and vowed I'd never go back," my mother told me later, sitting up in bed at her nursing home and chuckling at the memory.

"Why are you laughing?"

"'Cause I had to eat my words. We barely lasted a year. We moved to East Hills, into one of those brand-new affordable housing communities the government was building at the time. I got pregnant with you pretty quick, and things were good for those nine months. But as soon as I had you, that man turned on me like Jekyll and Hyde! He started drinkin' and yellin' and beatin' on me. He went around telling the whole neighborhood that I was a voodoo witch and that's why I was a gimp. Everyone believed him. No one would even talk to me." Here she trailed off, her eyes sliding away from mine and glazing over.

"So how long did this horror—"

"Not long. You were about to have your first birthday when he came home from work drunk one evening. You were in your crib and crying because you had a fever. Don't you know that man snatched you up, dangled you by one arm, then whipped you around and shook you so hard I thought your neck would snap."

"So what did you do?" I asked.

"I gotchu outta there in Jesus's name! I most certainly did! I packed your diaper bag and a suitcase and called Aunt Dot to come get me."

"But you hated—"

"I didn't hate her. I just . . . I didn't have anything or anyone else. Bill had become a danger to my baby. I had to protect you." Her eyes welled up, recalling this.

"Don't cry, Mommy. It's okay."

"No, it's not okay. Because I vowed I would never go back. And here after barely a year Aunt Dot was looking at me with that *I told you so* smirk on her face. But she was right. I had to eat my words."

It would be five full years before my mother was able to flee the Big House again. And so I spent those formative years in a home full of women: Mommy, Grandma, Aunt Dot, Karen, and Sharon. My mother and I shared the attic, which provided a modicum of privacy and the chance to bond as single mother and child, away from the toxic religiosity permeating the rest of that household and condemning our every human impulse and desire. This religiosity would form the bedrock of the internalized shame and self-hatred I would spend my life, up to this minute, trying to purge. The best way to hover above it is to focus on my art, to overwork myself, overbook myself all day, every day, so as not to find myself within the emotional chasm that only seems to widen as I age.

But you see, bedrock is almost impossible to displace—and if you dig down deep enough, you will always find it, lying beneath our every step.

* * *

In 1976, my mother and I moved into a two-bedroom apartment in the Hill District of Pittsburgh. This neighborhood has been a center of Black life in Pittsburgh for more than a century. August Wilson, the Pittsburgh-born Pulitzer-winning playwright, immortalized it with his Pittsburgh Cycle, which was set there. Rumor has it that the television series *Hill Street Blues* was inspired by it too, as its creator, Steven Bochco, is an alum of the famed Carnegie Mellon University School of Drama just down the hill. In any event, this move represented a hard-won independence and new beginning for my mother.

It meant a new beginning for me as well. In just a few days, I would begin the first grade at a new school. Much of my childhood is hazy in my memory, but I remember that first day of school with searing clarity.

I was frightened. But I was also excited. I loved the new outfits Mommy had bought me the day before, at the Sears & Roebuck department store. The Garanimals brand made it easy for me to coordinate my own outfits—all I had to do was match the animals on the tags. She bought me four matching sets: the giraffe, the bear, the lion, and the tiger. I wanted the monkey set too, but Mommy said no. She said she didn't want me wearin' nothin' 'bout no monkeys.

Mommy was sad. She was always sad. All I wanted was to protect her from the mean people who made fun of how she walked. She couldn't help walking the way she did. It wasn't her fault—she was born that way. And Mommy always said that God didn't make mistakes, so she was born just as she was supposed to be. Why didn't other people know that? Why wouldn't they leave her alone?

"Bow your head, boy—we gonna be late, and you know I hate a late spirit!"

"I'm ready!" I said, grabbing her hand and bowing my head.

"Father, in the name of Jesus, we thank you, Lord, for our life, health, and strength. We thank you for the clothes on our backs and the roof over our heads and the food on our table. We thank you for blessing us to wake up and see yet another day. Oh, bless your name, Jesus!"

Mommy's hands began to shake. Her whole body often shook. She had no control over it. The shakes just came. When she was sad, she shook. When she was happy, she shook. When she was nervous about something, she really shook. She was shaking all over today.

"Dear Lord, I ask you to bless my sweet boy on his first day of school. Give him strength, focus, and courage. Open his mind, Lord, and help him to learn and retain all of his studies—for we all know that education is the key to success in this life. And please keep him from all hurt, harm, and danger. These and all other blessings we ask in your name and for your sake—Amen."

"Amen," I echoed, giving her palm a final squeeze.

We walked hand in hand down Wylie Avenue to the school, a castle-like structure at the top of a sloping lawn. The kingdom was surrounded by a seafoam-green steel fence with spikes at the top and bottom. A lone baby doll dangled from the lower edge of this fence, its head impaled between the spokes and the ground.

As we made our way to the front entrance, where many moms and their kids were milling around, I could feel my mother's tension. Mommy got nervous around crowds and her shaking intensified. I gripped her hand to steady her, and she gripped mine back for dear life. People gawked as we walked by, children and parents alike, whispering and pointing as if we were some sort of sideshow act.

"That lady walks funny!"

"Ewww . . . she look retarded!"

The crowd parted like the Red Sea. My mother ignored the ruckus; she'd gotten real good at blocking out the noise. When we arrived at my classroom door, she reached down to brush some imaginary lint from my shoulder, make one last adjustment to my collar. "Come straight home after school, okay?"

"Yes, ma'am."

"It's a straight shot right back up the hill."

"I know."

"You feel comfortable by yourself? I could come back and—"

I cut her off. "I'm fine by myself."

People were staring at us. Her hand involuntarily clenched around my shoulder.

"Are you gonna be okay, Mommy?" I looked up into her doleful eyes and hugged her waist.

"Mommy's fine." She caressed the top of my head. "Don't you worry about me one bit, you hear me! Mommy's fine."

The first twenty minutes of the day were promising. The classroom was bright and cheerful. The teacher was a nice lady in a pretty print dress. I felt pleased by all the pictures and charts on the walls, showing the letters of the alphabet, the days of the week, the seasons of the year.

But before long, we were shepherded down the hall to the gymnasium, where a man with a whistle around his neck lined us up on a bench. He explained the importance of physical fitness and announced a start-of-the-year evaluation. He would call our names from a clipboard so we could each take an individual pull-up test.

The girls were called first. One by one, they climbed onto the wooden box beneath the pull-up bar and grasped it with both hands before stepping off into the air. Not one of them could pull herself up to the bar. The boys went next. The first boy managed to top the bar not once but four times. The rest of them followed, each with some measure of success. All the boys could do at least one pull-up. The tallest, strongest, and eldest boy—who had been held back . . . twice! and who had been among those mocking my mother that morning—did ten in a row, his motions fluid and beautiful. Even as I burned with the memory of him pointing and laughing at my mother, I admired the ease and confidence with which he repeatedly scaled the bar.

I was the last one called to complete the challenge. Gamely I grasped the bar as everyone else had and stepped off the box. And there I dangled, like the kitten in a poster I'd seen in the hallway. I pulled with all my might and kicked at the air in an effort to lift myself up, but within a few seconds, the dreadful realization set in: I wasn't strong enough to do it.

Acid flooded my stomach and flowed down my arms. This terrible disgrace couldn't be happening to me—it just couldn't. Surely I would be able to do at least one pull-up like all the other boys! I gave it everything I had, eyes wild, face twisted into a grimace, but to no avail. The kids exploded into savage laughter as I dropped to the mat in defeat.

"Ah ha ha, you little sissy punk!" sneered the tall boy.

Sissy. I'd never heard that word before. It seemed to suck all the air from my lungs. Sweat broke out along my forehead and beneath my arms as I tried not to hyperventilate.

"Boy, you shaking as bad as your mama!" It was true. My whole body was trembling. I felt sick and wanted to go home.

Word of my pull-up shame spread through the school like a plague. As the day wore on, it seemed no one would talk to me. In the cafeteria, I spread my lunch out on the table I had all to myself and ate alone. I had hoped this school would be different from the Big House, different from my neighborhood, different from kindergarten, but here too I was already an outcast. I suffered through the rest of the afternoon, holding on to what was left of my dignity, relieved when the bell rang to signify the end of the school day.

But this relief was short-lived. Outside the building, many of the boys from gym class had gathered, blocking my path. Were they waiting for me?

Waiting to mess with me? I'd told my mother not to pick me up, so I would have to walk past them by myself.

I summoned all the courage I had and made myself move in their direction, keeping my gaze on the ground as I drew near, and then suddenly, with no warning, the tall boy shoved me hard. I slammed into the ground and tumbled down the hill. I tried to stop myself but couldn't, the world a blur of grass and sky and dirt, and even within the confusion of my panic and pain, I was aware of the laughter floating down around me. All the other kids, it seemed, were ridiculing me. Hooting and hawing and snickering and . . . *BAM!*

The left side of my face banged into the bottom of the steel-spoked fence. After several dazed seconds, I tried to gather myself and rise, but I couldn't. I was stuck in place, impaled like an insect on a pin, with one of those spokes piercing my head. The dangling baby doll and I locked eyes. Then the world went dark.

I woke up in a hospital room with my mother by my side.

"Mommy?" I whispered.

"Shh, baby. You're okay now. You fell down the hill."

"I didn't fall."

"What happened?"

"A big boy shoved me real hard."

The pain on my mother's face hurt more than my throbbing head. Her voice cracked as she asked, "Why, son?"

I shrugged my shoulders. The left side of my head felt tight and sore, as if someone had taken a stapler to it. When I tried to sit up, the pain made me suck in my breath.

"Lay back, baby. You're okay."

"My head hurts."

"You got stitches."

I reached up to touch the sutures.

"Don't touch it! Doctor says . . . try not to touch it."

I started to cry. "I'm sorry, Mommy."

"You ain't got nothin' to be sorry about, son."

But I knew that I did. Whatever was wrong with me would be apparent wherever I went, and no fresh start would ever make a difference for me.

I didn't want to go back to school the next day, but my mother would have none of that.

"You have to, baby. You gotta get your education. It's your only way out."

"But I don't like it."

"I know. Mommy gets scared sometimes too."

"No one there likes me. They call me names. They want to beat me up."

"What names are they calling you?"

"Wimp. Pussy. Sissy."

Mommy looked away for a moment. Her lips pursed and her gaze turned inward. I could tell she was trying to find the right words to say. And then suddenly they seemed to come to her, for resolve came into her eyes and her gaze found mine again.

"They crucified Jesus, baby," she said. "You'll be fine."

There was only one place in the world where people looked at me with approval, admiration, and even respect. That blessed place was the Friendship Baptist Church Choir. My first solo had happened when I was five, at the annual Easter Sunday pageant, where I sang "His Eye Is on the Sparrow" in my clear and open-throated gospel boy soprano. That day had been a revelation. As I stood in the front of that sanctuary and let the song come through me, I had watched a ripple go through the congregation, like an electric current. Everything changed when I sang—something shifted in the adults around me and charged the very air in the room. The fear and shame left the grown-ups' eyes, and they all praised what they saw as my formidable gift from the Lord. God had graced me with the gift of song and that made me special.

After that solo, I was dubbed Lil' Preacher Man. Sister Walker, the brand-new music director, invited me to join the adult choir. And so, a year later, in the midst of my disastrous first-grade year, the one spot of light was the promise of the annual Mass Choir concert. For months I'd gone with my mother to all the Saturday afternoon rehearsals. I had learned my vocal parts with ease, and when the long-awaited day finally came, I was ready.

Trembling with excitement, I lined up along with the rest of the choir on the staircase leading to the sanctuary. Sister Walker had decided to trade our traditional choir robes for a simple black and white ensemble. The men wore black suits, white shirts, and black ties. The women wore black skirts and white blouses. The organ swelled and the choir members began our passage down the aisle, swaying from side to side on the two and the four. Sister Walker presided at the center of the sanctuary, facing the standing congregation as they welcomed us with sanctified fervor.

I was directly behind my mother and ahead of another sister in the choir line. I sang with everything I had as I marched down the aisle, my heart full of joy and my little chest puffed up with pride. *See, everybody? I have a gift. I can sing. Nothing is wrong with me.* My view was only waist high, so I gazed up with elation at the churchy high-fashion extravagance around me: the topcoats and pencil skirts, high waists and high asses, elaborate crowns and stick fans with the images of a haloed Martin Luther King Jr. or Black Jesus flashing in my periphery with every side step.

YANK! As sudden as a lightning bolt with no storm warning, I found myself jerked from this joyful procession into one of the side pews. At my cry of alarm, a hand was clapped hard over my mouth.

"Get out from underfoot of grown folks, boy!"

Terrified, I looked up and into the blazing gaze of Sister Freeman.

"But I'm . . . I'm Lil' Preacher Man . . . I'm supposed to sing with the—"

"Shut up, boy! Children are to be seen and not heard!" Sister Freeman took both my upper arms in her vicious grip and slammed me down onto the wooden pew.

Frantic now, I strained to catch the attention of my mother or Sister Walker, but no one noticed I was gone, or maybe no one cared. I let out a wail. Sister Freeman popped me in the mouth like I was a prisoner on a chain gang, and still nobody did a thing. Not my grandmother. Not Aunt Dorothy. Not even my mother, who stood in the front row of the soprano section, seeing me imprisoned by this stranger all the while. The concert went on without me as I sat trapped in the pew beside a monstrous woman I didn't even know, as if the violation weren't on full display in front of my family, the choir, the congregation, and Jesus himself.

Tears streamed from my eyes for the duration of the concert. Of all the painful betrayals I'd suffered in my young life, none had ever hurt as much as this one.

And yet this horrific incident left me with an essential and necessary lesson. A hard truth was driven into me that day, as indelibly as that iron spike on the elementary school fence: Just because a stage was rightfully mine didn't mean I would be allowed to mount it. Sister Freeman was the first person to yank me back from an earned place in the spotlight, but she would be far from the last. I learned that day that if I wanted to stand in that light, I would have to fight for it, wage a fierce and tireless struggle with all my heart and soul and might.

But for the time being, I was overpowered, overlooked, and all but invisible. Nobody had stepped in to rescue me and nobody would. My mother loved me, but she lacked power in this world as well; she didn't have much more than I did. I wept in that pew until my whole body felt wrung out like a rag, for in that moment I realized my tender self was already under siege. Marked and marginalized, sidelined, silenced, and set apart.

Unprotected.

CHAPTER TWO

He says I don't communicate. He says our relationship is toxic. Maybe it is. Actually—I know it is. We can't even be in the same room together without destroying each other in every way. The more he pushes the more I retreat. I'm at the edge of permanent personal destruction. I'm like one of those old, rickety houses that have secrets under the floorboards. Or just mess. Mess! Mess! Mess! I'm a fucking mess and I have no time to be messy. The shit is swirling around me way too fast. Interviews, photo shoots, benefit galas, The Twilight Zone, *hosting duties,* GQ Man of the Year: Germany— *Daddy's international now! Emmy wins and magazine covers . . . 2019 has been like being shot into outer space on the NASA* Challenger *in 1984. You know the one, the spaceship that blew up into a million little pieces right before the world's eyes. This is how my insides feel. Like a malfunction. Like I am churning into oblivion, with the potential to blow up. I think I might want to, and evaporate into thin fucking air! Like I was never even here.*

Breathe, Boo. Keep breathing. Life is good! You've made it this far, bitch, what chu gonna do now, just give up? You ain't no crazier than anybody else on this planet. You ain't nothing new. Get over yourself and get on with it. Put your fucking fifty-year-old big-boy pants on and pull it together. There's no reason that God would have brought you this far if there weren't a plan . . . Oh, here we go with the God thing. I don't even know if I believe in heaven, hell, eternity. I mean, think about it—eternity of anything sounds horrible! Grandma said, "You gotta believe in something or you'll fall for anything." I believe that. I believe in love. I believe in grace. I believe in dreams. I'm living proof that all these things exist. But this God thing. Yet again I feel abandoned by the concept. Always have. I feel used. God is used as a weapon to control. I don't like what humans have done to the idea of God. Maybe there is no God. Maybe it's just us humans down here fucking everything up, and when the universe is tired of the evolution experiment the world will simply implode.

How do I let him in? How do I truly learn to receive love? How can I trust that it will be unconditional, and if I'm feeling unsafe how can I communicate my needs? I can't do it like this anymore. I can't live with the patina of control. Balancing the professional and personal. I've been able to cope, compartmentalize, work it out individually . . . sort of. But here I am, a mess, and I don't like mess! I'm a fixer! I fix shit. But this . . . I can't fix it. It's been almost forty years of me trying to fix it. The worst part is, I know he's right. He knows me. He truly knows me, and to my continual private surprise, he even seems to love me. So why do I need to keep him at a distance? Why can't I let him in? If I'm honest with myself, I know I'm damaged. Unable to do this thing called intimacy. Always terrified by real love, always running, fronting, hiding. And I know why. Still more layers to peel. Never goes away, never becomes easier to bear. Not a day goes by. Not. A. Day. My healing is coming, my next layer of healing perhaps. He says I don't communicate. He's right . . . The next phase goes deeper . . . it must. The next level of healing is upon me. It's time.

* * *

After several months of careful observation, the Nice White Doctor delivered a verdict.

"Billy's a fine boy," he told my mother. "You just need to get a man around the house, to teach him to be more masculine." He said this as if a man were something my mother could acquire at will, like an item from a catalog, rather than a very long shot for a devoutly religious single mother with no income and a degenerative health condition.

And yet, within a year of receiving this prescription for my healthy development, my mother was standing at the altar with Mr. Bernie Ford, and I was walking down the aisle carrying two gold bands on a satin pillow.

Bernie was a kind man, and I was so thrilled to have him in the house that for the first few months, it felt like Christmas every morning. I had no memory of my own father; William Porter had made no reappearance in my life since my mother's departure. Instead, he had remarried and was raising three stepchildren across town. Other kids at school and in the neighborhood had daddies, men who drove the family car, did home repairs, knew their way around a toolshed, stood at the barbecue grill in the summer. I felt a deep pang inside whenever I saw a father and son throwing a football back and forth, organizing a home garage, or leaving town together on a fishing trip.

After Bernie joined our family, we had a man in the house too. It was like striking it rich, this sudden fortune, the continual sweet surprise of it all. Finally, after all these years, here was someone to ease my mother's way in the world: change the oil in her tank, bring her car to the shop, and haul the trash to the curb. He was both gregarious and gentle, and he took the time to teach me things, manly things like how to drive nails, mow the grass, change a tire.

I'd grown up surrounded by feminine personal effects: dresses, slips, hair curlers, lotions and perfumes and lipstick. These items intrigued and tantalized me, but Bernie's things excited me in a different way. Just having a man's items scattered around in our midst filled my heart with happiness. The suspenders flung over the back of a chair, the shoeshine box in the hall closet, his security guard work uniform hanging on the rack. I loved the various scents I associated with him: motor oil, fresh-cut grass, Old Spice deodorant. I loved his softly tattered work shirts and his meticulously pressed pants. I loved listening to him discuss the Pirates or the Steelers with our upstairs neighbors: his brother David, who lived in the second-floor apartment, and Mr. Ray, who resided in our third-floor one-bedroom apartment. I have to say in retrospect that Bernie was ahead of his time in terms of using one's home as rental units. Now don't get me wrong; our home was nothing fancy, and wasn't no "flipping" going on. But the rent from our two tenants was a great financial subsidy for the family.

The women in my family were done with men before Bernie came along. All of them—my mother, Grandma, and Aunt Dot—had been married at one point. They even still had their married names. But that was all that remained of their former husbands. I never even knew my grandfather's first name; they told me once but I forgot. Men were not to be mentioned, paid any mind, or trusted. But they trusted Bernie.

Once again, a man was the ticket out of the Big House for my mother. She and Bernie and I moved into the neighborhood of East Liberty just before I began second grade at Lemington Elementary School. Ours was a pleasant residential street on the border of a city park. Within its wide and tree-studded expanse was a full baseball diamond, playground equipment, and, best of all, a neighborhood pool. I could see it from my bedroom window, so I pretended that we had a pool in our own backyard like the white folks on television had.

My surroundings had changed for the better, but my social status had not. The bullying at Lemington Elementary was as prevalent and relentless as it had always been. By that time, it seemed to make no difference where we went or which school I attended. It was like I was marked in some way that I didn't understand, some way that invited abuse.

"Turn the other cheek," my mother always told me, in response to the bullying.

It started in first period every day. A boy named . . . let's call him DaShawn would catch my eye. He'd ball up his fist and mime the act of punching himself in both eyes to show what treatment lay in store for me. "After school, after school . . ." he'd mouth. From experience, I knew this was not an empty threat. Fear and dread would settle into my midsection, a familiar acid burn.

On this particular day, DaShawn tracked me down outside during recess. There I was, minding my own Black business, when he materialized before me with his sister and two other neighborhood girls flanking him.

The Jackson sisters lived on my block. They were the first kids I met when we moved to East Liberty. They welcomed me to the neighborhood with kindness and what seemed like true friendship. We swam in the pool every day, all summer long.

"You called my mother a bitch!" DaShawn flung at me.

"What!?" I said, flustered and scandalized. "No, I did not. I don't even cuss! Who told you that?"

The older Jackson sister crossed her arms over her chest and glared at me. "I did, you little bitch!"

"And I'ma fuck you up!" DaShawn huffed.

I was surprised that the Jackson sisters had been poisoned against me. Surprised and confused. They'd been so nice to me over the summer.

"I'll be waitin' for yo' ass after school, bitch," DaShawn warned.

In class again after recess, my concentration was shot. Everything felt like it was happening in slow motion. Just making my way to the pencil sharpener at the back of the room felt like slogging through quicksand. All I could think about was planning an alternate route home so DaShawn and the Jackson sisters wouldn't see me.

Why would that girl lie about me like that? I wondered. I'd been nothing but nice to her all summer. We played jacks together. She taught me to double Dutch jump rope. What changed? I wouldn't call anybody's mother a bitch. I didn't even know what that meant.

I was sweating. My heart was hammering. My hands were shaking so much I couldn't hold them steady for the cursive writing test. I loved writing in cursive. It looked so pretty, and my writing always drew high praise from teachers. But today I couldn't control the pencil and my cursive looked jagged and bad. Like Mommy's.

When the bell rang to end the school day, I dashed to the boys' bathroom and cowered in the stall, sitting on the commode with my legs drawn up and my book bag hugged on my lap so as to go undetected. My breathing was shallow. The sound of squealing children, fired up to be out of school, echoed through the halls. I heard locker doors slamming and feet pounding the corridors. I waited at least fifteen minutes, maybe twenty, until the cacophony subsided. When I finally found the courage to emerge, I crept outside and surveyed the school lawn. Thankfully I saw no one. And it was raining. Who would want to beat me in the rain, anyway? *But I ain't takin' no chances*, I thought, and set out to go the back way, which took twice as long. But here was something I hadn't counted on: autumn had stripped all the leaves from the trees, exposing my path to the watchful eyes of my predators.

"I see you, bitch!" DaShawn roared. I froze. I looked down to the playground below and there they were, waiting for me by the monkey bars.

I bolted through the brush, skidding and sliding on fallen damp leaves. Porcupine bushes poked their quills through my clothes. A bare branch whapped me in the face and threw me off balance. I slipped on the slick leaves and landed hard on my tailbone. Whimpering in pain, I went on sliding until I was halfway down the hill, wet, muddy, sweaty, my heart beating out of my chest, no time to spare.

DaShawn and his minions were racing me home from the other direction. I had to get there first. I pulled myself up from the mud and took off, hell-bent on getting to my side door first. If I could just get home, Mommy would be there. She'd protect me.

I yanked the chain holding my house key from around my neck. This was the home stretch. I was almost there. I looked up to see DaShawn looping the corner, with the Jackson sisters close behind.

I froze. He froze. We locked eyes.

And then, as if a starting gun had gone off, we raced to my side door. With the wind at my back, I took the lead, spurred by terror, but just as I reached my door and jammed my key into the lock, DaShawn shoved me hard from behind. The side door swung open and I lost my balance, landing face-first on the hallway stairs in front of me.

"Owwwwwwwww!" I howled. I grabbed my face.

"Billy! What in God's name . . . ?" I heard my mother's voice, high and frightened, from the other room. I turned around, and there DaShawn stood on the landing.

"Owwwwwwwww!" I roared. Guttural. Animalistic. DaShawn just stood there smirking. No alarm. No chagrin. Just amusement and disdain on his scornful face. "Whatchu gonna do about it—FAGGOT?"

That word again. Was that the word that made people turn on me? Riled them up like fight dogs? What did it mean? My head throbbed. I staggered toward the kitchen just as Bernie strode out of it.

"What happened to you, son?"

"They just wanna beat me! Why does everyone want to beat me up?" I said, weeping.

With fire in his eyes, Bernie crouched down until he and I were at eye level. "Hit 'em back, Billy! Go on out there and hit 'em back!"

I stared at him, wide-eyed and sniffling. "But Mommy says to turn the other cheek."

"I don't care what your mother told you, boy!" Bernie thundered. "You go right back out there and pop him in the mouth. Hit him back and he'll leave you alone!"

Hit him back? With what, my double Dutch rope? Nobody ever taught me how to fight—how to protect myself. Nobody!

Now my mother materialized in the kitchen. I registered the terror on her face—terror and something else, something like resignation. As if who and what I was were the actual issue here, not the violence unleashed upon me in response to it.

"Oh my God, you're bleeding!" she cried. Her voice scaled up and cracked with emotion. I looked down at my hands. All I saw was red.

I ripped my book bag off my back and hurled it to the floor. Then I stalked back to the side door to find DaShawn . . . still standing there! Sneering. Mocking me. And at the sight of his smug face, something inside me snapped.

I dove on him like the swan I'd seen on the nature channel, a male swan slaughtering an interloper. We flew off the four-step landing and hit the graveled driveway hard. The force of my full-body blow caught DaShawn so off guard that we rolled over and over before the momentum left him on his back, with the full weight of my eighty-pound body straddled on top of him.

Red! Red! All I saw was red as the blood dripping from my nose spattered DaShawn's face. I heard nothing. I saw nothing else. I just pummeled and prayed . . . pummeled and prayed.

Suddenly a voice pierced my trance, a shriek of desperation. It was my mother's voice, high and hysterical. *"Billy, stop! Stop, son, please stop! You're gonna kill him!"*

I snapped out of my crimson haze to discover DaShawn pinned beneath me, with the Jackson sisters looking on, frozen in terror and disbelief. My mother was wringing her hands, anguish in her eyes.

But beside her stood Bernie. The expression on his face was so unfamiliar to me that at first, I didn't know what to make of it. It wasn't until he offered me the slightest nod that I realized it was approval.

The faggot had won.

* * *

"Mr. Porter?"

I look up from my notes at the male flight attendant—Black and queer, a sweet young thing—hovering shyly by my seat. When he brings his hands together in a gesture of prayer, I can see that he's actually trembling. This slays me.

"I hope I'm not intruding on your privacy or time," he says. "I just wanted to tell you that I have been blessed by your presence on this earth."

Later he'll post on social media that I couldn't have been more gracious. As if I summoned my best manners and responded with tolerance to yet another interruption of my solitude and work. But what he has no way of knowing is that when I flash my brightest smile, and extend my hand to him, and thank him for his words and tell him it's people like him who keep me going, it's nothing less than my most sincere and heartfelt truth. These encounters lift my spirits and give me so much strength. I'm grateful beyond words for that faith and support. And I'm grateful also for the reprieve from my own dismal thoughts of the time when my nature was my liability.

* * *

My successful brawl with DaShawn cemented my trust in Bernie. He was already treated as a hero in our family. He'd won the trust of all its women. He'd rescued my mother from her role of Black-erella in the Big House. And now he seemed to be doing the impossible: making more of a man out of me.

For my part, I was eager to take direction, to prove myself the model apprentice. I adored Bernie and strove to win his praise. I understood he was there to guide me—to provide me with "man lessons"—and I willingly submitted to his instruction. He took the time to teach me basic skills. He taught me how to rake the jewel-toned fall leaves, how to trim the hedges, and how to salt and shovel our ice-covered sidewalk in the dead of winter so neighborhood pedestrians wouldn't slip and fall and sue us.

He taught me how to wash my own clothes. He taught me how to cook a mean hamburger—onions and green peppers in the patties, and seasoned with Lawry's Seasoned Salt. He helped me maneuver my way around a toolbox, educating my little seven-year-old self on the difference between a Phillips-head and a standard screwdriver. And when I was fourteen, about to enter high school, and it got way too weird for me to be rooming with a sister ten years my junior. My sister and I have always been close, but the age difference early on made it impossible for us to truly be real friends. I waited with bated breath for the day she turned sixteen and we could hang tight. But until then, Bernie and I built my own private bedroom in the basement. Imagine me with my measuring tape, goggles, power saw, and level, measuring to precision the wooden planks and framing out two new walls supported by the two outside, structural walls. Please try to picture my sissified ass measuring and sawing the faux-wood paneling that would become my bedroom walls.

Bernie taught me how to navigate public transit, so that when it was time for me to go to Grandma's house in Lawrenceville and help out with her lawn and hedges, I could get there on the bus. He taught me how to be self-sufficient, how to rely on myself so I wouldn't have to depend on nobody else but me. My man lessons were in full swing, and I was passing with flying colors. Bernie was kind to me. Bernie cared about me. So when he replaced my mother as my main source of comfort, I readily accepted that too.

For years, I had suffered from nightmares. The street and schoolyard bullies stalked me even in my dreams. When I woke up bawling, sheets damp with sweat, my mother would appear in my room and simply lie down beside me. She never spoke. No words were necessary. Her mere presence was the only solace I needed.

One night when I was seven I woke up whimpering, and Bernie came into my room instead of Mommy. Like her, he lay down beside me without a word. I was disconcerted at first, wanting her instead, but before long, his presence became a different kind of balm. Whereas before I had been lulled by her maternal warmth, I now felt surrounded and protected by masculine strength.

The first few times he came in, he simply lay beside me, just as she had. No words, no touching. Just the comfort of presence and proximity. Then one night, he rolled over onto his side and pulled me close to him, so that my back rested against his chest. Cradled close to his body, I dropped back into sleep within seconds, feeling as peaceful and blissed out as I had ever been. I loved having his arm draped over me, his heart beating against my back. I loved the freshly laundered scent of his white undershirt. No night terrors could touch me with Bernie beside me—not when I had a man's protection.

Then came the night when Bernie pulled me back from the edge of sleep by striking up a conversation.

"Do you know about the birds and the bees, son?"

I was seven. "I think . . . I think I do," I said.

"You think you do?"

"Well—sometimes I feed the birds in the park after church," I told him. "And I got stung by a bee last summer."

"You did?"

"Yeah. It hurt real bad."

"I bet it did. I'm sorry to hear that."

I loved this conversation. Never before Bernie had a grown man taken the time to talk with me in any depth. He asked me questions and he listened to the answers. He seemed interested in my opinions. That night, though, after a while he circled back to the matter at hand.

"Son, when I asked you before about the birds and the bees, I wasn't talking about the pigeons in the park. 'The birds and the bees' is a figure of speech. I'm talking about some of the things grown-ups do together to feel good. I brought some pictures to show you the kind of thing that grown men enjoy."

He produced an issue of *Hustler* magazine. My eyes widened at the sight of a near-naked white lady on the cover. She was wearing see-through panties and stockings that only came up to her upper legs. I knew it was the kind of thing my mother would consider sinful. Ladies were supposed to dress decently and not show too much skin, let alone any of their private parts.

"This is a *man's* magazine," Bernie said, as if he could read my mind. "It's the kind of thing we keep private, that womenfolk have no need to know about. In fact, it's like a special secret just between us men. Can you keep a secret?"

I assured him that I could.

We perused the pages of the magazine together and he asked which of the pictures I liked best.

"I like the ones with the girls *and* the boys," I told him. Indeed, the shirt-less men with their carved chests and bulging underwear were especially captivating, but I sensed that I should keep this information to myself.

He flipped to a page where a naked man reclined on a bed, receiving various ministrations from two scantily clad women. "You mean pictures like this one?"

"Why does he have hair down there?" I wanted to know.

"All men have hair down there. One day you will too. I bet you've never seen a big-boy penis in real life before. Have you?"

I shook my head.

"Do you want to see one? I'll even let you touch it and play with it if you're sure you can keep it a secret." He made this proposition sound like a special and tantalizing privilege.

"I'm sure," I told him excitedly. "Cross my heart and hope to die."

"All right, then. Would you like to see mine?"

I told him that I would.

* * *

No panic. No tears. Not right now—fluff up, bitch. Not on this plane. Not today. You can't be breakin' down on planes. Too many people know who you are and what you represent, and now everybody's watching. TMZ is lurking at airports and shit. Whatchu gonna wear? Whatchu gonna say? They cal-lin' you a role model now, they callin' you a trailblazer. There's no crying in trailblazing. You're that gurl now! People are being blessed by your presence. That flight attendant stopped by your seat to tell you so.

You're flawed and that's okay. Flaws make us human. Flaws give us grace.

Just breathe. Breathe. In and out . . . deep, cleansing breaths . . .

CHAPTER THREE

Middle school was a turning point in my life in many ways. For one, I was spending my days outside my neighborhood for the first time. Florence Reizenstein School, recently built on the border of East Liberty and Shadyside, was the biggest middle school in the district, drawing 1,600 students from a vast range of neighborhoods and backgrounds. It was thirty minutes away from my home, and I rode the school bus there along with many other kids from East Liberty.

Reizenstein was an interesting experiment, founded with the intent of providing a first-rate education to an integrated student body. Desegregation was the very worthy goal, but problems arise within everything we try in this democratic experiment we call America, and though kids of every color poured into the building from each corner of the city, we were soon separated in much the same way that we were outside those walls.

Upon our arrival at Reizenstein, we were given a series of tests—aptitude tests, IQ tests—that would place us in specific classes. As you might expect, the kids who had spent the last several years in poorer neighborhood schools were not as academically advanced as their privileged peers. So the Pittsburgh Scholars Program was overwhelmingly white, while almost all the Black kids were placed in the mainstream classes.

I was an exception. I was admitted to the Scholars Program. And this was a profound surprise to me. I'd had no idea that I was smart.

I was quite excited about this. My parents and grandparents had made it very clear to me, as a first-generation student of the post–civil rights era, that education was my only ticket out of poverty and violence, so I was very focused on making the most of mine. And for the first time in my life, at age eleven, I was really meeting white people and engaging with other cultures. I was excited about that too. But it also felt daunting and unfamiliar. Being one Black student in a sea of white faces was very intimidating.

Just as I adjusted to this level of separation—between mainstream classes and the Scholars Program—another layer of stratification emerged. That same year, the Pittsburgh Public Schools started a program called the Centers for Advanced Studies (CAS). It represented the very top echelon within the already advanced Scholars Program, and this group got to get on a bus every Wednesday and go somewhere else—a school called Banksville—for the entire day to study things I'm sure I could have benefited from, things that apparently someone thought I didn't have the capacity to learn.

I've since come to understand that my placement in that high-and-yet-not-the-highest tier was what crystallized this idea in my mind: that maybe I just wasn't smart enough. (Smart enough for what? I'm not sure. Just *not smart enough*.) I still carry this untruth with me. I've learned how to move through it, but that sixth-grade evaluation is where it originated.

Yet as much as it stung to be at once affirmed and denied in this way, it reinforced my drive, my conviction that I would have to work as hard as I possibly could to hold my own in the world. And because I was left with the sense that a rich cache of opportunities was being withheld from me, it spurred me to look for and create my own opportunities at every step. It drove me to cultivate my own agency and be my own advocate.

The first way this manifested itself was in the realm of phys ed. Gym remained the most dreaded part of my week, and unfortunately, it was now on the schedule every day except Wednesday, when we had a health class instead. Competitive sports still filled me with anxiety, but at this point, they were the least stressful aspect of the phys ed experience. Much more harrowing to me was the time spent in the locker room. My body was changing, and so were those of my classmates. Many of the boys were becoming men before my eyes. At every turn in the locker room, I was confronted with swelling muscles, chiseled limbs, hair where there had been none before. My own arousal was terrifying to me, and all I wanted was to hide.

Now, in the meantime, Mr. Lutz—the instrumental teacher—had invited me to join band because I played the alto sax. I loved music, and I cherished the experience of being in band. Mr. Lutz was a very warm and gentle man who seemed as if he was on my side. He recognized my creative drive and threw himself headlong into supporting it.

I speak of angels in my life very often—angels who dipped down and pointed me in the right direction. Mr. Lutz was one of them, and another was Mr. Highland, the gym teacher. He saw my panic and my distress. And when I asked him if it was possible for me to opt out of gym and use that time to practice my saxophone, he said yes. The only requirement was that I show up to health class once a week.

This was a godsend. It lifted a lot of anxiety and allowed me to be in a creative space more often. I was dedicated to my saxophone; I would go into the instrumental room and sit in the back corner and practice and practice. Music is healing, it had always been healing, and it was a space where I felt safe.

Once I'd experienced the blessing of leaving my neighborhood, it became harder and harder to return. I found myself trying to extend the school day in any way I could. There were a lot of after-school programs implemented by the Pittsburgh Public Schools. It was also the year that Ronald Reagan was elected president, so in the not-too-distant future, these programs would be dismantled and the people who were the most vulnerable would suffer. But at the time, they were still intact. There was a bound stack of after-school programs, at least three inches thick, filled with different activities that we kids could immerse ourselves in. I scoured the pages and came across a program called Reizenstein Musical Theater (RMT). I didn't know what a musical was, I didn't know what theater was, but *music* was in the title and I thought that perhaps it would involve singing, which I loved to do above all other things. So I signed up.

On the first day of RMT, the director, Ms. Schmidt, stood in front of the group and explained what a Broadway musical was. She was a compact woman with short hair and horn-rimmed glasses. She had a specific presentation that, later in life, I would come to identify as that of a lesbian, but at the time, I had no idea about this. I just knew that I liked her. She was strong, she was powerful, and she cared.

She told us that the musical chosen for the year would be Rodgers and Hart's *Babes in Arms*. The following week would be an audition. We could come in and sing a song—any song we wanted—in front of the group. And then she would cast the show. Each of us would get a part; each of us would have something to do. The entire show would be double-cast, which meant that no matter what, on one of the four evenings of the performance, every member of RMT would have a role in the show. As she spoke, I was filled with a jittery excitement because I knew I could sing; I knew I could ace this thing she was calling an audition.

We finished our first meeting, and when I walked outside, my grandmother and great-aunt Dorothy were there waiting for me. It was September 21, my eleventh birthday, and they had come to pick me up and take me on a special birthday trip. Grandma and Aunt Dot drove me downtown. We had a wonderful dinner, and then we went to Heinz Hall to see *The Wiz*, a Broadway show on a national tour. It was a surprise. I'd had no idea where we were going. And when the curtain rose and the actors began the performance, it struck me: *Oh my God, this—this!—is what Ms. Schmidt was just talking about. This is a musical!*

I remember thinking this coincidence was like magic—but the true magic was just beginning. I could not have been more mesmerized by the show. Of course I knew *The Wizard of Oz*; I was well acquainted with the plot line. But this version galvanized me. It was an African-American reimagining of the story with all Black people and an all R&B score written by the late Charlie Smalls with the book written by William F. Brown. I don't think I drew a deep breath for the entire two and a half hours. And then, at the very end of the evening, the character of Dorothy sang a song called "Home."

She stood center stage and belted out this song about a place "where there's love overflowing" that left me transported, breathless, and bereft all at once. When the lights came up in the theater, I was weeping. All around me, people rose to their feet and began gathering their things, filing toward the aisles, but I couldn't move. My grandma and Aunt Dorothy had to peel me from the seat and all but carry me to the car.

I woke up longing with all my heart just to hear that music again. And I wanted to sing "Home" for the audition the following week but didn't know how to find it and had no idea where to begin. So after choir class, I approached the teacher, Ms. Rhoda Arnold. She was another angel in my life. I told her about *The Wiz* and the song I wanted to learn. Two days later, she took me aside after class and handed me the cast recording from *The Wiz*, along with the sheet music. "This is for you," she told me. "Good luck with your audition."

I clearly remember standing there in front of her, stunned and clutching the shrink-wrapped vinyl album in both hands. The cover art featured a Black woman in silhouette, poised as if to take off from a starting block. Her hair and limbs swirled out behind her in a fantastical tangle. I remember my own joyful gasp of recognition: The image matched that of the *Playbill* on my dresser at home. I couldn't have been more surprised and thrilled if she had handed me the Hope Diamond.

I took the album home and listened to it until the grooves flattened. I learned "Home" and came in the next week and sang it for Ms. Schmidt and all the kids at RMT. Once again, I saw the faces of the people who heard me sing and felt the room soften. I felt hearts open. In that moment, I truly began to understand the power of this gift I had been given. I had no idea what I was going to do with it, but I knew that when I opened my mouth to sing, somehow the darkness lifted and all my shame went away.

The following week the cast list went up, and just as Ms. Schmidt had said, every role had been double-cast. Every role, that is, except for mine. There in the middle of the paper was my name all by itself: *Gus Fielding: Billy Porter.* I would get to play the role of Gus Fielding in *Babes in Arms* for all four performances.

There are no words for how I loved RMT: the shared sense of purpose, the way cast and crew became a tight-knit family, the sheer fun and escapism of becoming someone else for a few hours. The show opened at the end of March, and the actual performance was an experience unlike any I'd had before. Being onstage felt like home. It allowed me to breathe. The lights, the costumes, the orchestra, the audience: I had never known anything like it. I had never felt an exhilaration or a safety like this. I'd fallen wildly in love and there was no turning back.

By the seventh grade, I had become practiced in pursuing my own creative opportunities. I lost no time in signing up for musical theater again. This year, though, Ms. Schmidt had left the school and Mr. Lutz had taken over RMT. The production that year was *The Pajama Game*. We went through the same process: Auditions were held, the cast list went up, and once again every part except mine had been double-cast. The role of Hines was mine and mine alone. I had become the star of RMT.

I also chose to continue with band. Mr. Lutz made sure we had concerts outside of school all the time, and that was so much fun. We would play at different citywide activities, as well as Christmas and spring concerts all around the city.

And finally, Ms. Arnold found yet another couple of government-funded programs for me. The first was the All-City Choir, in which students from different schools would convene on Saturday mornings and rehearse with our choral mistress, Birdie Nichols. Ms. Nichols was a strong Black woman and a musical genius. She was all about discipline: showing up on time and being prepared. She taught us how to read music, how to be in a group, how to harmonize together—all tools that we would need in our regular lives. This woman was special. She was stern and she was tough. Some people might have used other words to describe her too, and I adored her. I loved the discipline and focus. I loved the fact that somebody cared enough to make sure I did the right thing. I cherished those Saturday mornings, and the wonderful feeling of having someplace to go and something to do. Kids need a place to engage, a place that makes them feel like they matter. It was such a gift and a blessing that those "enrichment" programs, rebranded "entitlement" by our cynical government officials, existed.

The second opportunity Ms. Arnold found for me took place on Saturday afternoons at the new Creative and Performing Arts (CAPA) high school. CAPA was a brand-new magnet school, a half-day program founded in 1979 by Dr. Harry Clark, an African-American scholar, educator, and prominent jazz musician on the Pittsburgh scene. CAPA was housed at Baxter Elementary School in the neighborhood of Homewood. The same building hosted a Saturday program called the Centers for the Musically Talented, and it offered free classes to anyone who qualified for admission.

Yes. Free classes. Free. Classes. I have to emphasize the miracle of this: *free music classes* for anyone talented enough to get in. Every Saturday afternoon, there was a staggering range of opportunities for us. There was a theory class. I had a private voice lesson. I had a private saxophone lesson. I had opera workshop, where I starred as Amahl in Gian Carlo Menotti's *Amahl and the Night Visitors*. I had a choir class. I had eurythmics. I had percussion class. I availed myself of so many facets of a music education that have shaped the artist I am today.

These opportunities don't really exist anymore. And I have to continue to talk about this, because that was the year that it all started to go away. Reagan was elected and all such programs started to fade. The care for others in the community began to crumble. Public education in America has been stripped away little by little over the last forty years, until only the most depleted, anemic version remains.

But during that time, throughout my seventh- and eighth-grade years, I would leave the house at 8:00 A.M. every Saturday and wouldn't come back until after 6:00 at night, utilizing what Bernie taught me about public transportation to travel to-and-fro all by my lonesome. This was the closest thing to heaven I had ever known. This program was for high-schoolers, but they accepted me in seventh grade, and I was hanging with all these high school students. For the first time in my life, I felt like one of the cool kids. I had found my people. Everyone respected me because I was talented. Everyone liked me. No one wanted to beat me up. This in itself was a stunning thing—*no one at this school wanted to beat me up*. It was all love. We were a tribe. We were bound together.

While things were undeniably getting better for me at school, they were worsening at church. By middle school, I had earned a reputation as a heretic. This particular trouble began in Sunday school when I was ten.

The teacher had told us that we were all made in the image of God, who loved us and knew what we were going to do even before we did it. This was confusing to me, so I asked the teacher, "If God loves us, and He made us in His own image, and He knows what we're going to do before we do it, then why would He create someone He knows isn't going to choose Him, only to send him to a burning hell for all eternity?"

There was a long and frightening silence. And then the teacher said, in a tone of pure rebuke: "You do *not* question God—and God is sovereign." That was her answer to me.

"What does *sovereign* mean?" I stammered.

"It means God can do whatever he wants to do whenever he wants to do it!"

Now, even at the age of ten, I understood this wasn't an answer. I would have preferred for an adult, any adult, to simply admit that they didn't know. But the question I asked dug way too deep for blind followers to allow. My question had marked me as a heathen and a sinner in my church community. Questioning God's ways was absolutely taboo and would not be tolerated on any level.

And yet this was not my most essential transgression. No, these troublesome inquiries paled beside the cardinal sin of homosexuality. It seemed that every time I showed up at church, the sermon would turn to the abomination of homosexual activity, of men lying with men. There was no apparent reason for this topic to surface so relentlessly. I couldn't help feeling that somehow they knew about me.

How could they know about Bernie? He said that it's a secret, one that's just between us. But now the preacher's saying I'm a sinner, that I'm lying with another man and it's wrong. What am I supposed to do now? I thought these were my man lessons, that doing as he directed would make me more of a man. That's what the psychologist said; that was the plan, right? Mommy and Bernie planned it because it was what the doctor prescribed.

As I tried to grapple with the idea that I would be burning in hell for all of eternity, I threw myself into my studies and back into theater. Those things still managed to bring me joy, but time spent at home began to feel more and more like a minefield. Because I would go home and play footsies with my stepfather under the table at dinner and do things with him in the middle of the night when he came home from work—though I didn't even know what those things were called. That man would be in my room, at the very least, two times a week for five years.

* * *

I can't stop crying. I guess this is the reason I've never allowed myself to go there. To the heart of the pain, the vortex. I have this terrifying feeling that if I let myself really go there, I won't come back from it. My heart hurts. My stomach is in knots. It's always in knots, that ain't nuthin' new, but the memories keep flooding in faster than I can process: My tummy was riddled with ulcers in the seventh grade. Nodes on my vocal cords by eighth grade. Couldn't talk for three months. Couldn't sing for six months. I did all the rehearsals for *Oliver* in RMT, cast in the role of Fagin, without singing until a week before the performances. I remember feeling like my voice wouldn't come back, like maybe it wouldn't be the same somehow. How would I fight off the terrors of this world without my secret weapon, my savior?

I feel like Mary Barnes. My freshman year at Carnegie Mellon the senior class mounted a production of a play called *Mary Barnes*. Mary was an English artist and writer who suffered from schizophrenia and became a successful painter. I sat in Kresge Theatre on the CMU campus and watched what seemed to be a very stable woman, a trained nurse who had served in World War II, check herself into an insane asylum. By the end of Act 1 she had regressed to standing at the top of the grand staircase naked and covered in shit. This image is seared into my memory, because even then, all the way back in the spring of 1988, I knew I had similar work to do. I knew even then that I was holding on to my sanity by a thread. And here I am all these decades later, at the height of my life and career—covered in alla my personal trauma shit!

My therapist has named the shit: grief! I never metabolized my grief, and my whole life has been filled with it. You gotta metabolize your grief, gurl. It's killing you. Literally. I saw myself as an adult. I split off from myself at seven years old and began to experience myself as a grown-ass man. I had no other choice. How was I to know that those sessions under the cloak of night with Bernie were wrong? I was seven.

I thought it was supposed to be good for me. I thought it was supposed to make me stronger, make me more masculine, and now the preacher was telling me I'd burn in hell for it. I started "accidentally" missing my bus after school. Now that I knew that my time with Bernie was sinful, I just wanted to stay as far away from him as I could. We had rehearsals after school three days a week, and on the other two, I just didn't want to go home.

After I'd missed my bus for several days in a row, Mr. Halapatz, the activities director, sensed that something was going on. He was another angel. He would let me do homework in his office until about 5:30, and then he would drive me home. This allowed me to miss Bernie, who worked the night shift from 5:00 P.M. until midnight. I missed him for an entire quarter, and then once RMT had come to an end for that year, I finally summoned the courage to confront him. One night, as he was leaving my bed, I simply told him, "I don't want to do this anymore. The preacher says it's a sin, so I want to stop."

Bernie had just risen, and he half turned to me as I said this. For a moment, the words hung in the air between us while I waited for his response, grateful for the dark that obscured both his face and mine. After a long, startled pause, he said only, "All right, then," and went on his way out the door.

And that was it—the end of an era. Bernie never came into my room again. One night went by and then another. One week and then two and then many. I realized that after all these years, it really was over, as abruptly as that—he wasn't going to return. And the relief of this was like the release of a chokehold from around my throat.

But it also had the unexpected effect of deepening my sense of guilt, adding yet another layer to my shame, though it would be years before I figured out why. If I could have made it stop anytime I wanted to, simply by asking, then I must have been in control the whole time. By not asking him to stop all those years, I must have been asking for the opposite—asking for what he did to me.

* * *

By the end of seventh grade, I had thrown myself headlong into performing in two musicals and familiarized myself with countless others by checking albums out of the Oakland branch of Carnegie Library. *Oklahoma!*, *Hello, Dolly!*, *My Fair Lady*, *West Side Story*, *Gypsy*, *Pippin*, *A Chorus Line*, *Chicago*, *The Sound of Music*, *Damn Yankees*, *Annie*, *The Music Man* . . . the list went on and on. Each of them sparked me in a different way. The lyrics were uplifting and comic and clever. They offered an escape from the moral rigidity and judgment of the church. They promised a wider and more life-affirming world than the one I was trapped in.

But it was impossible not to notice that none of them had been written with me in mind. There was nary a Black person in any original cast. *The Wiz* had been my first and last experience of Broadway actors who looked like me. I'd held that evening so close to me for so long, held on to it as tightly as I could through the months and years that followed, but I hadn't experienced anything like it again.

And then it was the second Sunday in June 1982 (an annual date that in some circles would be referred to as gay Christmas). I was alone in the kitchen, doing the dinner dishes while watching the Tony Awards on the small color television we kept on the counter. Tony Randall sat in a velvet high-back armchair and introduced a scene from one of the nominees for Best Musical, *Dreamgirls*. Then Jennifer Holliday, playing Effie, a singer ousted from the group for which she was the lead, emerged from the back of the stage. And when Holliday sang, I was struck into stillness. The back of my neck prickled, and it was as if I could feel the roots of my hair tingling. I cradled myself in a ball on the floor, stunned, my eyes transfixed on the screen.

From the first few moments of her solo, I knew I was bearing witness to something extraordinary. Holliday's performance was a tour de force of depthless grief and vocal virtuosity. There seemed to be nowhere her voice could not go. She was a tempest in a tantrum as she growled and howled and keened and bellowed *and squalled* her way through her spurned woman's scorching blowtorch of a swan song.

I had never seen anyone give so much to a role. Holliday's Effie held nothing back at all. I could hardly imagine the fearlessness required to wade so deep into what she knew of agony in front of a live audience. It was at once an act of sheer will and utter surrender.

And yet there was something in her performance that left me lit with recognition. She sang *the way we sang in church*. She sang in the gospelian style I was raised in. She had taken that high-octane, soul-belting, full-throttle gospel sound to the Broadway stage and brought mainstream audiences to ecstasies with it: I heard in the rapture of her audience a message expressly for me. I thought, *This can be more than just an extracurricular pleasurable activity in my life. I can do this musical theater thing too, and I can make a living from it.*

I knew that much in the moment, though there was so much more I couldn't know.

As taken as I was with Holliday's performance, I could never have imagined how long a foreshadow this song would cast across the next several decades of my life. I didn't yet understand that Effie, Holliday's character, was a singer being fired in part because she didn't fit the industry's idea of a dreamgirl: lighthearted and pretty, thin, sparkling and smiling, perceived by the dominant society as unthreatening, benign.

I wasn't familiar with the story line. Had no notion of what would happen next. From what I'd seen unfold on the Tony Awards stage, it looked like the end of the road for Effie: time up, game over. She had been dropped, abandoned, left on the side of the road. I didn't yet know that she would languish far from the limelight for many years, or that ultimately, like the phoenix, she would rise. And that when she did, she would do so as none other than her authentic self in all its glory: raw, real, full-bodied, full-throated, and Blackity Black Black Black.

There was no way to know, either, just how much I would come to identify with her message, delivered with the righteous ire of a thousand fire-and-brimstone-driven Furies—to the man she loves, yes, but also to the soulless, ruthless, dehumanizing industry bent on driving her out of the light:

> *And I'm telling you I'm not going.*
> *And you and you and you, you're gonna love me . . .*

CHAPTER FOUR

As middle school went on, I became practiced in the art of charting my own path. I understood very young that, at virtually all times, I needed to be figuring out the next five moves I had to make in order to survive and thrive. And as early as the seventh grade, I was aware that I was destined by the city's zoning laws to attend the notorious Westinghouse High School, located in the dangerous neighborhood known as Homewood-Brushton. Westinghouse was overrun with drugs, violence, and gang activity. Remember the 1989 film *Lean on Me*, starring Morgan Freeman as a tyrannical yet caring principal? Yeah, she was very that! I knew that if I were forced to go to Westinghouse, my faggot ass wasn't going to make it out alive. I had to find a way to go elsewhere.

Now, after being at Reizenstein and around white people for the first time, I started to realize how poor my family was and how much I didn't have. I also realized how rigid and restrictive my church community was. When you've never experienced an alternative to your own culture or circumstances, you don't always know there's something else outside of your bubble—that a different way of life is possible. But now that I'd been immersed in another kind of environment, and the opportunities that came with it, I made the conscious choice to stay in the light.

I also understood how the education system worked, because I was paying attention. I knew that if I did well academically, I would be offered the option of taking a foreign language. I knew that one of the choices was Russian. And I'd figured out—as improbable as it sounds—that taking Russian in the eighth grade was the key to my entire future.

Yes, that eighth-grade Russian class, of all unlikely things, was like Operation Save a Faggot, because I also understood that the best public high school in the city was Taylor Allderdice High School. It was in Squirrel Hill, where all the Jewish people lived, and had a stellar reputation and a top-ten national ranking, and I wanted to go there. Now, if I took Russian in the eighth grade and passed, the only high school in the city that offered Russian was Allderdice, so they would have to let me go there if I wished to continue my Russian studies. And not only would that get me out of attending Westinghouse, but it also meant that my personal transportation needs would be subsidized by the city. Because there was no school bus to bring me from my own neighborhood to Squirrel Hill, the Port Authority would have to provide me with an unlimited monthly bus pass for use on public transit. And this, in turn, would solve the problem of how I was to get to all the extracurricular activities that were piling up in my life. Because unlike the white folks I was runnin' with, my parents weren't driving my lil' booked and busy ass nowhere.

I hammered out this private plan during the summer between my sixth- and seventh-grade years. That's how far I was thinking ahead and how badly I needed to get out. I knew the only way to survive was to be outside my neighborhood as much as possible. I also set my sights on CAPA, the high school that housed the Centers for the Musically Talented, where I spent my Saturday afternoons. Many of my peers in the program went to CAPA for the latter half of the school day. So if only I could make my way there as well, I would have a ready-made group of friends waiting for me when I arrived. And I could devote half the school week to all my creative pursuits.

* * *

41

Of course, during that final year of middle school, I also signed up for musical theater again. And it was during this year that I had my first personal experience of the perils of traditional casting.

I'd learned that the musical this time would be *Oliver*. So I went to the Carnegie public library, did my research, and checked out the album. I learned Oliver's solo, "Where Is Love?," for the audition. I assumed that after two years of playing the second banana, I would finally be the lead.

And then the cast list went up. It read: *Oliver Twist—Eric Pearson*.

I never even bothered to look to see which part I was to play. Instead, I stormed directly down the hall to the instrumental room and burst into Mr. Lutz's office.

"Why am I not playing Oliver?" I demanded without preamble.

Mr. Lutz was at his battered metal desk, and he didn't even blink. As if he'd been waiting for me, as if we were merely picking back up on an ongoing conversation, he said, "Billy, you're playing Fagin."

"Who's Fagin?"

"Fagin is the villain."

"Why am I not playing Oliver?"

"Well, you're really not right for Oliver. There's an innocence that you just don't have. You're much more suited for Fagin."

"I deserve the lead, I've worked hard for it. I've paid my dues," I snapped. "And *FAG*in is not the lead."

Mr. Lutz regarded me with his gentle gaze. "Well," he said, "it's pronounced *FAY*gin, and Fagin *truly is* the lead."

"Well . . . the show's called *OLIVER*, not *FAGIN*! That don't sound like the lead to me!"

"Just go home," he told me. "Read the script and you'll understand what I mean."

I went home to read the script, which at that age meant counting my lines. That's when I realized that Fagin doesn't even enter the musical until the last scene of the first act. My throat ached with the indignant howl it held: *How, oh how, can this character possibly be the lead? This is some bullshit*, I cussed to myself, *but . . . whatever . . .*

But then I couldn't sing. I'd first had ulcers in the seventh grade, and now vocal nodes struck in the eighth. My body was reacting to the trauma I was experiencing, yet there was not an adult in my life present or equipped with the tools to even inquire why I was walking around with acid holes in my stomach. Maybe it was because I had seen a news report about the strange Gay Cancer that was killing gay men. Maybe it was because my pastor used his bully pulpit to curse the homosexuals as an abomination. *What is gay? What does* homosexual *mean?* I didn't even know, but I had a sneaking suspicion that I was that thing, that abomination. I looked it up in the dictionary, and sure enough—I was the poster child for *homosexual*. And to add insult to injury, my stepfather was doing the footsie thing with me at the dinner table during that alarming news report. He was still visiting my room at least twice a week, for a period of appoximately five years. I'm trying to sit with that. I'm trying to have compassion for Lil' Preacher Man Billy. Seven-year-old Billy . . . twelve-year-old Billy . . . he was all alone. *You were all alone, Boo. You were twelve years old and thought you were gonna die of AIDS, and you had nobody to talk to about it.*

The doctor said I couldn't sing for six months, was not supposed to speak at all for three. I had to carry a notepad with me everywhere I went to communicate with folk. I had to go through six months of rehearsals for *Oliver* without singing. I couldn't even try to sing until a week before the actual performances. My vocal cords were in distress. The throat scope showed my little saviors at the point of almost hemorrhaging. The doctor couldn't promise that I'd be able to sing again at all. I worried what Mr. Lutz would say, if he would replace me, what I would do if I couldn't sing anymore, how I would *survive*.

Well—I sucked it up, pulled my shit together, and suggested I be recast for the good of the production.

"I will have no such thing!" Mr. Lutz said. His trust and belief in me and my healing helped me to trust and believe in myself. I learned my part in silence, memorizing the text and etching the music into my psychic hard drive, and willed my body to heal itself. I ended up having an amazing time, and on opening night, I learned the meaning of a star entrance. See, sometimes you gotta make 'em wait! Fagin doesn't show up until almost halfway through the show. So by the time I glided out from the wings, everyone in that audience was waiting, with bated breath, for me. I walked onto the stage to a thunderous round of entrance applause. Lead or no lead, I was the star of the show, singing Lionel Bart's "Reviewing the Situation" an octave above the traditional placement, in my best Pittsburgh-cockney accent.

* * *

But after this impassioned three-year love affair with musical theater, my mama dropped a bomb onto my best-laid plans. *No, you may not go to CAPA high school,* she told me. *It might be fun but ain't no future in it. You're gonna do computers.*

Now in retrospect, I have to say this was rather visionary of my mother. In fact, I'm somewhat amazed at her foresight. There was no indication at the time that computers were going to be what they are today. An education in information technology would have been a very good investment, but I had no interest—so I defied her and went to the audition for CAPA anyway.

When I'd finished my song, I was accepted on the spot. "I'm sorry," I told them. "I can't come because my mother won't let me."

Dr. Harry Clark, the founder and first principal of the school, was in the audience. His brow furrowed in consternation. "Excuse me?"

"My mother will not allow me to enroll. She wants me to study computers."

I was startled when Dr. Clark stood up and began making his way down the aisle of the auditorium. "Come with me to my office," he told me, "and we're going to call your mother right now."

As I trailed him down the hall, I felt the sweat breaking out along my hairline and beneath my arms. *Oh my God, Mommy's gonna kill me. I'm not even supposed to be at this audition! She's gonna beat. My. Ass.* But I knew I needed to go to this school. The arts were not a passing fancy in my life; this burning love was here to stay. I'd found my passion and I was going to pursue it for all I was worth, fight for it with everything I had, to dream beyond my circumstance, to get myself out!

When my mother heard that I had auditioned for CAPA, she hung up the phone, jumped into her car, and was at the school within fifteen minutes. And I was so glad it was Dr. Clark and no one else who would be pleading my case to her. This formidable African-American luminary and scholar with a "Dr." before his name greeted my mother with the utmost respect, and then with the gentlest touch at the small of her back, he ushered her into his office.

When she was seated across from his desk in the chair next to mine, he leaned forward, locked eyes with her, and began to speak with a quiet and pensive intensity. "Mrs. Ford, your son has a gift. It's a gift that is so profound, so powerful and exceptional, that it could truly change the world. Some might say it's a gift from God. If it were to be squandered, it would be a catastrophic waste and nothing short of a tragedy."

"I just don't want to lose him to the streets. I don't want my son to end up in jail," my mother appealed. Her hands trembling. Her eyes watering at the thought of my systemic, inevitable demise.

Dr. Clark went through all the benefits of my joining CAPA: that it would keep me focused, that it was something I loved, that I would have ample time to change direction later if it didn't work out. My mother held herself very still as she listened to all this. When he was done speaking, her gaze seemed to turn inward, as it did when she was thinking hard, or consulting Jesus. I clenched my hands together in my lap as she pondered, not moving, barely daring to breathe. For those moments, it was so silent I could hear the clock ticking on the office wall.

Finally she seemed to return to us. She straightened her spine and lifted her chin. Her eyes met Dr. Clark's.

And she said yes.

* * *

I made a pact with my mother. As long as I did well in school, I could pursue any extracurricular activity I wanted. So freshman year was about solidifying my grades and making sure everyone understood that I was very invested in my academics. When it was time to sing, I had to ensure there were no limitations.

The first half of my school day was spent at Taylor Allderdice and devoted to all my academic classes: English, math, science, history, and of course Russian. Then at noon I got on the bus for CAPA. It was as if I'd found my tribe. It was a pure joy. CAPA was filled with the misfits and future faggots of America, and it felt like I was home. For the first time in my life, I was popular. The only drawback was that I was looking forward to the school's yearly musical, only to discover there wasn't one.

This was because the school was divided into departments, and all the departments were entirely separate entities. The first was drama, which was simply acting, doing plays. The second was music—and music alone. In this department, you could sing or you could play an instrument, and that was it. The dance department was all, and only, about dance. And then there was the visual arts department, for painting and sculpture and photography and stuff.

Having been the star of RMT in middle school, I felt the absence of musical theater very sharply. There was a void, and I made that clear to my teachers. I wanted to be in a musical! As I had for the last three years, like the actors and singers in *The Wiz*, like those glamorous members of the *Dreamgirls* cast on the Tony Awards. I wanted to be onstage!

In the spring of my freshman year, one of my teachers told me of a summer stock company in Pittsburgh called the Civic Light Opera (CLO), which put on productions at the grand Heinz Hall, the very same place I'd seen *The Wiz*. The minute I heard this, there was nothing left to decide. I wanted to be onstage and I wanted to be on *that* stage—the very same one graced by the entrancing performers in my all-time favorite musical. Wouldn't that be something?

The auditions for the Civic Light Opera were held on a Saturday morning. The fourth floor of Heinz Hall was teeming with candidates ready to sing. They were dressed to impress, with their hair all done up and their music laminated or pristinely tucked into folders. Some of them were accompanied by what I would soon come to know as *stage mothers*; some

46

brought their voice coaches, many of them well known to the CLO artistic staff.

I was good at auditioning at this point. And my song was still "Home." I wore my very specific church clothes and came with no connections, but if there was one thing I could do, it was sing, and I blew the roof off the joint.

I was invited to return the next Sunday for a callback audition. Callback auditions were new and confusing to me. What did that mean, and what would I be doing? *You're going to dance,* I was told over the phone. *So next week, bring clothes that you can dance in, and we will put you through a dance combination, and you'll also sing again.*

The next week, after begging my mother to let me miss Sunday service, I got on the bus and returned in what I truly thought was appropriate attire: a T-shirt and sweatpants. When I looked around the room, I saw lots of white children dressed in very expensive Capezio dance clothes—leotards and tights—and dance shoes. Apparently, there were special clothes and shoes for dancing. Who knew?

It didn't take me long to ascertain that I was not a dancer. As the choreographer stood in front of the room and taught us the combination in counts of eight, all the kids around me picked it up as if they had been doing it since the womb. *Waiiiit, are these people just picking this up right now? On this day? In this moment?* I didn't even know where to begin! I was completely out of my league. As the sweat poured into my eyes, stinging them with salt and hair grease, and my legs all but buckled beneath me, I knew I had blown it. *Well,* I thought, *this is the end. I'll never be a musical theater performer.*

The nice man running the audition separated us into groups of four. Each group then performed the dance combination in front of a board of judges as they looked on, pointing and whispering to each other. Post-dancing, there came yet another test. Everyone had to sing, again, but this time in front of our peers. We had to flex, let it all hang out for the people to see—and judge. I was thrown slightly off my game, 'cause the whole dancing thing was new and I had my fully drenched T-shirt and sweatpants ensemble to prove it. This communal audition situation was a very popular construct in the eighties—hundreds of prospective artists, sardined into overcrowded dance studios or music rooms, smelly from all of us pawns vying for our shot in the spotlight. Your competition could potentially be to the front, back, right, or left of you. You could experience debilitating nerves that could derail your possibilities for glory simply by hearing another person sing the same audition song as you, possibly better than you!

When each group had finished, we were lined up, shoulder to shoulder, across the room.

"If I call your name," the nice man said, "please step forward." And he began making his way down a list affixed to a clipboard. I stood there, barely breathing, praying to be called forward, willing him to say my name. But he didn't. When he came to the end, I felt a spasm of disappointment in my gut.

Next the man said: "To those of you whose names I called: thank you for your time. Thank you very much." A hush came over the room as the meaning of his words set in, and then slowly the dismissed began gathering their belongings: dance bags, lunch boxes, clothes. Some of the kids were crying. Parents came into the room to collect and console their children. Mine weren't there. I'd taken public transportation to Heinz Hall by myself. It had never even occurred to me that at least one parent was supposed to be here with me. My mother had no use for these pursuits, and my step-father had trained me to be self-sufficient. That free monthly bus pass from Port Authority was all I needed to get shit done!

The nice man addressed all the performers and parents who hadn't left. "Hello, everybody, my name is Joe Franze, and I am the founder and artistic director of the Civic Light Mini Stars. I wanted to find a way to engage the youth of our community through theater, and this is what I came up with." He went on to say that the Mini Stars would be ambassadors for the Pittsburgh Civic Light Opera all over the city. That we would be performing at different summer festivals, official government functions, and private parties. Rehearsals would take place on Sundays from noon to five at the Schenley Park Ice Skating Rink.

I raised my hand. "Excuse me, sir. I thought I was auditioning for the Civic Light Opera itself."

"Well, you are. You have. This is the Civic Light Opera, and this troupe is the Mini Stars."

"But I thought I was auditioning to be in the shows on the stage. The one downstairs, in Heinz Hall."

"Well, as a matter of fact, I was about to say that the Mini Stars is the troupe from which the CLO chooses children, if we need children in the mainstage shows."

Children? Why does he keep calling me a child? I am not a child; I am fourteen years old. I am a grown-ass man!

"How much do we get paid?" I asked next.

His eyebrows went up in surprise. "Our participants consider it a privilege to be in the Mini Stars," he said. "There is no pay."

Well, I knew this was not going to work. I wanted my Jordache jeans; I wanted my Chardons. I wanted my fashion, Henny! And no one was going to pay for alla that drag but me. There was also no way on God's green earth that my mother was going to let me skip Sunday service to rehearse with the heathens. I started to gather my things.

"Wait, wait, wait!" Joe Franze called. "What are you doing? Where are you going?"

"Oh, I can't—I can't be a part of this. I mean, you want us to do all these performances for free? And rehearse on Sundays? My mother ain't never gonna let me do that."

There was silence in the room as all the kids and their stage mothers looked on in horror. I can't imagine what they were thinking. This little Black boy, turning down this opportunity? Who does he think he is? But a moment later, I was out the door and heading down the stairwell. I hadn't gotten far when one of Joe Franze's associates, Paul Palmer, came running down after me. He asked me not to go, to think about it.

"I think it would be a very good thing for you to be around other kids who love and enjoy the same things that you do," he said. *Here he go with the kid thing again. Ain't no kid 'round here!*

"Well, my mother's not going to let me miss church, plain and simple. And I don't have any way to get to rehearsals. There's no bus that goes to the Schenley Park ice rink."

"Don't worry about that. We'll make sure you get to and from rehearsals. And we will talk to your mother and get her permission for you."

"Get her permission for me to work on Sundays? For free? Good luck with that!"

Angels. Angels! This six-foot-six gentle giant took me under his wing and brought me back to the room. And everything he promised came to pass. I'll never know how they got my mother's permission, but calls were made, conversations were had, plans were hatched, including with the artistic director, Joe Franze himself, escorting me to and from rehearsals and performances. And the experience turned out to be invaluable. My singing ability was never in doubt, but now I was being required to dance with a bunch of privileged white children who had been formally trained for years. I was late to this undertaking and I knew it. But I showed up and worked as hard as I could at every single rehearsal, and I practiced my dance moves on my own during every spare moment I had.

In the Mini Stars was a contingent of ten or twelve kids who all came from the same dance studio, the Center for Theater Arts in Mt. Lebanon. One of them was Kerry Nowe.

"Where do you study dance?" she asked me one day.

"Study it?"

"I mean, where do you take dance classes?"

"I don't," I told her. "I mean, I'd like to. But my mother has no money for things like that."

Her mother, Judy Nowe, overheard this. She was the founder and artistic director of the Center for Theater Arts. She offered me a full scholarship on the spot, and I gratefully accepted without having the least idea of how to make it work. Mt. Lebanon was a very lily-white and wealthy suburb of Pittsburgh. It could take up to two hours to get there from CAPA by bus. Could I get to class on time? Would my mother let me come home that late? I didn't know how I'd manage it, but it was free-ninety-nine, so I would find a way. Within a week, I was scheduled to go to the Center on Tuesday nights for a tap class and a ballet class, starting with the basics. I would arrive at the studio by bus after school, and I would need every one of the ninety minutes I had to get there. Then I'd get on the bus and hope to be home by 11:00 P.M.

But the white folks were concerned about me traveling on public transportation by myself that late at night. So the angels came together and hatched a plan. Billy Hartung was one of the other boys in my class, and we became instant friends. It was Billy Hartung's parents who volunteered to drive me home every Tuesday, even though it meant going all the way to the other side of town and back again. We would pile into the family pickup truck after class. On the way to the highway, we would stop at Wendy's, where I'd pick up a single hamburger, French fries, and my favorite, a Frosty. They drove me home every single week for two straight years. The care they showed this little Black ghetto-bound boy is something I will never forget, and I am forever grateful.

Billy Hartung went on to have an impressive career of his own, starring in *Footloose* and *Sideshow* on Broadway, as well as the film version of *Chicago*. He has since returned to Mt. Lebanon, where he lives with his beautiful family, works as the current artistic director of the Center for Theater Arts, and continues the family tradition of paying it forward by helping children activate and achieve their dreams through art.

As for me, not a day goes by in which I'm not grateful for my angels. And it's this gratitude that drives me to take part in as many benefits as I can, donate to a vast range of causes, and reach out to as many fans as humanly possible, especially the little sissy Black boys and trans kids all over the world.

It's been an inexpressible privilege to star in Broadway shows and on a hit TV series. I feel deeply honored to have won my Tony, Grammy, and Emmy awards. But every day I remind myself that nothing matters more than extending the legacy of the angels in my life. It's my devout conviction that if I'm not enabling and encouraging the underprivileged and the vulnerable, then I haven't justified their confidence in me, and I haven't done sufficient justice to their gifts.

CHAPTER FIVE

I f in middle school my talent had made me a star, in high school, it became clear that wasn't enough. I had to get better. Work harder. Improve as a dancer. And learn to act.

I spent my sophomore year of CAPA well outside my comfort zone. On the very first day, I was cornered by the head of the drama department, Peggy Hughes: a pistol of a woman with short-cropped blond hair. She was a bit of a broad, as we say in the business. She clutched a notepad and she came straight to the point. "I hear you want to be onstage. To act. To be in musicals. Here's what I propose: come to the drama department."

"But I'm in the music department," I told her. "I'm a singer."

"You're much more than a singer. You wanna be onstage, kid?"

"Well, yes—yes, I do."

"Leave the music department behind. Come and try the drama department for a semester."

Ms. Hughes said she'd put me in her production of *Our Town* by Thornton Wilder—I'd never heard of it—in the role of Mr. Webb, and promised I could head back to the music department if I didn't like it. Well, I thought that was a wonderful proposition. So I showed up and realized that, once again, I was late to the game. I had no idea what I was doing.

That year, I would learn that acting was not just about memorizing a set of lines and projecting them with clarity and flair. It wasn't just a high-end version of mimicry, either. It was very much about the actor's level of humanity and empathy. It was a profound form of communion with the character you were playing, as well as with the audience. Finding an honest, heartfelt path between yourself and your character was just one aspect of the work.

Ms. Hughes was an incredible acting teacher and director. She really worked with us and cared for us and helped us understand the many ways *Our Town*—which on the surface seemed quaint and sentimental, an homage to conventional values—was a radical departure from traditional theater and a very subversive work. It was a remarkable introduction to acting, because it hurled me straight into the fire. I didn't have a single crutch at my disposal. There was no curtain, no scenery, no props. No glitzy costumes. No high drama, no comedy, and—most terrifying—no singing. At the end of the semester, though I had not been in a musical, I sensed that Ms. Hughes's intuition had led me in the right direction—that the drama department held a set of lessons that would be essential for me. I decided to stay, and I transferred from the music department for the duration of my time at CAPA.

I also remained committed to my ever-more-demanding dance regimen. One of my friends at CAPA, Curtis Clark, was an extraordinary dancer and a continual inspiration to me. There were also a couple of teachers at the school who had started their own studio downtown. Buddy Thompson taught jazz dance, and Leslie Anderson taught ballet. Buddy and Leslie knew me from school, so I gathered my courage and approached them about the possibility of training with them at their own First Side Studios—even though the tuition was beyond my means. They could not have given me a scholarship faster. Angels. The angels who were in my life . . .

So now I rose at 6:00 a.m., attended *two different* schools, then took the bus downtown, where I took three or four dance classes per evening. Then I'd take the bus home, wolf down a very late dinner, do my homework, and try to be in bed by 1:00 a.m. Only to wake up five hours later and do it all again. Can't have nothin' if you don't work for it. I learned my work ethic from the generations before me. My aunt Dorothy always told me, "If you stay ready, you don't have to get ready." I was getting ready for the world, and I was willing to do whatever it took.

And I reminded myself it was also the only way to get the fashions I required.

To this end, Curtis told me of a job he'd had the previous summer performing shows at Kennywood, the amusement park that's been a mainstay in the Pittsburgh area since 1899. He was planning to work there again during the upcoming summer, and I resolved to join him if I could. As much as I'd enjoyed being a Mini Star with the Civic Light Opera, I knew I needed a real summer job once school let out, one that paid real coinage.

The communal auditions were held in the instrumental room of the music department at Duquesne University. All the hopeful applicants— dancers, singers, musicians—were, once again, all in the same room, sizing up the competition, ready to devour, giving us *Lord of the Flies* realness. I was still singing my good old faithful audition song from *The Wiz*, and I had added "Be a Lion" to expand my repertoire. If it ain't broke, don't fix it.

Because Curtis had worked there the previous summer, he already knew the entertainment directors and he was clearly a shoo-in. I wasn't quite as confident, because I knew dancing still wasn't my strong suit, but I'd been working at it, so I was as ready as I could be at that point.

I sang; I slayed. I danced and . . . I was all right! I didn't embarrass anybody, including myself. Curtis and I were offered slots on the spot.

Being that I was only fifteen years old, I needed special permission from a guardian to subvert child labor laws. My mother was happy to sign, thrilled I had a job. I was making $4.25 an hour, working from noon until 11:00 P.M., Tuesday through Sunday. We put on six shows a day, four of them different. Most of the cast were of college age and from out of town. They were lodging in a motel about ten minutes from the park. To this day, I'm not sure why my mother allowed me to stay there too. I guess she realized how much easier it would be for me to get to work. I think Mommy was just happy that I wasn't on the streets or causing her any problems. I was a good kid, passing all my classes and making my own money. And the summer was unfolding without a hitch until she got a phone call from a member of our church, a distant cousin. As it happened, the local news station had come to the park to do a story on Kennywood, and part of the segment included B-roll clips of one of our shows.

Now, the movie *The Blues Brothers* had just been released, and we were performing a number inspired by the film. I was flanked by two girls in trench coats and fedoras, and I was serving a huge green afro wig, squalling out Aretha Franklin's "Think" for the children. I was having the time of my life, but apparently this sense of fun was not shared by our church, which dispatched an ambassador to berate my mother, telling her that my performance was a shame before God.

A shame before God. I was fifteen years old and working nearly seventy hours a week, making money and alleviating financial pressure for my family. And I was a shame before God.

My mother wasn't having it. "Really? That's what you have to say to me? Well, allow me to remind you of what your son was doing when he was in high school. Having babies! My child is fifteen years old and going to work every day. He has money in his pocket now—spending money for himself. So unless you'll be taking on the responsibility of paying for all the things he needs? Take that mess somewhere else."

It's so interesting to me that my mother clapped back on that occasion. She wasn't always like that. But this time, she took up for me. She understood that I was in a good place, the right place. Even now, I can only wonder: What was shameful? The singing? The dancing? The wig? I don't know what it was.

Actually, I know exactly what it was. Everybody always sensed the queer. The fag. The something wrong that needed to be fixed. And the haters were losing their control over me.

* * *

As my relationship with theater was deepening, so too was my relationship with dance. And during my junior year at CAPA, no one provided me with more guidance in this realm than Lenora Nemetz.

"Bob's going to love you," Lenora would tell me. "He is going to adore you. I can't wait for you to meet him. So we have to get prepared."

She said this to me as we stood in front of the mirror in dance class. It was just me and her. She had pulled me into the room alone. There was a free period; we had some time. She wanted me to mimic her in the mirror. Legs turned in, feet pointing at each other, left arm wrapped behind my back, all the way to my right leg. It was awkward twisting my body up like a human pretzel. I started to cramp.

"The cramping goes away," she said. "Bob Fosse's work is very specific. It's about the individual. It's about the interpretation. It's about the story. The simple twitch of a finger, the back pulse of a booty, can be worth a thousand words."

Lenora came into CAPA during my junior year. She was teaching there as a guest artist. Lenora was a star in Pittsburgh, because she had gone to New York at seventeen years old and, by nineteen, she was understudying two of the most formidable musical theater performers in history. The show was *Chicago*; the ladies were Chita Rivera and Gwen Verdon. Lenora was a Fosse girl. She had learned from the master, the actual master himself.

Fosse was a galvanizing choreographer, who fascinated and spoke directly to me for a range of reasons. The first was the fact that the most iconic aspects of his work were inspired by his imperfections. Because he was losing his hair, hats became an integral part of his pageantry. His shoulders were rounded, giving rise to his signature slouch. He didn't like his hands, so gloves made their way into his numbers. He was pigeon-toed and couldn't achieve the kind of turn-out expected in ballet, so he developed a style in which the legs are turned in and the feet point at each other. I was intoxicated by the way he had spun his "flaws" into stylistic gold. It felt like a message for me: that my own "flaws" and vulnerabilities might actually be arrows pointing straight to the heart of my power as a performer, and— dare I say—my artistry.

Also freeing to me was the overt eroticism of his style. Throughout my formative years, I'd experienced so much sexual repression from my church community. But here was an undisputed master celebrating sexual expression, embracing it, enjoying it. After so much self-censorship, I was now being encouraged to dispense with that kind of moral rigidity, and it felt electric.

I believe Lenora intuited all this—the many different ways Fosse could inform, shape, and save me. She saw beyond my talent. She saw into my heart and soul. I loved Lenora with all my heart and I still do. For whatever reason, I was special to her. It was personal to her, to make sure that I got through and got out.

* * *

In the meantime, as my dancing improved, so did my compensation rate. Once I'd had a taste of how it felt to be paid for performing, I was on the lookout for other paying gigs. Enter Don Brockett and his local production company. Don was a Pittsburgh celebrity, best known for playing Chef Brockett on *Mister Rogers' Neighborhood*. He was the master of what we call business theater, or industrial shows, which meant he would put specialty shows together for companies, to promote their new products. As a result, he was always seeking talented entertainers.

In the spring of 1986, Don announced a big job for an international printing business. The breakdown read: *Don Brockett seeking one actor/ singer/dancer. Must be able to engage a live audience. Must tap.*

This was a three-person gig. Two performers had already been cast: we'll call them Man 1 and Woman 1. These were two more Pittsburgh kids done good. Woman 1 was a formidable tap dancer who had moved to New York City to be in the original cast of a big, splashy Broadway musical. For some reason she was back in Pittsburgh. Man 1 had moved to New York as well, where he'd starred in several splashy Broadway musicals, and now he too would often return to Pittsburgh, in the capacity of director/chore- ographer. His reputation preceded him. Everyone was in love with him.

I was coming from morning high school classes, so I was late getting to the audition. The audition room was crammed with about two hundred people, all vying for that one gig. Man 1 was teaching a complicated tap- dance combination, fast and intricate. I flung my bag down, got my tap shoes, and threw myself into learning the combination, or trying to. The room was so packed, I couldn't see a mirror and I couldn't see Man 1, so I tried to pick it up by watching the people in front of me.

"Change lines!"

This happened in dance classes and auditions as a rule, to counter over-crowding and level the playing field. It let everyone have a chance to learn the combination directly from the choreographer in front of the mirror. As I moved to the front of the room, I caught a glimpse of Man 1 for the very first time. His hair was dripping with sweat. He sported a soaked tank top and every muscle in his body glistened.

He was the most handsome man I had ever seen in person. He had old-school matinee idol looks and could easily have held his own in any Holly-wood movie. He was dark-haired and blue-eyed with chiseled features and a glorious body. And his bottom was adorned with the very popular Capezio Lycra spandex dance pants with a seventies flared bell-bottom that clung to his tree-trunk legs and crotch in all the right places. He took my breath away. But I wasn't going to let that Lycra spandex bulge get between me and my money, Henny! No ma'am. My focus was clear. I was present and accounted for and ready to snatch this gig.

They divided us into groups of eight, and I nailed that tap combination. My two years of free classes out in Mt. Lebanon, with the white folks, were paying dividends in real time! They called us back to sing, and I knew I was a shoo-in.

I had heard the others. They were mainly dancers, most of whom couldn't carry a note to the grocery store.

I booked that gig as Man 2, and now I was in a dilemma once more. I was sixteen years old, a junior in high school; accepting the job would require me to miss two days of school. But miss those days I did. And why? Because a bitch was 'bout to make some coin!

It would require one week of rehearsals in the evenings. Three days of performances in Baltimore, Maryland. Travel, meals, and lodging would be paid for, we'd each receive a $30 per diem, and I would earn a whopping $1,500 for the entire gig. Now, please remember: This was 1986 and I was sixteen years old, so that was a lot of Jordache jeans.

Rehearsals were very relaxed. It was just the three of us. They treated me like an adult, because, essentially, I was an adult. They weren't my parents; they weren't my babysitters. I was sixteen going on thirty. I saw myself as a grown-ass man. This was by necessity and, in retrospect, quite problematic. I had to be grown way too fast in my life. I grieve for that little boy who never knew innocence.

Man 1 taught me how to dance like a man. He showed me how to get down into the floor, how to ground myself, how to be strong. But his instruction did not come from a place of disgust for the way I was presenting myself naturally. He didn't shame me for not being masculine enough. He was merely imparting his knowledge to me, like the natural teacher he was. And much to my surprise, when he was done with me—I danced like a man! Whatever that actually means.

Man 1 and I hit it off. He instantly became a mentor to me; it was the natural progression of things. Every night for two weeks after rehearsals it was just me and Man 1. He would drive me home to the hood and we would sit outside in my driveway and talk and talk and talk for what seemed like hours. I found in him a mentor . . . and a crush. I was shook.

On the way to Baltimore, as I sat alone on the Amtrak train, I realized this was my first out-of-town gig. We would be staying at a hotel. Would I have my own room? Would I be sharing one with Man 1?

Oh my God, if I'm rooming with him, what am I going to do? I can't be anywhere near this man without getting a boner. I can't be sharing a bedroom with him! He'll know, he'll know the minute I walk in. Am I going to see him naked? All I can think about is him kissing me, rubbing on me, grinding on me. I want that. I want it so bad, but it's an abomination. I need to block it, block it out of my brain, block it out!

I checked into the hotel. I couldn't even bring myself to ask the front desk what arrangements had been made, like, if I had a roommate or if I was bunking alone. I just went to the room, in which there were two queen-size beds. The uncertainty made my heart flutter. It was 4:30 P.M. We had rehearsal in the convention room at 6:00 P.M., so I told myself I would know soon enough.

But then I heard the click of a key in the door. "Hey, handsome!"

And there he stood. Like a vision in Technicolor at the foot of my bed. As if he had just walked out of the pages of my *International Male* magazine. Fear and excitement washed over me like a rushing, mighty wind. My prayers had been answered. Man 1 was my roommate.

That evening, back in the room after rehearsal, Man 1 rolled himself a joint and offered me a toke. I politely declined, because *just say no to drugs*. (Isn't that cute?) He asked me about my life, my family, my church. I admired this man. He was doing what I wanted to do, living the dream I had for myself. He had lived in New York City and worked on Broadway. He was friends with and had been mentored by Michael Bennett, the genius mastermind behind *A Chorus Line* and *Dreamgirls*. I was in the presence of greatness.

"You want to trade massages?" he asked. "My muscles are in knots. I'm sure yours are the same."

"Sure," I said, trying to sound natural.

"Why don't you give me one first?" He took off his T-shirt and lay face-down on the bed. He was wearing a pair of gym shorts and no underwear.

"I've never really done this before. I'm not sure what to do," I confessed.

"Just straddle my butt, dig your elbow into my shoulder, and work your way down," he instructed.

"Okay."

I did as he directed. I straddled his butt, immediately got a boner, and jumped off him like his body was on fire.

"What's the matter?"

"Nothing! Nothing, I just have to go to the bathroom right quick. I'll be right back."

I ran to the bathroom and stood there trembling. My dick was rock hard and my underpants were wet and sticky. How fucking embarrassing is this? I locked myself in the bathroom for at least ten minutes, maybe even twenty, trying to get my breathing under control, willing my boner to go down.

When at long last I came back into the room, Man 1 said, "Why don't we start with you? Just lie down."

As instructed, I lay facedown on the bed. He straddled my butt and began to knead.

How can I describe the miracle of those hands on my body? Of lying beneath this man, the focus of his undivided attention? He went to work on the muscles of my neck, moving eventually to my shoulders, his elbow niggling beneath my shoulder blade. His strong fingertips pressed into each vertebra, releasing fear, releasing shame, finally releasing in me something that felt like hope. Maybe it's strange to say, but there was hope—that maybe someone understood what I was going through, and could help me believe that my same-sex desires weren't wrong, that they were just as natural and essential as my heartbeat.

When he rolled me over, I was no longer ashamed of my arousal. My erection strained at the opening of my new Capezio jockstrap and dance pants. His mouth was warm and he engulfed my entire shaft in one motion. It didn't take long for me to blow. Like half a minute. If that.

He went to the bathroom and got a warm washcloth. When he returned he was fully naked. Gently he wiped the semen from my stomach and crawled into bed with me. We spooned. I felt his own erection press into the crack of my ass. It was larger than mine, thicker than mine. It was like Bernie's, and from long experience, I knew what to do.

He had been so kind to me. It was only right to return the kindness, wasn't it? The size of him almost gagged me. But as with Bernie, I willed myself to relax, to breathe through my nose and take it all in.

And after what happened in the next thirty seconds? I didn't feel so embarrassed anymore. I realize that in today's times what happened to me in that hotel room in Baltimore was wrong. We didn't know that then, though. We little gay boys didn't get to have regular coming-of-age experiences with our peers, for many of us had to hide our true nature from one another. Very often our sexual exploration and liberation came by way of older, more experienced men teaching us how to love ourselves without shame. Man 1 was an important figure to me in my journey toward self-acceptance, so in other words—it was then, and has always been, all good!

CHAPTER SIX

*D*id this muthafucka just low-key ask me to suck his dick? Really!?!? I
came to him for guidance, I came to him at my mother's behest. Homosexuality is an abomination. I get it. I hear it every week from the pulpit, from
our government, and every place and space I go. Religious and government-
sanctioned homophobia is all I know. I been prayin' for the Lord to take this
out of me my whole life. I didn't ask to be born like this, but I was, and God
don't make no mistakes, right? So why is my mere presence on this planet so
reviled? My mother is concerned about my salvation. I understand that. It's
all she knows; hell, it's all I know. She asked me to go to a preacher to talk, to
pray the gay away. I was all for it. You think I wanna walk around this earth
living an abominable life? I wanna get into heaven just like the rest of them.
I don't want to lose my mind, but I'm holding on to my sanity by a thread. I
may need to let these church folks go. My stepfather molested me for years and
nobody did anything about it. Not one person around me was holy enough to
step up and protect me, and I'm the abomination. And now this muthafucka
essentially just asked me to suck his dick! He's a preacher, he was supposed to
help me pray the gay away. Clearly, I gotta save myself!

* * *

In the spring of 1986, I saw in *Backstage* magazine that *Dreamgirls* was hosting open-call auditions in Chicago. Reading that ad was like being touched by lightning. I felt the electricity in my bone marrow. And from that moment on, it was as if a fever had taken hold of me. I had to be there. I'd find a way. I would somehow get to Chicago and audition, so I could be in *Dreamgirls* and out of my house forever.

The audition was on a Friday morning. I don't remember why, but by sheer chance, I had that Friday off from school. I also had spending money from the many jobs I'd worked up to that point. So I told my mother I was spending the night at a friend's house.

That Thursday evening, I packed an overnight bag, took a bus to the Amtrak station downtown, and bought myself a round-trip train ticket. Then I rode that train all night, for thirteen straight hours, all the way to Chicago. I arrived Friday morning with my sheet music, my dance clothes, and an address. I soon found myself at the top of a huge prewar skyscraper overlooking Lake Michigan. The floor was empty, or so it seemed to me. And then I found the room. No one else was there.

I couldn't believe it. Nobody wanted to audition for *Dreamgirls*? No one understood the impact of this musical on me . . . on the world? I sat on the floor for about fifteen minutes, and just as I was about to give up, two men showed up, one Black and one white. I would soon learn that the white man was Vinnie Liff, founder of Johnson-Liff casting in NYC. The Black man was Weyman Thompson. He had not only played the character of Curtis Taylor Jr. in the national tour of *Dreamgirls*, but also was what we would call the resident director of the piece. Michael Bennett, the director-choreographer, had handed over the reins to Vinnie and Weyman to preserve the integrity of the work as first-class productions were now being staged all over the world.

As soon as the pianist arrived, I was called in for my audition. I belted out "Just Once" by James Ingram, one of my favorite R&B ballads. When I finished singing, Vinnie Liff gazed at me with an expression that made me uneasy. I'd seen that look in a thousand pairs of eyes. It was the gaze of an adult in the presence of a precocious child.

"That was quite something, young man," he said. His tone alarmed me further. It was gentle and paternal and somewhat patronizing. "Your voice is simply amazing. How old are you?"

I felt I had no choice but to lie. The breakdown specified that applicants had to be eighteen to twenty-five. I was sixteen.

"I'm eighteen, sir."

"That's . . . wonderful," he said carefully. "And . . . did you have the day off from school today?"

"Oh, yes, sir. I did."

"Where do you go to college?"

"Well, actually, I'm still in high school," I told him. "I'm a senior." Another lie. I was a junior.

"All right. Then where do you go to high school?"

"I attend Taylor Allderdice and the Creative and Performing Arts high schools in Pittsburgh."

His eyebrows shot up. "You're from Pittsburgh? Then why are you in Chicago? Do you have family here?"

"No, sir."

"You just happened to be in Chicago?"

"No, sir. I—I came for the audition."

He leaned back in his seat with a sidelong glance at Weyman. "You came . . . from Pittsburgh . . . to Chicago for *this* audition? (What I came to learn later was that Actors' Equity, our actors' union, requires Broadway producers to have open casting calls every six months whether they need to or not. So—they really didn't need anybody. This was just one of those required calls.)

"How did you get here?"

"I took an Amtrak train last night, and I just arrived this morning. I came straight here, and I'll be getting back on the train to return to Pittsburgh once we're finished."

Vinnie let out a long, low whistle. "Wow," he said. "That is some kind of dedication, son. It's going to serve you well."

"Thank you, sir."

"Well, I wish I could offer you a job on the spot, but the reality is that, as talented as you are, you're just a little bit too young."

"But I'm eighteen!" I said, hoping I didn't sound as frantic as I felt. "The breakdown said the age range you're looking for is eighteen to twenty-five."

"Yes. Yes. I get it. You're 'eighteen,'" Vinnie said. "However, you are far too young for our show. But I want to tell you something." Now he looked me straight in the eye and spoke with a low, level intensity that I knew was heartfelt and sincere. "Keep going. Your talent is extraordinary. And with a drive like the one you've shown us today, you will be fine. Continue to work, continue to train, and come back to us real soon."

His words were kind, but they were no comfort. I knew no argument I could summon could possibly change his verdict, but I stood there for another moment anyway, tossing ideas about in my mind for some way to alter this disastrous outcome. It couldn't all be over just like this, could it? After I'd come all this way? My heart felt like a trapped bird beating its clipped wings inside the cage of my chest, and I could feel the hot tears building behind my eyes. Somehow I managed to hold it together as I took my leave of the audition room.

But I wept all the way home.

* * *

Upon my return to Pittsburgh, I threw myself back into my studies. I knew that I had to get better. I needed to get out of my circumstance. And if I wanted to succeed, I knew I needed to be the best. Like Mommy always said, "You gotta be ten times better than your white counterparts to even get in the room!" There needed to be no question when I arrived at an audition, any audition, that I was the only one who was right for the part.

One night, after a very late evening class at First Side Studios, I had a decision to make. I could take a single bus straight to my neighborhood, which would leave me with a ten-minute walk to my house. Or I could take two buses, the second of which would drop me just a few steps from my door. The risk of the latter plan was that, during the transfer, I would have to wait for the second bus in Homewood, one of the worst neighborhoods in the city. But on that particular night, I was too exhausted to care. I'd taken six dance classes that day. My legs were trembling with fatigue, my body depleted. I just wanted, as my auntie used to say, to "crawl up under the bed"!

So there I stood at 11:00 P.M., under the bridge, waiting for the 74A bus to take me home. Within a few minutes, I noticed a gang of boys across the street, walking up the hill. The first sight of them didn't inspire any real alarm. But then, after having walked several blocks in the opposite direction, they crossed to my side of the street and headed back in my direction, and suddenly I understood they were coming for me.

What I'll never forget about that moment is how fateful it felt. There was no surprise at all. I'd been waiting for, bracing for, this moment all my life. The whole world had told me from my earliest memory that I had it coming, so how could watching them walk straight at me feel like anything but a foregone conclusion? I had no energy to fight back. Not even a will to run. There was nothing to do but let them come.

"Yo," the ringleader said as they closed in on me. "Don't you go to that faggot school up the street?"

I knew he meant CAPA, which was in the neighborhood.

I met his eyes with fire in my own. "I don't know what faggot school you would be referring to."

I was feeling myself. I wasn't gonna be a fucking pussy for these people anymore.

"You know what faggot school I'm talking about, faggot," he spat.

The boys surrounded me. There were six of them.

"I go to CAPA high school, if that's what you're referring—"

BAM. It felt as if I had been slammed across the face with a two-by-four. I hit the ground. They punched, they stomped, they slurred. "This is what you want, faggot. This is what you get, faggot. This is what you get for getting smart, faggot. This is what you *GET*, faggot!"

After several blows to the head, I lost consciousness. I don't know how long I lay knocked out on the sidewalk. When I woke up with my face against the pavement, I was alone. And I was cold—so cold, bone cold, though winter was over. It felt like I'd been run over and then dragged along the cement. My head was throbbing, my body battered.

But what hurt the most was the first thing I registered when I pulled myself up on one elbow. There was a gaggle of people across the street—onlookers, observers—who had watched the whole thing and done nothing. They were still standing there, looking at me, and now they walked off without a word. No one so much as asked if I was all right or tried to help me in any way.

Slowly I struggled to my feet and dragged myself to the gas station a few blocks away. In a phone booth near the pumps, I called my mother. Blood dripped from my face and spattered the metal floor of the booth as I asked her to come pick me up and bring me to the hospital.

My mother cried when she saw me. I hadn't seen my own face yet, but soon I would see that it was a mask of dried and oozing blood. My eye and jaw were swollen and my face was black-and-blue.

The diagnosis was a black eye, a fractured jaw, and a fractured rib. All the doctor could do was tell me to go home and heal. "Just get some sleep, and for the next few days, try to rest as much as possible," he directed. "You should be healed in about a week or two."

What kind of healing? How do you heal from living every day of your life in a society so hateful and dangerous you can't even walk down the street in peace? How do you heal from something like that?

The next morning I was slated to star in CAPA's annual recruitment show, an abridged version of *Much Ado About Nothing*. Just as in my middle school days, my role was mine alone. No one was assigned to be my understudy. The show would be seriously compromised if I stayed home.

At 6:00 A.M., I woke up as usual and made myself breakfast. My mother, baby sister, and I were silent as we sat at the table together. MaryMartha Elizabeth Ford is my sister's full name. We call her M&M for short. She's ten years my junior. We have different last names because we have different fathers. Bernie was hers. She was so young during alla this. I didn't want her to be freaked out by my bruises and wounds. I wanted to show her strength and resilience. So I made the conscious decision to keep the shit movin'.

When I gathered my things to go, I saw the terror in my mother's eyes. Her whole body was trembling as she said, "The doctor said you need to rest. I think you should stay home today."

"I can't," I told her. "Mommy, I can't. If I stay home, they win. I'm not goin' out like that!"

I felt her eyes on my back as I made my way to the side door. But when my hand was on the knob, I turned and spoke over my shoulder. "I'll never stop doing what I'm doing. I'll never stop being who I am," I seethed. "They don't like it, they're going to have to kill me."

And then I was gone.

That day was a turning point in my life. It marked the moment I stopped caring about making anyone else comfortable with who I was. I performed in front of hundreds of schoolchildren that afternoon with a black eye, a bruised face, and a fractured jaw. If someone asked me what happened, I told them the truth. But even more telling was what I left unsaid. The mere fact of my presence and participation carried a clear message to everyone around me. And that message was: I am in your midst, without apology. I'm here to stay. I'm here as I am. And if you have a problem with that— *fuck you!*

I would go on being precisely who I was. I wouldn't let anyone take my life or my work away from me. Never again would I apologize or hide, or attempt to be something I wasn't.

I wanted everyone to see my face. To take in the blood and the bruises. Bear witness to the hate and the cruelty. See what the world does to a person who's different.

Look at it.

Own it.

And, y'all, fix that!

CHAPTER SEVEN

As my junior year of high school wound down and I turned my sights on the summer, I was hoping for an upgrade. Within my previous job at Kennywood, I'd performed those six daily shows outside, under a high tentacled ride known as the Monongahela Monster, separated from the audience by a moat—and spotlit by the sun. As temperatures rose, the direct sunlight and sweltering heat became more and more oppressive.

The upgrade I hoped for would let me perform in a different park with a higher budget, where I could dance indoors. I had seen the performance venues at other parks: Cedar Point Busch Gardens, Kings Dominion, and Geauga Lake. Child, these people had *shows*. With costume changes—real costumes, and a wardrobe staff (our Kennywood costumes were mainly culled from the Gap, and I had to wash them by hand every night and hang them to drip-dry because the motel we were housed in had no laundry facilities). Disney, along with all these other parks, had started holding auditions in Pittsburgh for their upcoming summer seasons.

I would get a permission slip from my mom to leave Allderdice early and go downtown for these auditions. I loved to audition: It was the chance to prove what I could do. I still love it. When the children doubt your ability, the only thing you can do is prove them wrong, and that happens by the slayage you serve in the audition room. The one that slays, stays.

But every audition was the same. I would sing and be called back. Dance and be called back again. Then I'd be kept with a small group of performers until the very end of the audition day, when the casting staff would tell us, "Congratulations, you are all in our files and we'll be casting very soon. Expect to hear from us."

I waited for months. But I never heard from any of the other venues. When May came around and I hadn't received any offers from the other amusement parks, I accepted the offer on the table and went back to Kennywood. It was all good; it was fun, and it was what I knew. So there I was: biding my time with my six shows a day, staying at the motel, and then one morning when I arrived at work, it was apparently Family Day at Kennywood, because Mommy, M&M, and her father, Bernie, had come to enjoy the park and watch me perform.

At first it was a nice day. The family was together. They saw my shows. But then during a break, the three of them separated. My stepfather and my sister, who was now six years old, decided to rent a paddleboat for half an hour while my mother waited in the outdoor audience area. It had become harder for her to walk unassisted. Though she would eventually need a wheelchair, she still got around with a walker then. But right now she wanted to rest.

So I left her in her seat with a funnel cake, cheese fries, and a Pepsi. On my way to the dressing room, I spotted Bernie and M&M paddling their boat in the moat between our stage and the rest of the park. And very suddenly, at the sight of them together, a great wave of nausea broke over me. I had no idea why. I ran to the nearest trash can and emptied my stomach of the lunch I'd just eaten, and then I just stood there, trying to make sense of the state I was in. What in the world was going on? What was wrong with my stomach and why was I trembling and sweating?

And then I saw them again, caught another glimpse of them as they paddled into view. *Oh. Oh. Oh my God. He touched me. Oh my God, I was naked, he was naked, we were in my bed and he was touching me. His dick was in my mouth. Oh. My. God!*

And then right on top of these thoughts came another that was more terrible still, displacing all the others. *What is he gonna do to her?*

It didn't occur to me in that moment that somehow I'd managed to go four straight years with no awareness of the abuse. I'd blocked it out, disassociated myself, hadn't remembered it at all. I'd separated myself from the trauma and compartmentalized it in order to survive. And now it had all come flooding back to me because I saw my sister—my sister at six years old—with him. This man who was supposed to protect us. What was that? Who was he?

Somewhere within this vertigo of confusion and unanswered questions, I had a singular sliver of clarity: I had to take care of my sister. I had to know she was going to be okay. I didn't know whether my stepfather was a repressed, closeted gay man or an equal-opportunity pedophile, but I couldn't afford to wonder without action a minute longer.

And so I told my mother. Right then and right there. I went directly back to where she was sitting on that bench and said, "Mom, Bernie molested me."

My mother looked at me, her face a blank of shock and incomprehension. "What?"

"Bernie sexually molested me."

"What are you talking about?"

"For years. It went on for years. From age seven to twelve. It happened all the time. And . . . *I'm gay!*"

The back of my sweet mother's head blew off! She had no way to process this information. She had grown up in a sheltered religious environment where this kind of thing was never talked about or acknowledged. It happened all the time, but no one ever spoke the words out loud. I spoke them out loud.

"He touched me, and more. And I'm not telling you this because I want you to do something about it now. I mean, there's nothing to be done. For me, I guess. But I'm telling you so you'll watch out for M&M. You need to protect your daughter."

Then I had to bolt back to the dressing room to change my costume, lest I miss my next show call.

And that was that. We never spoke of it again, or at least not for a very long time. They watched me perform over the course of the day and then went home as if nothing were ever said, as if this new information had no significance.

But nothing was the same for me. The lever of memory had been pulled, and there was no escaping the cascade of images that came to me unbidden at all hours of the day, no matter how hard I tried to shut them out. I was thankful, so thankful, that I could live at that motel all summer. But after that—somehow, some way—I had to make it through senior year.

As I had so many times before, I hatched a plan for my own survival: no contact. I would fastidiously avoid any contact with Bernie. When I got home in the evenings, I'd enter the side door of my home and go directly downstairs to the bedroom we built together. I would sequester myself there until the following morning. And then I would leave again.

Bernie's schedule had him leaving the house for work from 4:00 P.M., returning around midnight. So, as it happened, I never had to see the man. I went for a period of months, from September through March, in which I saw my stepfather a total of four times, and even then, it was just in passing. I made sure I was never in the house—that my schedule was so packed I never had to see anyone or think about anything. Wake up, go to high school, then to CAPA, then to dance classes. Or a job, if I had a gig. Or a party, if it was the weekend. I would do anything to avoid going home.

Senior year had gotten off to a rough start when I was inadvertently placed in an AP calculus class I had no use for and no reason to take. When I filed a request to be transferred out, the guidance counselor was at a loss for where to put me instead. I had already fulfilled all the academic requirements I would need to graduate. So I very gratefully accepted a study hall, which allowed me forty-five extra minutes in my impossible schedule in which I could study or sleep.

Alexandra Berger was the first person I met in study hall. Allderdice was a big school, and I had never seen this girl before. She was so pretty, with warm blue eyes and long, curly brown hair. We were both artists. I think that was what drew the two of us to each other.

Study hall became our time to talk. About everything: life, love, family, hurt, disappointment, pain. Within the first week, she told me about her older brother. "He goes to NYU," she told me. "He's in the theater program."

And somehow, though nothing explicit was said, I was pickin' up what she was puttin' down. Alex's brother was gay, and she sensed that I was gay too, and it was okay.

Soon afterward, I asked her to be my date to the prom. I didn't want to send anyone mixed signals and I didn't know who else to ask. She was pretty, she was my friend, and I knew we would have a ball. She said yes and another potential problem was solved.

Alex was the last of her siblings left at home, and her parents had just moved to an expensive contemporary home on Mount Washington with floor-to-ceiling windows overlooking the resplendent Pittsburgh skyline. The family went out to high-end restaurants once a week. Alex was allowed to bring one guest, and that guest was always me. Not just once or twice but every single week for a year. Angels. *Again!*

Martin and Judy Berger were the kindest of parents. They were present, they listened, they engaged. They worked their asses off to give their kids the childhood opportunities they likely never had. I think back to my time with the Bergers so fondly because they didn't know it, but they were teaching me skills I would need, including fine dining. How to order. Which fork or knife to pick up first and how to tell a red wine glass from a white wine glass. I had so many questions that were answered over the course of those evenings. What was a haricot vert, a filet mignon, a balsamic reduction? What was arugula? Alex and her family have been lifelong family friends ever since. They were supportive of me from the start, and I will never forget it.

* * *

Midway through my senior year at CAPA, Peggy Hughes all but yanked me into her office one afternoon. Lenora Nemetz was already there.

"What is it?" I said. "What's the matter, what I do?"

"We heard you think you're going to New York City once you graduate."

"Yes, that's the plan."

"Well, you're not. You're going to Carnegie Mellon."

"That school down the street?"

"That school down the street has one of the best drama departments in the country," Peggy snapped.

Lenora chimed in. "Billy, you're immensely talented. You're one of the best singers I've ever heard, and now you're a phenomenal dancer as well—"

"But every time you open your mouth to speak, it's a disaster," Peggy shaded.

And then in unison they declared: "And you must learn how to act!"

"Well, okay . . ." I said, taken aback. "I mean, I trust the two of you . . . and I do want to learn to act. But if I do go to college, I don't want to go here. I'll apply to somewhere outside of Pittsburgh. I want to get out of here. I need to get out."

"The program at CMU is a conservatory," Peggy told me. "It will be as if you're not here. They will take all of your time. You'll start at eight in the morning and end at midnight every night for four years. Trust me. Not even you will know you're in town. Auditions are in a couple of months, so we need to get you prepared. One classical monologue; one contemporary monologue. One dramatic and one comic. Two songs to sing, and you'll take a dance class. That's the audition. There are a couple of other schools you should apply to as backup. We'll let you know what they are shortly."

"Well, how am I going to pay for all this? College is expensive."

"There are ways. There are loans, grants, scholarships. And you are a candidate for all of them."

My audition for CMU was at the drama department of the university itself. I performed my two monologues for one of the acting teachers in the program and my two solo songs for one of the voice teachers. I took a dance class with the head of the dance department. And as I was collecting my things to leave afterward, a tall older gentleman approached me.

"May I speak with you for a moment?" he asked.

"Absolutely."

He pulled me into a side room, the orchestra room, filled and stacked to capacity with instruments. "I just wanted to inquire as to which other colleges you're applying to, and how seriously you're considering ours."

"Does . . . does this mean I've been accepted here?"

"Well, unofficially—yes."

I stood there for a moment, stunned and overcome. Then I repeated this information, trying not to sound as incredulous as I felt. "I've . . . definitely been accepted . . . at CMU? On the spot, right here, right now?"

"Yes," he said again. "We would love to have you at Carnegie Mellon, and it's my responsibility, as the head of financial aid, to find out how we can assist you in accepting."

"Well, I'm glad you asked that," I told him. "Because the school that gives me the most money is the school I'll be attending."

He asked if I'd been accepted anywhere else. I had: the Cincinnati Conservatory of Music and Northwestern, but neither had come through with a financial aid package yet.

He smiled as if this was good news. "Then we would like to be the first."

My mother wept with emotion when I was awarded enough scholarships and grant money to pay my own way to college. I was the first in our extended family to be college-bound. She had put the highest priority on my education, and now it seemed her dreams were being realized. As for me, I felt a profound sense of validation. I'd fought for the chance to pursue my heart's delight, and now that investment was underwriting my college tuition.

By mid-spring, I was more or less in a continual state of elation. My immediate future was secure and my permanent escape from home was in sight. The end of the school year held a sense of liberation and abandon.

And then, after a Saturday evening gospel choir concert at my church, I pulled up to the house at about 2:00 in the morning. It had been an electrifying night of gospel music and worship, followed by socializing with cousins and friends for many hours afterward. We did this all the time—attended some church function and then headed over to the closest Eat'n Park, a local twenty-four-hour diner franchise where we sat and talked and fellowshipped with each other, sometimes long after midnight. I had no curfew to speak of, especially when I was at church and my mother knew where I was.

So I thought it strange, when I pulled up in front of my home, to see every light ablaze inside the house. I had succeeded in essentially hiding from my family for the past six months. My schedule was so full I'd scarcely seen any of them. But when I came in now, my mother accosted me in the living room. She was in a near frenzy. "Where have you been?"

"I'm sorry?"

"Where have you been? It's two o'clock in the morning!"

"I . . . I was at church," I told her, bewildered. "You knew where I was."

My mother was agitated. She was shaking and sweating and filled with rage. "Don't talk back to me! Where were you?"

"I was at church," I said again. "I was hanging out with the gang. We went to the concert and then to Eat'n Park afterward like we always do."

"Don't backtalk to me!"

"I'm . . . just answering your question," I said. "You asked where I was and I told you. Why are you yelling at me?"

"It is two o'clock in the morning. You have Sunday school tomorrow morning. You need to be on time! I can't believe you would come in here this late."

"I always come in this late after gospel concerts! I'll be up for Sunday school—you don't need to worry. I know that's what you want and I'm on it."

"It's not what I want," she snapped. "It's what the Lord requires of you."

"Okay."

"Boy, you know what time it is?"

I heard his voice. And there he was in the doorway. Bernie, my stepfather, in his boxer shorts and no shirt, his grossly distended belly hanging over the waistband. He was holding a belt by the buckle, and it dangled at his side. "Boy, you know you ain't supposed to be coming up in here this late. What is wrong witchu?"

I had no words for him, but it seemed he had more for me.

"I'm about sick of you, comin' in and out of this house as you please, cain't speak to nobody, acting like you grown, acting like you run things around here."

I summoned all my will to not say a word or react in any way. I didn't understand the drama unfolding around me, but I felt the need to resist being swept into it.

My mother's eyes were wild. She was wringing her hands and rocking back and forth.

"You see that time over there . . . ?" Bernie persisted, pointing to the clock on the mantel. "Two-thirty A.M. That means you just got yourself three months' punishment. No television privileges, no extracurricular nuthin."

"Oh, so you tryin' to parent somebody now!?" The words heaved out before I could snatch 'em back.

"What you say to me, boy? You think you grown enough to talk back to me?" He cracked his belt.

I stood firm and looked him straight in the face. "Oh, you gonna beat me now? That's what you think you're gonna do?"

He cracked the belt once more and stalked toward me. I was immovable. We squared off, eye to eye.

"If you hit me, you better kill me," I said.

He blinked but didn't back off. "What you say? What you say to me, boy?"

"If you hit me, you better kill me."

Silence.

And then my mother shrieked, "Tell him!"

I turned to her in alarm. "What?"

"Tell him! Tell him what you told me at Kennywood! Go on! Tell him what you told me he did!"

"Uh . . . no . . . no, this isn't the time—"

But even as I was sputtering, Bernie broke in. "Whatchu talkin' bout? I didn't do nothing to this boy! I didn't do nothin' to him that he didn't have coming to him!"

"That he didn't have coming?" my mother repeated, dumbfounded.

"Something's wrong with him! Something ain't right with him in the head! He ain't right, somethin' about him ain't right. I didn't do nothing to that boy he didn't have coming to him. It's a lie. He's lying to you."

"Lying about what?" I flung at him. "See, you just told on yourself."

This hung in the air for a moment as Bernie registered his mistake, but soon enough he recovered himself and resumed his rant. "He's a liar! He wants to destroy us. He wants to break up this family!"

"What family? This family is a farce."

"You will respect me in my house! So help me God, you will respect me and you will respect your mother if you ever plan to set foot in my house again."

I looked around the room: at my mother, my stepfather, this home that held so much trauma. "My mother will always have my respect," I told him. "But you? You mean nothing to me."

And I turned without another word, went downstairs to my room, and locked the door.

Within two months' time, I would move out to work at Kennywood for one final summer, to be followed by college in the fall. I don't ever remember speaking to Bernie again, until that day in the hospital.

CHAPTER EIGHT

"You okay this morning?" my husband asks me.

If I'm being honest, I'm in a fog. I've been in a fog for months. It's like . . . every moment of every day I'm swatting away demons from the past.

I'm not sleeping well. My mind doesn't stop. I have to take a white-lady pill and chase it with a nip of tequila or scotch or something. Something to knock me out. So as to rest.

But apparently I'm not resting so well. My heart hurts. I can't breathe.

Over three million cases of coronavirus in this country and rising. People are dying. Hundreds of thousands of people have already died. They lie to our faces. The facts no longer matter. We've been quarantined, sheltering in place for months. Fifty million people have filed for unemployment. The economy has tanked. George Floyd is dead. The people are rising up.

Thesamethesamethesamethesamethesame. Sixty-one thousand new reported cases in twenty-four hours.

I can't catch my breath. My head hurts. My heart hurts. It races.

"You okay, babe? You were tossing and turning all night. You stole all the covers. You nailed me in the head with your elbow."

"No. I guess I'm not so good." The tears stream. "I'm not so good at all."

* * *

It seemed like I auditioned for every summer stock theater in the country in my sophomore year at Carnegie Mellon. My entire musical theater class loaded ourselves in cars and stormed the Civic Light Opera ensemble auditions in downtown Pittsburgh. CLO was the big get. It was one of the last true summer stock companies left. Which meant six shows in six weeks. Those who were blessed with that gig were set up for the entire year. It offered a total of seven weeks of intense work. There was a singing ensemble of ten and a dancing ensemble of ten—five men, five women for each, twenty ensemble players in total. The ensemble, aka the chorus, were the constants of the season. They populated the background of all six shows, while the principal players were jobbed in for specific leading roles. Some of the lead actors were cast in multiple roles in a season, but for the most part the leading players were transient.

To be in the ensemble of Pittsburgh CLO was the highest of the highs in terms of prestige, 'cause not only did one acquire their Actors' Equity union card (which would allow them into Broadway auditions in New York), but after the seven-week musical theater marathon they also got one year's worth of medical insurance!

I had been a CLO Mini Star when I was fourteen. I only did one year and then booked that gig out at Kennywood park that paid a qween. Every year in between, I would put myself through the grueling two-week audition process. Young hopefuls would flood the Benedum Center rehearsal spaces from musical theater programs all over world! (Mainly just the tristate area and a smattering of performers from up and down the East Coast, but, I mean, the shit was coveted.) And politics-wise, once you were in, you were in. Which meant if any ensemble member wanted to return for subsequent seasons, they were usually automatically grandfathered in. Now let's add the racist infrastructure that allowed for only two—yes, count 'em, *two* chocolate chips out of twenty slots. And those two slots were already filled with Pittsburgh natives Denise Sheffey and David Jennings Smith. They both were trained in opera and, I believe, were arts educators in the Pittsburgh public school system during the academic year. These dolls snatched those two slots and kept them for decades! Which meant my little sassy Black ass never had a shot. 'Cause while my Caucasian counterparts were generally vying for eighteen slots, I was gunnin' for two—that were already quota filled! Ooooh, but a bitch was determined. Because after serving my time as a CLO Mini Star for the year of our Lord 1984, shuckin' and jivin' for the white folks for free, I felt I was a shoo-in for the ensemble when I got old enough for sure. Right? They at least owed me that, right?

The age requirement for the CLO ensemble started at eighteen, for insurance purposes I'm sure, but in my previous experience with employers, getting them to bypass those pesky little child labor laws was my forte, so I began auditioning for the CLO ensemble when I was sixteen. For three years in a row I would drag my happy ass on down to the Benedum Center rehearsal spaces and let them put me through my paces.

I had sailed through all the levels and layers of cuts and callbacks for the previous three years—never booking the actual gig, but I was a pro at the process. This made me very excited, as I now was able to usher in my classmates. My class at Carnegie Mellon was filled with some of the most talented people I had ever met. Ty, Natalie, Jeff, Tami, Natascia, and Jack. The CMU crew came to snatch wigs and get gigs. We all made it through the first cut, the singing. And then we danced. We all made it through the dance cut and were invited back for the final callbacks the following weekend.

At the time, I was playing the role of Mary Sunshine in the Pittsburgh Playhouse professional company's production of *Chicago*. It was a principal role, and I was sharing a dressing room with one of my mentor/angels, Joe Franze—remember he's the founder of the CLO Mini Stars. He's the man who gave me one of my most important learning opportunities. He drove me to and from all the Mini Stars rehearsals and performances, and here I was, a mere five years later, sharing a dressing room with him in a professional production while being a full-time student, making real coin.

I had gone into this CLO audition process fully deciding that if I didn't book the gig this year, it would be my last time tryin'. I was beginning to see the truth. Best man in the room wins? Best person for the job gets the job? Not so much. And as this may come off shady or prideful, I had the luxury of being in the room with my competition and seeing what they had to offer, and I can truly say humbly and with grace that there was no reason I shouldn't have been booking these gigs.

In retrospect, I shoulda known something was up when I sang my sixteen-bar cut of "A Piece of Sky" from *Yentl*. In Barbra's key!

"Are you aware that you're singing flat?" the musical director for the season fired.

I was caught off guard.

"No, I was not aware, because I don't sing flat."

Is this bitch trying to come for me? Is he trying to read my singing?!

There were two other people in the room. One was the artistic director, Charlie Gray, and the other was Wendy Bobbitt on the piano. Wendy was my personal accompanist in my private voice lessons at CMU. I looked to her. Her face was beet red with bewilderment.

"Am I missing something? Was I singing flat, Wendy?"

I caught sweet Wendy off guard. But I know she knew me. She heard me sing every week in my voice lessons. She was the musical director for the Mini Stars. Surely she would help me shut this shit down!

"I didn't hear anything flat, no. You were right in the center of the pitch to my ear over here," she mumbled, barely audible.

"Would you like for me to sing it again? Maybe something is off with the echo in this gigantic room."

"Yes, please. Let's hear it again," he snarked.

I sang those bitches under the ground! There was no way for them to set me up, make it my fault. This is what began to happen to me, and it would be a thorn in my side for decades. There have been many times in my career when I deserved jobs I didn't get—for various reasons: too Black, too gay, too specific, too much. But weep not for me; I'm not the only one whose had these types of challenges. This business is a bitch, and as my friend Nathan Lee Graham always says,

"This business is not set up for you to fail. It's set up for you to quit!"

I ain't goin' out like that!

At the final callbacks the following weekend I and my CMU compadres made our way down to the Benedum. After six hours of a grueling audition day, everyone was brought into the third-floor rehearsal room for the final cut. Everyone who makes the final cuts does not necessarily get the gig, but whoever doesn't make it goes on file as alternates for the season if one of the ensemble members has to drop out. We had just finished doing a very simple jig to "Get Me to the Church on Time" from *My Fair Lady*. It was the dance combination for the singing ensemble, so, truthfully, with all them classes that the white folks was givin' me for free—the little pedestrian jig they served us was a piece of cake. I aced it, and of course I would make it through to the final cut. I was standing next to my sista-girlfriend Patricia Phillips. She was mixed-race and had broken through the racist glass ceiling and been in the ensemble for three years already. Her racially ambiguous slot was solidified. They called names. In alphabetical order.

"Pat Phillips, John Preston . . ."

I started to hyperventilate.

"I just got cut," I whispered to Pat. Tears already streaming.

"No, you didn't, that's not possible." She tried to comfort. She was in the room. She saw my audition. Cutting me just didn't make sense to anyone with functioning eyes and ears.

"They just cut me. The names are in alphabetical order. I gotta go!"

I grabbed my things with my head down and rushed out of the audition room and locked myself inside a bathroom stall. I didn't want to cry. Those bitches never deserved my tears. But I was gutted. I was embarrassed. Every one of my classmates made it through to the finals, and they cut me.

Why was I crying? Why did I care? I knew there was a world beyond CLO. I knew it was some bullshit. But it hurt so bad. I just wanted my Equity card, just wanted my ticket out. But . . . nothing. I was called back to the end of every audition. I was "put on file" and never heard a word. Always the praise. Never the gig.

A few months earlier, a musical director at a Disney theme parks audition pulled me aside and told me the truth. This musical director was from Pittsburgh. I had worked with him. He knew my gifts.

"Don't ever come back to Disney. In my inside opinion, they will never hire you," he muttered to me in a covert corner outside of the audition room.

"Why?" I gulped.

"You're too good for them. You're too special. They don't want special. They want bland, mediocre, people who fit into . . ." He trailed off.

"White!" I barbed. The color drained from his already alabaster face.

"They want somebody white, right?" I barbed. And after a deep breath, the musical director simply answered, "Yes. White." And he was called back into the audition room.

There was a knock on the stall door.

"Billy, it's Ty. Let me in."

Ty Taylor was the other Black boy in my class at CMU. We were instantly brothers from the first time we laid eyes on each other at a dormitory welcome party freshman year. He is still one of my besties to this day. He fronts a rock band called Vintage Trouble. He's a fucking rock star! Always has been.

"Fuck them! You don't need this CLO bullshit! You know it's bullshit, right?" He hugged me tight.

"I don't understand. What did I do? Why do they hate me so much?" I wept. Ty cupped my face in his hands. Forced me to look into his eyes.

"You know what this is about. Neither one of us is gonna get this gig. They already have their quota. Now you get to go and enjoy the rest of your day and not waste your time. Come over tonight after alla this mess and I'll cook us some dinner."

The following Tuesday night as I beat my face for the gods to play Mary Sunshine in *Chicago*, Joe Franze entered our dressing room and sat down beside me. He rubbed my shoulders and in a very optimistic, reassuring tone said, "It took me ten years of auditioning to get into CLO. It will happen for you. In due time."

I looked at the reflection of this beautiful soul in the mirror. My mentor, my friend. And as I put the finishing touches on my character's drag queen face, which one reviewer described as reminiscent of a young Diahann Carroll, I simply stated, "I don't have ten years of my life to waste. Thank you, but no."

* * *

"Your voice is too high for the American stage and you'll never work."

I sat, stunned, looking dead into the eyes of the new head of the Voice and Speech department at Carnegie Mellon. She was a broad of a woman;

I always liked that. Strong women were in my wheelhouse. But this was something else.

Earlier that day I had received a letter from the school at my apartment—the apartment that I paid for with my own money—addressed "to the parents of William E. Porter II." These "letters" were a big deal back in the day. Nobody wanted to get a letter. Fat letters to the girls were a big one. Butch-it-up gay letters to all us sissified qweens. And, of course, the more traditional progress-report letters, which came in tiers: 1. Warning. 2. Probation. 3. Final probation. 4. Advised to withdraw. Now, make no mistake: "advised to withdraw" means "yo' ass got cut!" Dismissed. Sent back to wherever you came from, soiled in "you'll never be a serious actor" loser shame.

Being a freshman or sophomore in the School of Drama at Carnegie Mellon in the eighties was like being a target in the dunk tank at a carnival, always on guard to be dropped. My freshman class at Carnegie Mellon started with about sixty students. Four years later we graduated seventeen. The system was brutal. The struggle was real. Anything could get you lettered; anything could get you cut. Even things you had no control over. Like my queerness.

Mine was a "final probation" letter for Voice and Speech, and it had arrived out of the blue, with no warning. No nuthin'. So I paid a visit to the new department head, and I couldn't believe what I was hearing.

"I suggest you take a year off. Maybe take up smoking. Go to New York—you may get yourself a job and not even *want* to come back!"

Is this bitch for real. Is she really trying to come for me? Kick me out of this place? I put four years aside to learn my craft. To prepare myself for living the life of an artist. This is the place that's supposed to teach me how to do that. I know I'm not the greatest actor in the world, but I'm here to get better. I'm here every day, on time, working my ass off to do whatever it is I'm supposed to do, and I'm on final probation?

Telling me to pick up smoking . . . I'ma punch this bitch in her neck! 'Cause now she's fuckin' with my scholarships and grants. I have to keep a particular GPA to keep this money so I can stay in this program!

Hot tears streamed down my face, sending a false message that I needed her comfort or some shit. She reached out to touch my hand. "Are you okay?" I snatched it back.

"Don't touch me! Don't condescend. Don't pretend that you care. First you tell me that I'll never work on the American stage, and in the next breath you say maybe I'll get work and not even want to come back. Which is it?" My body was trembling.

"Well . . . I mean—I didn't mean that you won't work at all, it's just the *type* of work you'll do," she deigned to say, tossing a bitch crumbs, I suppose. I had to shut that shit down.

"Listen, if my voice is 'too high for the American stage' now, in December, that means that it's been too high since we started working together in August. Correct? So why am I just hearing about this now?"

She gagged! These white people aren't used to being questioned, being called out on their bullshit.

"I have been to every single class this semester. On time! I have engaged. Why am I only hearing of this now? And with *final probation*? No warning letter, no probation letter first?"

She got that red-faced thing that white folks get again, that skin change very often brought on by embarrassment and shame.

This bitch has no idea . . . I am not the one!

I leaned in for this next part.

"And just so we're clear, it costs twenty thousand dollars a year to attend this university, and when the bill comes due, it comes to me! I pay these bills! Not my momma, not my daddy—*me!* So if you feel like something is wrong with me, something I need to fix . . . if my voice is *too high* for the American stage, I pay you people to fix it! So do your job!"

My next stop was the office of the head of drama, Liz Orion. I stormed past the executive assistant and swished and swirled right up to her desk. She was clearly frazzled by my rage. I did catch her off guard.

"What is this about!?" I said as I slammed the probation letter down on her desk. She feigned amnesia.

You're the head of the department. Y'all have y'all's meetings about us all the time, so you know damn well what I'm talking about.

"And now I'm getting a C-minus in talking and a B in singing!? I know my acting ain't so great and I'm working on that, but this attack on my voice is unacceptable!"

Liz perused the letter. "Billy, this is just a formality. Please don't take this personally."

I swear to God, the back of my head was gonna blow off!

"My scholarships and my grants to attend this school depend on me keeping my grades up, and I pay these exorbitant bills by myself, so it *is* personal, 'cause this is fuckin' up my shit! So, formality or otherwise, I'ma need this fixed! Now!"

"Well, what would you have me do?" Liz hemmed.

"First, you need to get her straight. I don't deserve this grade and you know it and she knows it."

Liz sat silent. Contemplative. Sobered. "I'll handle this."

And that was it. I stood up to the bullies; I looked them dead in their eyes and I won. But I wasn't finished.

"And one more thing . . . this B grade that vocal hack of a woman masquerading as a voice teacher has given me also needs to change. A B . . . in *singing*? I'm gonna need that upgraded to an A, and I need to be transferred to a different voice teacher for next semester."

A B in singing . . . ? For real . . . ? The fucking nerve!

Why is it always my fault? When folks don't understand me, they just go on the attack. Trying to silence my voice, squash my natural instincts. Anything I say, how I walk, how I sit, how I move my hands and arms are all in the attack zone. I miss my angel Myrna Paris. She was a great voice teacher. She heard me sing and embraced the voice I have. I met her in the ninth grade and she nurtured me. She honored what she did not understand and truly leaned into helping me heal from my vocal nodes and learn how to use my unique vocal power in a healthy way.

Lee Cass was another angel. He spent the entire first semester of my freshman year at Carnegie Mellon researching my voice. He was amazed that my voice could do the things it could do. The heights it could reach, with full belting power. He would stand in front of me with both of his hands on my throat as I sang the highest and the loudest that I could. Perplexed and intrigued, he set out to figure out this extreme vocal type that he had never encountered before. End of freshman year Lee came to me, so excited. He had found the diagnosis, a logical, definitive description of my voice—in a book!

"You're a tenorino!" he exclaimed in his basso profundo that rattled the walls. "Which means you're the highest of the highs that a man can be. And though you're considered to be in the counter-tenor and castrati-tenor family, your voice is not a light, falsetto, head-voice sound. You can belt up there naturally and healthily." Rather than try to shape me into something safe, something he knew, Lee celebrated me for my gifts, for who I was.

* * *

I spent the summer in between freshman and sophomore years working at Hartwood Acres, performing in their summer stock season, which included a featured role in *Tomfoolery: The Music of Tom Lehrer* and then a minor role in John Guare's *House of Blue Leaves*. I say all this to let y'all know that I was livin' and giggin' and even though my family was a mere twelve-minute drive from campus, I took no initiative to see them. Especially Bernie. I figured after our last confrontation I should probably exit . . . stage *out!*

On the spring morning of April 19, 1989, my phone rang at 5:30. Now this was back in the day when telephone etiquette dictated that if your phone rang after midnight, something was up. I picked up the phone groggy and annoyed.

"Hello?"

"Hey, son, I know it's early and I'm so sorry to be calling, but your father is in the hospital."

"Who . . . ? Bill . . . ?" I asked my mother with irritation.

My father . . . ? Please. Father of what? Last time I saw him was at that Thanksgiving dinner with his new family where he made me drink red wine (for the body of Christ) and I threw up and he beat me and locked me in a bedroom where I picked up the phone and called you to come and get me. So why on earth would you think I would care about this man?

"Not Bill. Bernie."

"He's not my father. Don't call him that!"

"I'm sorry. I know, I'm sorry. Listen . . . I know you two have had your issues—"

"Issues?! Oh, that's what we're calling it now?"

"I don't know what you want me to do. I don't . . . I'm trying to . . . I'm just calling because I thought you might want to go and visit him in the hospital."

My heart started racing. I couldn't stand being in the same room with this man for the last five years. In what world would my mother really think that I would want to visit him, alone, in a hospital!? She went on to tell me the story of how he came home from work acting strange. He went and lay across the bed for about an hour or so while she prepared dinner. As legend would have it, he came into the kitchen, asked my mother to call 911, put on his coat, and stood outside on the corner to wait for the ambulance. By the time she drove herself to the hospital, early test results showed that he had suffered a minor heart attack, and they were gonna keep him for observation.

"Well, is he all right!?" I popped.

"Yeah, looks like he's gonna be just fine."

"I have class all day. I can't miss. Tell him I said hello."

I hung up the phone. I was sweating. My body was trembling. I couldn't catch my breath; I couldn't get back to sleep. So I got up early and prepared for class. I worked on my scene for Voice and Speech dialects class. High British. My favorite. I've always felt like a high-mighty-white-woman in a previous life, so my friend and classmate Eric Woodall and I chose the Gwendolyn and Cecily scene from Oscar Wilde's *The Importance of Being Earnest*. I couldn't focus in my morning classes, my afternoon classes, or any classes for that matter. I finally called my mother and asked her to come and get me on my lunch break to take me to see him. He was groggy when I came into the room, hooked up to lotsa medical machines. Mommy made me go in alone. So there I was, sitting beside the hospital bed of the man who . . . who . . .

"Hey, son."

"Hey." I bristled.

"So good to see you."

"Good to be seen."

Bernie shifted in his bed a bit, trying to sit up. I helped him. He squeezed my hand in his and looked me in my eyes,

"I'm proud of you, son. I'm proud of who you are. Keep being you. Don't ever let anybody take that away from you."

"Okay . . . ? Thank you . . . ?"

I don't know what I'm supposed to say. Was that an apology? Is he trying to atone? He's never spoken to me like this, ever. I've never heard him speak with this kind of emotionally focused language. I didn't think he had the capacity. Maybe there's a chance for a healing . . . maybe . . .

"You take care of yourself and we'll talk more when you're outta this place, okay?" An attempt at being comforting.

"I look forward to that day." He smiled. Present. Vulnerable.

The rest of the school day is a blur. I remember being assigned to the stage crew of Henrik Ibsen's *Peer Gynt*, a five-act play that would be performed over the course of two days. We were in tech rehearsals, which can be torturous, especially when you've spent the last two school years paying your dues: building sets, hanging lights, sewing costumes, running crew . . . Nobody wanted to run crew, which meant you had to sit backstage, or in a light booth, or swing from a grid high above the audience operating a spotlight for the duration of the performances. This was my last stage crew assignment. It's a long play, about white people (most everything is about white people), staged in the abstract, which meant the crew was integrated into the performance. That meant I had to put on a ridiculous Norwegian pantaloon situation and wave a huge piece of thick aluminum in the air to produce what would sound like thunder. Needless to say, my heart wasn't in it. All I could think about was Bernie . . . and our conversation, dare I say connection . . . ? A space to heal . . . ? I'm here for that. Ready to broker forgiveness. Talk about the why. Break the cycle. Maybe get to the bottom of alla that mess.

Mommy kept me abreast of how Bernie was doing. She said he was getting better. She said they were ready to move him out of the ICU and into a step-down unit. My phone rang at 5:30 A.M. the morning of April 20, 1989. I knew before I even answered the phone what the news would be.

"Bernie's dead." My mother spoke in a fogged whisper.

"What? How?"

"The doctor said he had a ruptured ascending aortic aneurysm."

"What's that mean?"

"I don't know. It was a massive heart attack, from what I can gather. The nurse told me he was crackin' jokes all day. Had the entire floor in stitches. She told me she gave him his last dose of meds for the day around nine P.M., and by the next morning he was gone . . ."

* * *

I have this wall; I have this block. I can't have sex with someone I'm in love with, or who is in love with me. I can only fuck strangers. This is not a good thing for a marriage. He loves me. I know he does. I can feel it, but I can't receive it. Don't know how. I want to know how. I'm tired of this. It's been forty years! Just forge ahead. Keep it moving. Never look back. I've been so good at compartmentalizing my trauma, and that has served me for decades. My art saved me. Kept me focused on something tangible . . . ish. I want to trust love. I'm trying. I'm trying so hard. This pandemic has had one silver lining: I've had a minute to breathe, to take stock, to look at my life from an observatory position and make some changes. Deal once and for all with the Bernie of it all, the fact that he dumped his shit on me, whatever it was, and then died. He peaced out. Leaving me, leaving the family, with the wreckage. Shit I still gotta deal with in my fifties. I'm so tired I don't know what to do. This trauma therapy is hopeful. My therapist made me count. She's asked me how many times Bernie came to my room. I told her at least twice a week. She said, "I'm no mathematician, but two times a week, fifty-two weeks a year, for five years . . . That's over five hundred times. It's time you metabolize your trauma and grief." We been sheltering in place for months now. I've managed to stay sane. We're managing to heal ourselves inside of this pandemic. I have been and will continue to tell anybody who will listen that "the world stopped so that we could heal our marriage!" Lemonade outta lemons, right . . . ?

* * *

The summer between my sophomore and junior years at Carnegie Mellon's School of Drama, I couldn't get any summer stock work in my hometown or the surrounding areas, so I decided to come to New York. My college roommate Natalie and her family offered me a sofa in their duplex in the Bronx for a few weeks—I think that's the last time I was even *in* the Bronx until filming *Pose* season two, when production moved from Brooklyn to Silvercup Studios there.

Anyway—I figured if I wanted to be in show business, I would have to get out of Pittsburgh and come learn to navigate the big bad city, learn the subways, the audition spots, the temp agencies. I was not in the actors' union yet, so there was a process for being seen at auditions. Actors' Equity had created a loophole that would allow non-Equity actors to sign up at the beginning of the day on a wait list. The idea was that after all the Equity actors had been seen, they would move to seeing non-Equity actors on said wait list. The challenge was that if the show was popular, all the day's slots would be filled with union actors and we, the riffraff, who had been waiting patiently since the 6:00 A.M. sign-up time, were shit out of luck. I was obsessed with the trade paper *Backstage* (I had been receiving my weekly subscription in Pittsburgh since I was fifteen). It came out every Wednesday at midnight, and I would scour its pages, circling my dreams with a highlighter. I couldn't see any reason why I wouldn't be cast in one of the musical theater obsessions of the time, be it *Les Miz* or *Phantom of the Opera*, but they weren't hiring Black folk for those shows back then. Tommy Tune had a duo of happy darkies "daba-daba-dabing" over at *Grand Hotel*. And Mrs. Huxtable (the inimitable Phylicia Rashad) replaced Bernadette Peters in *Into the Woods*, but that don't count. She was America's momma. She transcended race. She put butts in seats. So here I was, nineteen years old, trolling around New York City trying to find my life. I ran out of money in a month and decided to Greyhound it back to Da'Burgh to . . . I don't know; I really didn't know what I was going to do. But on the subway to Port Authority with alla my luggage in tow, I found an audition in *Backstage* for a summer stock production of *Joseph and the Amazing Technicolor Dreamcoat* that would be performing in the town of Montclair, New Jersey, just thirty minutes outside of the city. Rehearsals would start in two weeks, and I was already late! I checked my luggage in the holding section at the Port Authority terminal on Forty-Second Street and marched two blocks west to where the audition was being held. I joined the dance call midway through and slayed the children. I was asked to stay and sing. I informed the people in power that I had a Greyhound to catch and needed to sing first. They let me sing, and then offered me the job on the spot! I bussed home to Pittsburgh for two weeks and came back to live with my college buddy Ty Taylor and his family, who just happened to live where? . . . wait for it . . . *Montclair, New Jersey!!!* Can you even imagine how perfect? Talk about the Universe conspiring for our good!

First day of rehearsals. Michael Del Bianco was the sassy one. The sexy one. Overflowing with life's joys and possibilities. It was a split cast. Union actors vs. non-union. And the room was split in that way too. Being non-union is like walking into a school as the new kid, in the new town, midyear. No one talks to you. You're treated like you have the plague, and all you want to do is disappear. Delby crossed over the aisle. He came over to me on the first day of rehearsal and proclaimed, "Well, aren't you just the sweetest little chocolate morsel." Delby was strapping. Delby was gorgeous. Delby was my first Fairy God Gay. I didn't know shit from shinola; my clothes were cute, but I didn't have a place to wear them. Until now. The fourth Sunday in June was coming up. High Holy Day for the Gays—and Delby had a plan. A group plan. He made it plain that we were all to meet in front of St. Patrick's Cathedral on Fifth Avenue and Fiftieth Street the following day at 11:00 A.M. "Don't be late, bitches!" I was late. Wasn't no GPS smartphones back then. A bitch had to write directions down on a piece of scrap paper and hope for the best. I walked up just as our group was beginning to march down Fifth Avenue.

People were chanting on the sidelines with banners: *Homosexuals are possessed by demons. God hates America. God hates fags.* I felt like I was in slow motion. I had always known what the church thought about me. My family made that clear. They had just not spewed the hate in such a direct way. Well, aside from declaring that AIDS was God's punishment for the gays.

One sign had the word *GAY* placed vertically like an acronym: *Got AIDS Yet.* I couldn't breathe. There was a big mass of back-and-forth chanting. I bobbed and weaved through the valiant crowd, but I couldn't find my friends. I was just about to leave when Delby grabbed me by my arm: "I told you not to be late, Qween! Here!" And in one motion he swooped a T-shirt over my head that said SILENCE = DEATH, dragged me by the ear to the front of a group chanting *"Act up, fight back, fight AIDS,"* and we were off. At war. And I was enlisted. We marched down Fifth Avenue. (It's a march, not a parade! Get that shit straight!) I went from theater queen to gay activist in 3.5 minutes flat and never looked back. And we been fighting ever since. Thirty years later . . . ? Those of us who did survive know how to fight to the death. Past it. But we don't know how to live . . .

* * *

That September, Delby threw the 5th Annual Miss America Beer & Sock Extravaganza. You know the queens always have to have a theme. I took a Greyhound from Pittsburgh for the weekend. What is a Miss America Beer & Sock Extravaganza, you may ask? She's exactly what she sounds like. I walked into Delby's apartment and there was a mountain of rolled socks in the middle of the room. "What are the socks for?" "You'll see," he said. Fast-forward to the "Talent" portion of the televised beauty pageant. You can see Miss Kansas's mouth moving in her ventriloquist's dummy act. *Blam!* A barrage of socks pelts the TV screen. The queens taunt, "What's the matter, bitch? Too many dicks, too little time? We want Vanessa Williams back!" If Darcel Wynn from *Solid Gold*, Rick Astley, and the entire male underwear model section of *International Male* had a baby . . . this was the baby shower. The qweens would caterwaul all over each other. It was simply heaven!

A week before Thanksgiving 1989 I got a call from one of the *Joseph* boys, who said Delby was asking after me. I needed to come see him.

"See him where?"

"He's at St. Vincent's. Room four-fifteen."

Ground zero. Fuck. I didn't even know he was sick. I went alone. I caught the Greyhound. His food was outside his door on the floor. I picked it up. Went in. He didn't hear me. He was glued to the TV. He was camouflaged in purple lesions. Skin paper-thin to the touch. He was maybe a hundred pounds soaking wet. So weak he could barely muster the energy to speak. He didn't know who I was. I kissed him. He smiled. He knew. I fed him. He struggled to swallow. I rubbed cream all over his body. I snuggled into bed and held him as we watched *The Golden Girls*. Dorothy Zbornak was his favorite. Laughing turned to hacking . . . and hacking . . . and hacking. Violent. Chilling. I was nineteen years old. A bona fide soldier. I called for the nurse. She was kinder than the nightmare stories I had heard. It was time for me to say goodbye. I kissed him again. He thanked me. "I love you." "Ditto," he said with a smirk. He mumbled something barely audible.

"What did you say?"

"Remember to live . . ."

Two weeks later he was gone.

CHAPTER NINE

C ivil rights icon John Lewis has been "called on to see the Lord," as the old folks would say. I had the blessing of meeting him on a couple of occasions. Once backstage at the Human Rights Campaign dinner back in 2016, back when we all had hope, back when the world seemed sane. It looked as if we were finally going to elect a female president. Who the fuck else would it be? Hillary Clinton dedicated her life to public service. She spent eight years in the White House with her husband. She became a senator for the State of New York. And then lost the presidential nomination to a Black man. For eight years we had a Black president. I still have a hard time believing that actually happened. And this post-Obama-lyptic blacklash is in direct response to the fact that white folks had to take orders from "the nigger" for eight years. And yes, I said nigger! 'Cause their actions say it all!

My second chance meeting with civil rights icon John Lewis was at the 91st Academy Awards ceremony in 2019. The night Ms. Porter broke the internet in that Christian Siriano tuxedo gown seen—and gagging the children—the world over. They call it iconic; I call it "all in a day's work." In any event, I was invited to be a host/correspondent on the red carpet for ABC. The network had called to talk about the dress a week prior. It all happened very fast; I didn't even get the invitation until two weeks before the gig. It just so happened I was the first individual ambassador for New York Men's

Fashion Week, representing the Council of Fashion Designers of America (CFDA), at that very moment. And as luck would have it, Christian Siriano had me sitting front-row with all the celebrity ladies. My brain was on overdrive. What was I going to wear to the Oscars? This is my Idina Menzel/John Travolta-said-my-name-wrong-on-the-Oscar-telecast! I remember seeing my Broadway sista-friend representing Frozen with a performance of "Let It Go," and the businessman in me logged the moment. I actually said, to myself out loud, "Somebody needs to say my name wrong at the Oscars!" It's showbusiness's biggest night. The Super Bowl of the arts, if you will. I remember dreaming and scheming with my drama classmates back in the eighties while having Oscar watch parties, vowing to wear a gown instead of the traditional penguin suit, and here I am. The time is now. I thought I was joking. I never thought I would have the option of wearing a gown to the Oscars, but here we are. This is the moment the universe has been preparing you for. This is that moment—to do all the things you've been claiming you've wanted to do for all these years. And as I was captivated by the breadth of Christian's design aesthetic of inclusion and diversity, it came to me . . . If the first shot the world sees of me is a close-up that looks like a traditional black velvet tuxedo, and then the camera pulls out to reveal a full-on antebellum hoop skirt/gown situation—all the world's edges will be snatched! And snatched they were. And even with alla that, I never could have predicted the impact that the image of a Black cis-gendered gay man in a gown at the Oscars would have. I now speak of my life in halves: B.O/A.O., Before Oscar/After Oscar.

In any event, there I was at Oscar rehearsal, and my personal segment producer handed me the five prepared questions for my interview with Congressman Lewis—yes, I was to interview John Lewis! My hero! Unfortunately, I must say I was gobsmacked by the frivolity of the prepared questions and I made my displeasure known.

"I can't use any of these questions," I declared to my white producer.

"Why? What's wrong with them?" he asked, with true concern.

To which I replied, "I will not be that Black faggot in a gown at the Oscars who is bestowed the gift of being in the presence of civil rights icon John Lewis and asks him what kind of movies he likes to watch in the movie room on Capitol Hill!"

How very dare they. I don't care where we were or what we were doing; there was a lack of respect inside the molding of those questions that I found disquieting and offensive. This man was a walking piece of history. He carried an entire movement in his being. These facts must be honored.

"Well, what would you ask instead?" my producer offered.

I thought for a moment about the state of our country. I thought about Election Night 2016 and the trauma and terror I live with every day under this administration. I thought about the young John Lewis marching arm in arm with Martin Luther King Jr. across the Edmund Pettus Bridge and risking his life for the freedoms that I, a gay Black man in America, get to benefit from. I thought of Congressman Lewis's plea on the floor of the Senate in favor of marriage equality, and on the night of the Oscars I proudly asked:

"Congressman Lewis, I know the Oscars may not be the time or place for politics, but I must ask you, for those of us who are feeling activist, resistance fatigue—what would you say to us to encourage forward momentum and engagement?"

Congressman Lewis's eyes lit up, he gave me that knowing look, and he clicked right in. "We can neva give up! We can neva give in! We must resist! We must fight for what's right. Equality for all!"

. . . or something like that. I don't have access to the ABC archives so I can't give you his words verbatim. All I know is, I got to touch the hem of his garment, and that is enough.

Congressman Lewis's words are on my mind. This death count just keeps rising. And our government continues to act as if it's not happening. This Orangina muthafucka is showing the world, through his actions, that he cares nothing for the people. He would rather we die than have the entire country wear a mask. Wearing a mask during this pandemic has become a political act, and half the country supports this fool.

Every day the virus gets worse and worse and the administration disseminates misinformation to the people, like injecting bleach to cure the virus . . . I mean—you can't make this up. But it's the people who are in danger. We the people suffer. Essential workers, frontline personnel . . . ? Lots of Black and Brown folks in those jobs. And Black, Brown, and poor people are dying at a disproportionate rate, and nobody in power does enough to stop the spread. No national plan. No mandates. Y'all are on your own.

AIDS, AIDS, AIDS . . . that's all I can think about. This is how they treated us. Like we deserved to die. Like AIDS was God's punishment. The generation we lost. The artists, the friends, the family, the church member who they said died of cancer when I knew damn well what he died of. I could tell just by lookin' at him. Everybody could tell. There was a look. A very specific look. The weight loss. The shortness of breath. The wasting. The Kaposi sarcoma lesions . . .

* * *

Billy Wilson was covered in them. I had gotten that "you need to get to the hospital now" call again. Billy was my favorite teacher at CMU. He was there for us Black kids. He was an adjunct professor, and from what I can remember about his history, he'd started as a ballet dancer in Europe somewhere. He was married to a woman and had two children. His daughter Alexis was two years ahead of me in the drama department at CMU. Through the years he had become a well-sought-after director/choreographer, choreographing and setting ballets for prominent dance companies here in America and abroad—companies like Alvin Ailey American Dance Theater, Dance Theatre of Harlem, and Philadanco. His Broadway offerings included *Bubbling Brown Sugar*, *Eubie*, and the all-Black cast of *Guys & Dolls*.

The myth, the magic, the legend that was King Billy Wilson reverberated through our hallowed halls a full semester before he would grace us with his glory in the spring of 1988. I was a freshman, and generally freshmen were not given access to the special professors. But my class was fierce. We had the largest number of musical theater majors the university had ever seen, and we did *not* come to play. Our assignment for our first class with Billy was simply to prepare an A and B selection for him to choose between upon meeting us. I prepared "Pity the Child" from *Chess* and "A Piece of Sky" from *Yentl*. Billy chose the latter. And I let him have it! Having spent the entirety of my freshman year quite cognizant of the skills I lacked in other areas, with acting class being my main source of insecurity, I leaned into my superpower, my singing voice. My weapon against all danger. My shelter in times of storm. I blew the roof off the joint with my offering. *Have I mentioned I sang that shit in Barbra's key?*

"So what," Billy eviscerated. I was in shock.

"I'm sorry?" I stammered.

"Did I stutter? I said so what?"

"Okay?" I muttered. Gutted. Longing for guidance.

"Listen, you have one of the best voices I've ever heard. You can sang! But you don't know what you're singing about. You need to figure that out. Next!"

And that was that. There was no special "Black people" treatment from Billy Wilson. I don't know why I would even think or hope for such a thing. Billy tough-loved us Black kids, almost to the grave. He made sure to care for us without babying us. He demanded our best every day, all day! Full-out was our only form of communication and/or connection with Billy. He was known for snatching solos from folk who thought they were fine holding back, saving it for the stage or quite simply "marking" in rehearsal. You got one warning. "I need to hear it," he would advise, peering over his glasses. "If I can't see it in the rehearsal room, what makes you think I'ma trust you to deliver on the stage!" Another angel. Challenging us all to excellence. Preparing us for greatness.

Now here I was again, at ground zero, St. Vincent's in Greenwich Village, saying goodbye to yet another friend, another mentor, another angel. A Black man in my life who loved me as I am. His meal sat on the floor outside his room. He was asleep when I arrived. I didn't want to wake him; he looked so peaceful. And for those of us who lived through the AIDS crisis—there was no peace. Just . . . death. I spent twenty minutes sitting silently by his side. Trying to feel the pain. Maybe understand what to do with my rage. Billy died within the week. There's not a week that goes by when I don't think of him and how he tough-loved me to be the best version of myself even when the bar was preposterously low.

"You're gonna have to hold yourself to a higher standard, 'cause most people around you won't be able to tell the difference, whether you're fakin' it or not. Don't fake it!"

* * *

I told my mother no. It had been three years since I had set foot in a church. My art was my church. My god was within. I was on the road to reconciling my gayness with the hate spewed from the bully pulpits of my childhood. Religion is man-made. Spirituality is divine. *Oooh, that's good . . . stay with that . . . keep questioning.* See, I learned early on that questioning religion garnered two abrupt responses: shaming and/or banishment. I had already been shamed and banished for asking a question about the reach of God's love in Sunday school class when I was ten, and wearing a green afro wig and singing an Aretha Franklin tune at Kennywood park when I was fifteen, so there you have it—no love lost. I actually enjoyed the unspoken exile. I count myself as one of the lucky ones, one of the ones who broke free from what very often can be a life's worth of debilitating stagnation. I've seen it. I felt it happening to me. The Christian othering, the soul-salvation bullies. The shame that keeps one bound up in a prison of their own mind for a lifetime. The hypocrisy of church folk was dangerous and deadly to me, and I could see that fact plain as day. Mommy couldn't. She was caught up in the spell. She had nothing else; it was all she'd ever known. "You gotta believe in something, or you'll fall for anything," she would say. The Bible seemed to comfort her. Going to church two to three times a week plus twice on Sundays was the way she surrendered to her lot in life. i suppose church was a space to hope. To pray for that blessing. To pray for and believe that the Lord would provide a physical healing that never came. Can you imagine . . . ?

In the fall of 1988, Archie Dennis, founder and pastor of the Lord's Church, requested my presence to offer an A and B selection at the Pittsburgh Believers Convention. Fun fact: Pastor Dennis sang in the choir that backed up Aretha Franklin on her live gospel album, *Amazing Grace.* The point being that Pastor Dennis was an amazing, trained singer, and an artist at heart. He enjoyed a good gut-bucket church squall just like the rest of us, even though he was bougie. He was classically trained. He studied opera. Yes, Pastor Dennis was one of the first African-American preachers in Pittsburgh to dream big, break with the traditions of the storefront Black church, and create something that looked more like what we saw the white evangelicals doing on television. The likes of Jerry Falwell, Billy Graham, Jimmy Swaggart, Oral Roberts, and Jim and Tammy Faye Bakker. Those pioneers managed to organize, mobilize, and commercialize religion, and Mommy was mesmerized by the word of the Lord squawking through those white men from inside that idiot box. I wasn't having any of it. My past had cured me of any desire to receive validation or care from the so-called saints of my congregation or any man-made religiosity. I looked around at twelve years old and realized there wasn't an adult in my life who was equipped with the tools to help me, support me, see my pain, see my abused and wounded soul. *No, not one.* So by nineteen, operation "save-a-sissy" was in full swing!

Something in my spirit was screaming, *Bitch, why would you even think about doin' some stupid shit like that? A megachurch, during a weekend convention? With over three thousand sheep waiting for the shepherds to lead them . . . ?* But my mother was so sweet, attempting to be supportive of me. She tried with all her might to understand this artistic wild child she had birthed. A few years prior to this event, she'd dragged me to a special service at this very same church when they were hosting visitors from a church in New York. Apparently this church was founded by all show-biz folks, and my mother was on the lookout for a church home for me to attend when I would inevitably move to the Big Apple. The only problem was, when I met these New York, show-biz church folk and started talking to them in person, I came to find that none of them were still in the business. They all spoke like Stepford Wives in a somewhat monotone fashion, with glassy eyes and a bit too much religious "compassion." I was not bothered or fooled, but I was excited to see my mother happy about fusing my art with my possible salvation—because as I was getting older my relationship to the church and the people who populated the church was strained and phony at best, and I wasn't good at hiding my disdain. They saw me as an abomination, I experienced them as hypocrites, and there was no love lost on either end. My mother observed this and was worried about me. I love her for that.

Church folk can be the worst. Church folk can be petty and mean. They can make a person feel worthless, empty, and alone—all in Jesus's name. They were always shady to my mother. Lots of folk treated her like she was stupid because of her disability. She was othered in the only space she felt remotely safe, the only space she knew. I understood and respected the importance of the space for her, which is why I tried to stay in the church for as long as I could, but by the age of sixteen, I simply couldn't take it anymore. I felt used, 'cause I was fine with everybody when I was singin' in church, but the minute anybody found out I was singing outside the church I was branded "not of God." I felt like I had a scarlet *S* on my chest that screamed *sissy sinner.* I would become so enraged every time I had to sit quietly in the pews while every single pastor, preacher, minister, missionary, evangelist, and prophetess condemned "the homosexuals" as an abomination to be cast into the pits of hell for all eternity, and said that AIDS was God's punishment for choosing that sinful lifestyle.

It's not a fucking choice, you assholes! And good people are dying for no reason. People I know, people who are my friends, people who live by the principles of Christ more than any of y'all up in this sanctuary. And all y'all holy Christians stood by and did nothing about the shit I endured at the hands and . . . cock of my stepfather, for five years, and none of y'all did nuthin', none of y'all saw nuthin'? Nobody sensed that anything was wrong with a twelve-year-old riddled with stomach ulcers? Nobody thought to pry, to ask me why? Nobody thought it strange that I had nodules on my vocal cords at thirteen and couldn't sing for six months, couldn't speak for the first three? Nobody? 'Cause the Holy Ghost is gonna fix it? And I'm the sinner? Pastor up here having a Saturday afternoon delight in his back study with my mother's best friend, and when they get caught, Pastor literally with his pants down, she has to apologize in shame in front of the entire congregation while he sits on his pulpit-throne with no accountability or consequences required or applied. I see y'all. I see alla y'all.

Like my grandma used to say, "You can't be so holy that you're of no earthly good!" None of these church folk were any good for me, so I was on my way out of the church. I found my art, or my art found me. However you slice it, I had been blessed to be given a gift that allowed for me to step outside the confines and strictures of my religious bubble and find the space to dream beyond my circumstance.

So the nail in my church sissy coffin was the weekend of Pastor Archie Dennis's Believers Convention. This was a Friday-to-Sunday Christian weekend retreat replete with all-day breakout sessions and evenings dedicated to special services with guest preachers and various Christian and gospel music acts. I had agreed to appease my mother and accepted Pastor Dennis's invitation to sing—he'd called to ask me personally. There were a few thousand people in attendance, and at this point in my church singing life, I had been burned way too many times from relying on the unknown musical acumen of whatever musician was in the building. So I wised up, cut my losses, and began bringing musical tracks, which I would purchase from the local Christian bookstore, to accompany myself. I have high musical standards and learned from experience that not all church musicians are at my level. No shade. Just facts.

My mother was sitting up in the front. She loved sitting in the front. Third pew, left-center, was her favorite spot. I was a bit tardy, as I had scene study rehearsal that morning. I slid inconspicuously into a pew three-fourths of the way back in the makeshift sanctuary. It was a Sunday afternoon and I had the star musical slot of the closing service, right before the sermon. This is always an important moment in a church service, because it's the moment that is meant to open up the hearts and minds of "the saints" and prepare their spirits to receive *a word* from the Lord. I showed up. I sang my two songs: Sandi Patty's "Upon the Rock" and Larnell Harris's "How Excellent Is Thy Name." I used my voice to anoint the congregation, as I had learned to do starting with my first solo at Friendship Baptist Church when I was five. My plan was to slip in and slip right on back out so I could get back to my schoolwork.

A white preacher woman was the guest closing speaker for the convention, and the moment Pastor Dennis introduced her, she rose to the raised pulpit and she spoke directly to me:

"Brother Billy, I need to talk to you for a minute."

Thousands of congregants went silent. You could hear a pin drop. My stomach sank to my toenails. Her voice cut through the silence like daggers through my heart. I been to this movie before. I knew what was coming. I couldn't move my body.

"Come on up here and sit on this front pew." I was paralyzed. "Come on now, be obedient to the word of the Lord."

I stood and slowly plodded down the center aisle of the convention center to the front row, alone, emotionally naked.

My mother's eyes were downcast as I passed her on the way to my crucifixion. She had done this to me again. She had put me in harm's way in Jesus's name. I finally reached the front row. I sat, obedient and pissed!

"Brother Billy, the Bible says in Matthew 7:14, 'Because strait is the gate, and narrow is the way, which leadeth unto life, and few there be that find it.' Brother Billy, the Lord told me to tell you that every time you come into the house of the Lord you are to sit in the front row. You wanna know why? Because if you sit in the front row every time you come into the house of the Lord, it will keep you on the straight and narrow!"

This bitch think she slick!

"You have been blessed with a great gift, and it is to be used for the edification of God's glory. Anything else you try to do will fail."

Is this bitch cursing me now? Somehow she thinks God has chosen her to be the judge and jury of my life? Well, I got news for you, Honey—quiet as it's kept, I have my own relationship with God, and He or Her or They or Them or Whatever doesn't need a third party to communicate with me. I have a direct connection to spirit—TRUST!

Of course, my mother feigned oblivious-realness when I confronted her about the pastor crossing the line. Once again, she couldn't see the blatant attacks on my humanity; and I say *once again* because she was too on the inside to see the microaggressions wielded at her own self, so how on earth was she ever gonna see offenses hurled onto other people? How was she going to see that every time I set foot in a church building, somebody would inevitably be shamin' and blamin' the gays?

"That woman outed me and cursed me all in the same breath, in front of all of those people, and I need you to know that I know exactly what she meant to do. But I'm not the one. As of right now, I will be removing myself from harm's way. I won't be attending any more churches with you anytime soon."

She cried, "I'm sorry, son."

"No need to be sorry. It ain't your fault. But I'm done—and I mean it."

She got it. She knew. Even if she didn't have language for what was happening to me at the time, she knew deep in her spirit that how the sanctified saints treated me was wrong. From that day forward she has never asked me to go to church with her again.

I let my mother off the hook on this one. Actually, I let her off the hook for everything. Including not leaving Bernie when I told her of the abuse. I mean, what was she gonna do, right? She was disabled. She didn't have no job, couldn't get no job. Who was gonna take care of her and my little sister? What I didn't realize at the time was that I was unconsciously testing her, testing the waters to see if she could or would choose me. Unfortunately, at the time, she didn't have the tools. I'm proud to say that eventually she found them. However, in this moment, her apology would have to be enough.

* * *

Jordan Thaler has been a casting director at the Public Theater, formerly the New York Shakespeare Festival, for over thirty years, and he's a CMU alum. He came to school the first semester of my junior year to do an audition workshop/masterclass discussion with us. We weren't really performing; it was just an informal and informative talk about all that would be required of us to become working actors in the business of show. Unbeknownst to me, Jordan was casting what we call a specialty role for a new William Finn musical called *Romance in Hard Times*. He was looking for an understudy to cover the role of the gospelian, high-in-the-rafters, extreme-singing character played by Victor Trent Cook. I had seen Victor win *Star Search* on television a couple of years prior. He sang down! He is a unicorn, much like myself.

During the previous summer while playing the role of C. C. White in a summer stock production of *Dreamgirls*, my good friend James Stovall had spoken to me about a show he was doing in the fall and how I would be perfect to understudy Victor when the time came. The time had come, and how fortuitous that the casting director just happened to be a CMU alum, and just happened to be coming to my school, to talk to my class specifically.

I was caught off guard when Jerry Dantry, the drama department's musical director, asked me to meet him backstage at the Kresge Auditorium and bring my audition book—Jordan wanted to hear me sing. Jordan was kind, and warm, and encouraging. He is Jewish and a surprising fan of Black music, and by that I mean we talked contemporary gospel. He knew my very specific gospel music heroes: the Winans, the Clark Sisters, the Hawkins Family—Walter, Tramaine, and Edwin, the latter well known because he had a crossover hit with the classic "Oh Happy Day."

I served Jordan Barbra Streisand realness with my ol' faithful, "A Piece of Sky" from *Yentl*, and he was shooketh. He just wanted me to keep singing. I don't remember what else I sang from my book, but I gave a mini-concert that day. Here was somebody with power in the business who was responding to what I bring to the table with amazement. He embraced all of me, just as I am. I was offered the gig. My rehearsals were set to begin the day after the start of winter break, and the goal was to move the show to Broadway. Can you even believe it? Just a year before, I had been maligned by that Voice and Speech bitch tellin' me my "voice is too high for the American stage," and here I was, headed to New York City to work at the prestigious New York Shakespeare Festival on my five-week winter break from school—because of my high voice!

WERK! Broadway, here I come, and the rest of you can suck it! Neva liked you bitches anyway!

I took the Greyhound bus. I don't remember where I stayed. I think I couch surfed for about five weeks. Five weeks is all it took, 'cause when those reviews came out—baybee, I'd never experienced a show closing so fast. Now, in Joe Papp's brilliance, he'd found a way to preserve his New York Shakespeare Festival's (now the Public Theater's) commitment to developing and producing new work. In an effort to protect the creative process and thereby create a safe space for artists to create, Joe Papp extended the preview period for all of the theater's shows. For those who don't know what a preview is—it's when a cast performs in front of an audience while still working on the piece, to fix, change, and adjust things based on how the audience responds. The audience is the last component of live theater, the last scene partner, if you will. The audience will always tell you what's working and what is not. Preview periods for Off-Broadway shows were historically very short, like a week to two weeks at the longest, and during previews for a Broadway show, the ticket prices used to be 30 to 50 percent cheaper than what a normal ticket would cost.

Critics have a lot of power in the theater. Specifically, the *New York Times*. A bad review can obliterate years, decades even, of very hard and personal work and shut a show right on down! I've never understood why a critic gets to become a critic. There are no prerequisites. I believe one has to have been in the theater or studied theater to understand the blood, sweat, and tears that go into creating something from the page to the stage. However, in this day and age a critic simply gets to come in, once all the work has been done, and give their make-or-break opinion. An opinion that, in my opinion, doesn't always hold any weight or make any sense. Most critics at high-profile papers at that time, and even still today, are white men. White men who have never had to exist outside of their immediate, privileged comfort zone. Nor have most of them ever been onstage. Everyone's entitled to their own opinion, and I'm not saying that every critique should be good if the piece one is critiquing isn't. What I will say, however, is that there is a difference between being respectfully critical of something that ultimately doesn't work and just being a dick! Anyway, the highly educated and powerful Frank Rich was the reigning theater critic/executioner at the time we opened *Romance in Hard Times* on December 29, 1989. I will not give any credence to the review; suffice to say, we closed two days later, on December 31.

In the two weeks I had to lick my wounds before I had to go back to school with my tail between my legs, I picked up a *Backstage* magazine and read about an open call for the Broadway megaproducer Cameron Mackintosh's new hit show *Miss Saigon*. Sir Mackintosh came onto the Broadway scene and changed the game entirely. He was a visionary. He was like a modern-day Florenz Ziegfeld or David Merrick, a Svengali of the theater who changed the face of Broadway forever. Prior to Cameron, Broadway musicals sat heavily on the shoulders of star-driven talent, thereby banking on the power of the star to succeed. Cameron changed all that. He made the star of the show the show itself by employing techniques from the traditional branding space. So instead of the marquee saying "Gwen Verdon in *Sweet Charity*," there were just the iconic yellow cat eyes with pupils that, if you look closely, are dancers' bodies, for *Cats*. *Les Miserables* is branded with a little homelessy-looking girl whose face is blended in with the French flag waving behind her. *Phantom of the Opera*'s is a simple white mask. And *Miss Saigon* . . . a breathtaking piece of calligraphy art that looks like a Vietnamese letter, a girl's face, and a helicopter all at once. All iconic. All internationally recognizable. Cameron Mackintosh created what we in the business now fondly refer to as the British Invasion. Before Cameron, a Broadway musical had a shelf life based on the star who was in it. Cameron blew that business model to smithereens, breaking house records with shows that have run for decades all around the world. *Phantom of the Opera* is still running on Broadway, nonstop for over thirty years! *Werk!*

I got to the Equity building at 6:00 A.M. to stand in line. First come, first served. There were so many of us there that the standard sixteen-bar cut of our songs was trimmed to eight. *How am I gonna make an impression with only eight bars? I know, sing till the power of the Lord comes raining down.* "Pity the Child" from *Chess* was a popular "pop" song that was acceptable to theater creative types. And just so we're clear, when they ask for "pop" voices in the theater, they are simply talking about men and women who can sing extremely high . . . and white. They want a "white" pop sound (but more on that later). They cattle-prodded us in herds of ten at a time to stand outside of the audition room with paper walls so thin you could hear every single note of your competitors' auditions. I was tenth in line. Six out of the nine before me sang "Pity the Child." *Fuck!*

The specifications for what makes a good audition song are so exacting. You have to find a song that you can have a sixteen-bar cut of (translation— about thirty seconds). It needs to have a beginning, middle, and end, so that it feels complete and you don't just stop singing in the middle of a phrase or idea. It has to show that you can act. It has to show off your voice in the best possible light. It's a lot of pressure and the pickins' are slim; thus, when you find a good one, *everybody* sings it. "Billy Porter?" The audition attendant called my name. *Well, here goes nuthin'* . . .

Baybee, when I tell you . . . I. Went. Off! The music markings say "ad-lib" when you get to that last note. And ad-lib means sing whatever you want. So I went full gospelian church sissy on those bitches! I thought I did good. I was happy with myself, but as I passed by a girl talking on a pay phone on my way out, I overheard her say, in that way that only privileged white girls who live, breathe, and eat musical theater, with stage mothers who have transferred their failure-in-showbiz trauma onto their daughters, who are extremely talented but you just wanna punch 'em in the neck . . . That bitch was on a pay phone, speaking in that pitch where you *know* she wants everyone to overhear: ". . . there was this guy who was singing 'Pity the Child' all gospelly. So inappropriate!"

It was like the rug had been pulled from under my confidence. *I just made a different choice than alla the white boys who went in and sang it the same way the white man from London sang it on the album. That's not what* ad-lib *means. Ad-lib* means sing what you want. Make it your own. Fuck her! I know I turned that out.

The following Wednesday when I was back in Pittsburgh, back in school at Carnegie Mellon, I finished my very long day and walked home. My answering machine was blinking. I pressed the button: *Beep!* "Hello, I'm calling for Billy Porter. I'm so-and-so and such-and-such from the casting office of blah-blah-blah. Just calling to let you know that you've been called back for the ensemble of *Miss Saigon*, and your audition is scheduled for this Sunday at twelve-fifty at 890 Broadway."

There was no time to take in the good news. I had to plan. How was I gonna get to New York in four days? *I don't have much money, I'm gonna have to take the Greyhound bus. I hate that fucking bus. It's just nasty. This is my ticket. This will get me outta here for good. I'm running out of money and I don't know if I'll be able to afford to stay here for senior year anyway. Go git dis gig, bitch, and you'll never have to ride a funky Greyhound bus again.*

I took the overnight trip. The bus left from downtown Pittsburgh around midnight and arrived in Manhattan around 7:30 A.M. Dropped me off right at Port Authority, right in the middle of Times Square, in the winter of 1990. Second Sunday in January. This is Times Square before Disney moved in and cleaned up Forty-Second Street. The main drag was still littered with sex shops, and peepholes, and drug dealers and addicts and homeless folk. There were four theaters on the block between Broadway and Eighth Avenue all burned out and boarded up. Midtown West is called Hell's Kitchen for a reason. Most Broadway fans, post-shows, would come out of the theater and hail cabs to get out of the mangy Theater District as quickly as their mostly white, affluent feet could carry them. You hear many New Yorkers wax poetic about how amazing the city was before Giuliani "cleaned it up," before Forty-Second Street was Disney-fied, but real talk, I started going to New York in the late eighties, and the clean-up that happened was good for the city and good for Broadway.

The eight-story building at 890 Broadway at East Nineteenth Street was a belt and shirt factory until choreographer Michael Bennett bought it for $750,000 in 1978 with the money he made from *A Chorus Line*. He converted much of it into a rehearsal space to develop theatrical works. It was a prewar building with the biggest rehearsal spaces I have ever experienced. Like half a football field in size, with very high ceilings and huge warehouse doors. A mock-up of pretty much any Broadway set, no matter how big, could be constructed in these rooms so the creative teams in collaboration with the actors could really create work at the highest level. The building was like gay summer camp. Every Broadway show that was worth its salt rehearsed at 890, several shows and several floors at any given time. The elevators were manual and only held maybe eight people at a time. There was a lot of waiting in the lobby, especially those with late spirits, and a lot of using "that elevator!" as an excuse for lateness. It would turn out that I would rehearse *Miss Saigon*, *Five Guys Named Moe*, and *Smokey Joe's Cafe* in these hallowed rooms, but on this second Sunday in January 1990, I was one of two actors called back from the previous week's open call, where it was reported that at least fifteen hundred men came to throw their hats in the ring, and now here I sat in the waiting room with the next tier of Broadway boys—*men* would be more accurate. They were men; I felt like a little boy. They all had Broadway credits already. I did not. Many had been invited through agents. I didn't have one, really. I mean, I was "working" with a very small mom-and-pop type agency that my friend James introduced me to, but I wasn't really *in* yet. I was the newbie. The youngin'. The kid.

They called me in and I walked into the room, where there were at least twenty people behind the table. I had no idea who any of these people were, but I knew they were people I should know. I waved to everyone and greeted the room. They volleyed pleasantries back at me as I glided over to the accompanist to talk him through my sixteen-bar cut of "Pity the Child." *If it ain't broke . . . ? I got a callback singin' in all my sissified gospelian glory, so take that, bitches!* I heard a voice speak from behind the table: "We'd like to hear the entire piece this time, Mr. Porter."

OMG! Thank God I brought the entire song and not just the sixteen-bar cut. Thank God I know the whole song—or do I . . . ? Fuck, what's the top of that second verse? I responded, trying to sound like I knew what I was doing, "Okay great, let me just take a little gander at this lyric for a split second, I wasn't actually expecting to sing the whole song."

"No worries. Take a moment to prepare," the kind voice behind the table replied.

Though I didn't know it at the time, that kind voice from behind the table was the casting director, Vinnie Liff, who I had auditioned for in Chicago years before. I sang those people under the ground; I acted with intense madness and mania, histrionics and apoplexy. When I was finished I received a simple "Thank you. Well done!" And that was that. I caught the next Greyhound bus back to Pittsburgh to be on time for my 8:00 A.M. Voice and Speech class the next morning.

By April, I hadn't heard anything from the *Saigon* people, and there was also international controversy swirling around the production that was scheduled to transfer from London, with Jonathan Pryce and Lea Salonga reprising the roles they originated across the pond. This practice had become a bit commonplace with these transfers to Broadway during the British Invasion era: *Les Miserables* starred Colm Wilkinson and Frances Ruffelle, playing Jean Valjean and Eponine. Michael Crawford and Sarah

Brightman came over with *Phantom of the Opera*, and now it was obvious that the Olivier Award–winning actors of *Miss Saigon* would be coming to storm the Broadway barricades. Only one problem this time: Jonathan Pryce is not Asian, not one bit. And for the yearlong run in London, Mr. Mackintosh decided it was a good idea to tape Jonathan's eyes back using prosthetics to make him look Asian. You gotta remember this was 1990, and the conversation was just starting to change.

To be clear, Jonathan Pryce is an amazing actor and a dear friend of mine to this day—and he was a revelation in the role of the Engineer. But he was playing the role in "yellow face," and a new day was dawning. The Broadway community was in the throes of "nontraditional" casting conversations. People of color trying to work in the theater were even more marginalized then than we are today, very often reduced to one Black man and one Black woman per musical ensemble, sometimes one Asian, sometimes one Latinx, and never anybody disabled (shout-out to the first actress who uses a wheelchair for mobility to appear on a Broadway stage, Ali Stroker, who won the 2019 Tony Award for her portrayal of Ado Annie in the revival of *Oklahoma!*—disabled people get horny too!). Black performers were generally relegated to musical revues, the "it ain't over till the Big Black Lady stops the show" role, or the "magical Negro." Comic relief, enslaved people, maids . . . micro- and macroaggressions may have gone undetected in white privileged eyes, but they were a daily reality for us. An army of BIPOC talent was having no more of this, and in conjunction with our union, a conversation was birthed. Now there was a directive to theater directors, choreographers, and producers to address the disparity in hiring practices surrounding people of color. Racist casting practices were being called out. In 1991, Tommy Tune was essentially forced to hire at least one Black girl to be a follies girl in *The Will Rogers Follies*. Just one. And Jerome Robbins, the genius and notoriously racist director/choreographer, was rumored to have said that Black people didn't have the facility to execute his choreography . . . now my good girlfriend Lisa Dawn Cave was cast in the first national tour of *Jerome Robbins' Broadway*, the only Black woman out of the cast of more than sixty (Greta Martin was the one chocolate chip in the Broadway production). In a note session just prior to opening on the tour, Mr. Robbins informed Lisa Dawn that he was having the costume designer add arms and legs to one of her skimpier costumes, because her dark skin was pulling focus. When Lisa found the courage to raise her hand and ask *the master* why, his response was, "I didn't want to hire you people in the first place!"

* * *

In 1990 you would have had no problem finding a dumbass to say "there was no Asian-American actor qualified to play the part," but that was disrespectful, hurtful, and simply not the truth. Rumors of a possible cancelation were swirling around the world for months. Daddy needed a job post-graduation, so I carried my happy ass right on down to Heinz Hall in downtown Pittsburgh for a *Cats* audition in April 1990. I had auditioned for multiple companies of *Cats* in New York over the past two years plus. I would always make the cut, always make it to the end, get filed, and then never hear anything back. I was an audition whore and always came to slay! I was "typed-out" after the double pirouette (which means the creatives line up all the potential actors/dancers across the stage and we are asked to execute a double pirouette on both sides). This moment is not only to determine "type," which is a yea or nay simply based on one's appearance, but also to ascertain technique. If you fall out of your double turns, you're probably in the wrong place. I executed my double turns to perfection, both sides. I was cut! As I was gathering my belongings, confused and embarrassed, a voice called to me from the audience.

"Mr. Porter, could you stay for a moment?"

Wait . . . did somebody just call my name? I think I heard my name. But they just cut me, so why would they be calling my name . . . ? Boy, that don't make no sense. You must be dreami—

"Billy . . . ?"

Bitch! Snap out of it! They callin' you!

I walked to the lip of the stage with my right hand hovering over my eyes so as to block the spotlight blinding my eyesight, only giving me a silhouette of our jury and judges.

"What are you doing in Pittsburgh?" a very kind, faceless voice asked from the void.

Is this a trick question? Why am I being targeted?

"Umm . . . I'm from here. I live here."

"Oh, I see—we thought you lived in New York."

"I'm still in school here. I grew up here and I'm a junior at Carnegie Mellon!"

Who are these people and why do they know me?

Another voice spoke. British. It was David Caddick, the music supervisor of all of Mackintosh's shows, and he was there with Vinnie Liff (that casting director fan of mine since the Chicago *Dreamgirls* audition). "We don't think you're right for *Cats*," Caddick said, "but we do think you're right for *Miss Saigon*. We were wondering if you might be able to return later this afternoon to sing for us?"

Well . . . look at God!

But I had already auditioned for *Miss Saigon* back in New York, and then there were all those rumors that Mackintosh would pull the plug. "Word on the street is *Miss Saigon* is canceled," I scoffed.

"Don't believe everything you hear," he voiced with an English lilt.

"Everything will be sorted out in due time."

Werk . . . WERK!

"What time should I return?"

"Come back around three. And I was wondering if you could sing something a little less R&B?"

And there it was. Just as I suspected. That microaggression. The dismissal of my very nature, my history, my heritage, my soul. The cast breakdown in *Backstage* says "pop/rock" voices. Turns out what that really means is—sing it like the white boys would sing it. Period!

Oh, but I got sumthin' for these bitches!

I returned to Heinz Hall at 3:00 P.M. to sing. Dressed in my Sunday best, I strutted to the grand piano that was center stage. I placed my music in front of the accompanist and then stood, firmly planted in the crook of the piano with my right hand resting on top for classical effect. I nodded for the accompanist to start. I proceeded to summon the spirit of Luciano

Pavarotti and sang "Nessun Dorma" from Giacomo Puccini's *Turandot*. In perfect Italian. It was a full gag! Edges were snatched! Gauntlets were thrown down!

Don't try me, bitches. 'Cause you just might git yo' feelins hurt!

"Well, I suppose my question has been answered," David Caddick said with a grin.

"Yes, sir. It has!"

* * *

From April to August, I heard no word from that chance meeting, that impromptu audition. I was living in mega-musical limbo. Junior year ended. I worked summer stock. Money had run out, and paying for my senior year at Carnegie Mellon was becoming more and more of a tricky proposition. I needed a gig! And then, the Actors' Equity Association put their foot down and refused to give Pryce a visa, and Cameron called their bluff. In August 1990, Miss Saigon was officially canceled. *FUCK!*

I couldn't afford to live off-campus anymore, so I had to return to live with my mother and sister in my dank and musty basement bedroom. When I left that house, I'd vowed, just as my mother had once in her youth, that I would never return. But here I was, with my tail between my legs, grateful to my mother for taking me in. And not only did she take me in, but she also committed to driving me to school and picking me up late at night so I wouldn't have to depend on wishy-washy public transportation.

The first senior show of the season was *A Chorus Line*. I was playing Richie—the Black one. Film director and Carnegie Mellon alum Rob Marshall, whose credits include *Chicago*, *Memoirs of a Geisha*, *Nine*, and *Into the Woods*, to name a few, was our director/choreographer. He and his partner, John DeLuca, set the show on our class with Michael Bennett's original choreography, staging, direction, and intention. During the first week of the run I got the call from New York. *Miss Saigon* was back on, and the final callback was scheduled for a Sunday, the day after we closed. I packed my overnight bag and after our closing-night performance went straight to the Greyhound station to catch the midnight bus to New York.

The final callback was at one of those rows of smaller Broadway theaters on Forty-Fifth Street between Broadway and Eighth. Old-school style, like you see in the movies! We sang in the morning. We danced early afternoon. They sent us away at the end of the day saying we would hear something within the week. I went back to Pittsburgh, and every time the phone rang my heart would race. My future was hanging in the balance. My coins had officially run out. I would have to drop out of school for my final semester no matter what the outcome. I waited a week and a day.

It was the Monday morning before Thanksgiving, 1990. 10:05 A.M. I was asleep. The phone rang. I popped up with a start, waited to hear if my mother . . .

"Bill, it's for you."

I ran upstairs, picked up the rotary phone on the kitchen wall.

"Hello," I whispered, wiping the sleep from my eyes.

"Hey, Billy, this is Vinnie Liff from Johnson-Liff casting, and I wanted to officially offer you a track in the ensemble of the original Broadway company of *Miss Saigon*.

Mommy stood in the doorway in her nightgown, with bated breath, excited and scared.

I hung up the phone, tears streaming down my face . . .

"I got it!"

Mommy praise-danced and intoned.

"ThankyouJesusThankyouJesusThankyouJesus!"

And there it was. I did it. I survived my childhood. I got out! I formally moved to New York City on December 27, 1990. I packed my bags and got on the Greyhound. Rehearsals for *Miss Saigon* were set to begin January 11, 1990, and they did. My second semester of senior year was counted as a paid internship, and I took a personal day from the show to fly back home and graduate. I'd promised myself that if I booked that gig, I would never ride a Greyhound bus again. Haven't even seen one since.

CHAPTER TEN

I t was New Year's Eve and the ensemble boys from *Miss Saigon* were taking me out! We had started rehearsals on January 11, 1991, and opened
on April 11 of that same year. We were nominated for eleven Tony Awards.
We won three, all in the acting categories. Best Actress in a Musical went
to newcomer Lea Salonga. Best Actor in a Musical went to the controversial Jonathan Pryce, and let me just say this one more time so we're all
clear: Jonathan Pryce's performance as the Engineer in *Miss Saigon* was a
revelation, *and* I'm grateful that the controversy surrounding a Caucasian
man playing this Asian character cracked open a space where actual Asian
actors have benefited from access and opportunity that they were historically blocked from for so long. Best Featured Actor went to Hinton Battle.
This was his third win. He had also taken home the statue for *Sophisticated
Ladies* in 1981 and *The Tap Dance Kid* in 1984.

Hinton was a hero to me. He exploded onto the scene when he was
only sixteen years old, snagging the role of the Scarecrow in *The Wiz*. Hinton was a dance prodigy and originally made his mark in the business
through that lens. *Miss Saigon* marked a turning point for him, or at least
for those of us on the outside looking in, since he was being honored for a
performance where there was no dancing required at all. For a young Black
dreamer such as myself to have Hinton's example of Black excellence all up

in my face every day was so inspiring. I had just arrived and I had big plans, huge dreams for myself. We lost Best Musical to *The Will Rogers Follies*, directed by Tommy Tune. Good musical. Amazing staging. But nobody asked me my opinion, so I'll just keep my opinion to myself.

I moved to New York with every intention of being a star. I wanted to be the male Whitney Houston. I just knew in my heart of hearts that I had the talent, skill, and craft, the *it* factor. I just knew my little faggoty ass was poised for stardom. Fame, if you will! I wanted to be famous because I thought that fame would bring me validation. Understanding perhaps? Love, even? I don't know; it's hard to say. I knew what my family thought of me, my church, the Black community, whatever; I was just out here all on my own, with no safety net, no blueprint. I thought if I could just prove that white preacher lady wrong, the one who cursed and shamed me from her bully pulpit in front of thousands of people, wielding the Bible as if it were an AK-47 . . . If I were on the top of the charts, a household name, on the cover of magazines? Maybe the *gay* would fade away. Maybe my success could transcend my abominable sin. The plan was to take Broadway by storm. Win a Tony, then star in a sitcom centered around me, like Nell Carter did after winning Best Featured Actor in a Musical for *Ain't Misbehavin'*. She also won a Primetime Emmy Award for her reprisal of the very same role on television in 1982. I watched that filmed production of *Ain't Misbehavin'* on PBS, and never missed an episode of *Gimme a Break!* I can still sing every word of the theme song to this day.

So, here I was, debuting in one of the biggest musicals to ever hit Broadway, with advance ticket sales that broke all previous box-office records, and even though my gig was technically called an "internship," which usually translated into "free labor"—a bitch got paid! Do you hear me?! I think it was, like, $1,200 a week! That was triple what Bernie was making when he died. I had stumbled across his tax return, and his salary for the entire year was $21,000. Can you even imagine? Just so we're clear—$21,000 ain't neva been a living wage in my lifetime.

I'll never forget my first day of rehearsals for *Miss Saigon*. I walked in and saw all my Asian castmates, or, as they were referred to, "The Orientals." Yes, you heard right. We didn't know, and this was new to me. I had only a couple of Asian classmates in high school. Asians were white folks, as far as I was concerned. I thought Latin folks were white too. Suffice to say that anybody who didn't have chocolate skin, to me, was white. Now we know. *Now* I know better, and "When you know betta, you do betta . . ." Thank you, Maya Angelou!

Barry K. Bernal saw the overwhelmed look on my face and introduced himself to me immediately. It was clear I was a newbie, and Barry was already a pro. He was kind. He was the morale builder. He was hot! Like, muscle-man make you tingly and sweaty on *the inside parts* kinda hot. Like, if they were casting actual Asians to play the "Oriental" roles in films, he would be a movie star! I would soon learn that he'd been cast in the role of the villain Thuy. An unlikely villain, indeed!

"What's with the Black girl resting face? You should be smiling, sweet thang! Today is the first day of the rest of your prepubescent life!" Barry gave me the warmest hug, and then with one hand inverted, fingers down on his hip, and the other arm flung up like Vanna White revealing those letters on *Wheel of Fortune*, he exclaimed, "And just FYI, we're not called Orientals anymore—we're *Gaysians*!" Barry became another one of my Fairy God Gays.

I don't remember much about that time, because I was too arrogant to appreciate what was happening to me. I made my Broadway debut at twenty-one years old, but that was three years later than I had planned. As far as I was concerned, I was already behind the eight ball. I was late! I had convinced myself that I only had one decade to become the star I dreamed of being.

Barry was activated by the plague and the effects AIDS was having on our community. He spearheaded our cast's participation in the fifth year of the Broadway Cares/Equity Fights AIDS Easter Bonnet Competition. Broadway shows and national touring companies all over the country participate in a six-week fundraising competition where volunteers and cast members hold red buckets after each performance and collect donations for the cause. Some shows sell autographed *Playbill*s, posters, and props. Other shows offer auctions to meet the cast backstage or to win a one-night-only walk-on. At the end of the six weeks, each show is invited to participate in the two-day Easter Bonnet Competition. During this competition, performers from participating shows perform specialty numbers that present each show's unique Easter Bonnet. There are two winners: one for presentation and one for most money raised. Barry and a couple of other ensemble cast members were the architects of our entire contribution—and we won, Best Presentation and most money raised, at $62,582.67. It had been an exhausting year for me personally, just trying to wrap my mind around the fact that my friends were dropping dead. Like flies. In the streets! Good people. Loving people. My friends. Being reduced to sexually perverted stains on the fabric of society who deserve to die. That's how we were treated by mainstream and religious society.

How does one live with the burden of that? When you know that the self-appointed moral leaders of the world think you should be dead. Hmm. No wonder we don't know how to connect, we don't know how to love.

It was New Year's Eve and all the Gaysians were headed out to ring in the New Year at a club called the Roxy. The Club was a safe space for us. We were insulated from the rest of the world under our mirror ball of inclusion, solidarity, and love. Nobody was an outcast at the Club. Gay, straight, Black, white, all races, colors, and creeds. Nobody was judged, for anything. I was offered my first hit of ecstasy that night, and I instantly understood what all the fuss was about. Numb the pain, erase the plague, tell death to fuck off—if only for just a few hours. Maybe we got out of hand. Maybe we spiraled into a mirror ball of addiction. We didn't know. We were just—trying to *remember to live.*

Miss Saigon opened on April 11, 1991. Barry left the show at almost the year mark. He summoned me into his dressing room and told me privately why. He got the diagnosis. The death sentence. He wanted to spend his last days with family. Shortly thereafter he disappeared. He died on October 31, 1994. He was thirty-one years old. Nephi Wimmer, another *Miss Saigon* ensemble member, died in 1993. And there were many more. You know . . . that's what happened. Folk would silently just dissipate, dissolve, disappear—and soon fade from the memory of those of us left behind. It was too much to hold, too traumatizing to internalize every day all day. So we partied.

A few months into my run in *Miss Saigon*, I auditioned for several leading-role understudy positions, including Chris (the love interest), John (the best friend), and the Engineer (the Jonathan Pryce role). *Man, did I have balls!* Later that day, Mitchell Lemsky pulled me aside. "I just wanted to tell you how impressive your auditions were today. You were the absolute best. Unfortunately, there's no real growth for you here at this time. You're just not right for any of the understudy slots. But please know you have me in your corner, and I'll do everything I can to champion on your talent."

I didn't move to New York City to be in the back, lurkin' in the shadows under Asian coned cullee hats. I had visions of superstardom dancing around in my head. So Mitchell's truthful assessment of my place and possible growth, or lack thereof, with the company coupled with his encouraging words pushed me to find spaces for myself where I could be *seen*. You know what I mean . . . ? Like, for realz. 'Cause I didn't come to Broadway to play. I came to slay.

One of the first spaces I found myself frequenting, outside of my eight-shows-a-week Broadway schedule, was the cabaret scene. I can't remember who introduced me to the scene. Maybe it was the summer I spent in Montclair, New Jersey. A big group of us drove into New York on a Saturday night and parked directly outside the piano bar Don't Tell Mama on Forty-Sixth Street and Eighth Avenue (also known as Restaurant Row). We put our bags in the trunk and went on to have a festive evening of dinner, Broadway show, and gay bars that weren't carding. When we returned to the parked car, the trunk had been broken into and our bags were gone. To this day I never leave anything in the trunk of my car in Manhattan—or anywhere, for that matter—*ever!*

In any event, the piano bar was discovered, and that was all a bitch wrote! Every night till last call at 4:00 A.M. you could find me at any number of piano bars around New York City. Don't Tell Mama in Midtown was a seven-days-a-week situation. Monday nights were poppin' at the Duplex down on Christopher Street in the Village, and on Thursday nights I could be found underground at Rose's Turn on Grove Street, only a hop, skip, and a jump across the street from the Duplex.

"Don't wait for anyone to give you permission to practice your art. You must always be practicing, even when no one's listening—and most of the time, no one's listening." George C. Wolfe would drop that knowledge to me much later in my career (like decades later), but when I look back over my life and how I showed up and showed out in those first years of my career in New York, I know I was already inhabiting that ideal.

I would use the piano bars to try out new material, instinctively practicing my art and trying to make people listen. Literally. For example, victim ballads were still very popular at the time, and I found it to be very therapeutic to bleed my loveless life all over the crocked patrons. And if you could calm down a raucous piano bar at the height of the evening's frenzy—replete with a singing bar- and waitstaff, drunk patrons singing along with the soloist, banging on any number of instruments from tambourines to cowbells to maracas to kazoos—if one could stun *that* kind of crowd to silence, one's street cred would ascend to that of a god among men. Silencing the room with my superpower became my specialty.

Peter Gloo was the premier pianist at Don't Tell Mama and my first New York City crush. He was older, in his mid-thirties. I think I was about nineteen when we met. He had a crush on me too. He was handsome in a very *Leave It to Beaver* kind of way, white, kind, with ice-blue eyes shielded by a simple pair of round horn-rimmed glasses. Every piano bar piano player had their own style. Some were strictly Broadway babies and the evening would lean more into show tunes, with the accompanist sight-reading whatever piece of music was placed in front of them. And sometimes you got those *play-by-ear* kinda cats who couldn't read a stitch of music but could play almost any major pop song of the twentieth century—tunes by James Taylor, Billy Joel, Carole King, and Annie Lennox, with a little Stevie Wonder, Aretha Franklin, Whitney Houston, and some Motown classics thrown in for good measure. I found tunes I could sing with all the accompanists in town, but Peter Gloo was my favorite. It was the way he looked at me. How he spoke to me. He saw my fear, my loneliness. He was lonely too, and word on the street was that he was known to like "chocolate." Yeah, you guessed it—he liked Black boys and that was a *thing.* 'Cause quiet as it's kept (or maybe not so quiet these days), the LGBTQ+ community can be just as racist as the rest of the country, so as a young Black queen living in America and working in predominantly white spaces, there was always the unspoken race situation to navigate.

My fast ass tried to get Peter to have sex with me for years, but he wouldn't. I couldn't understand why. He kept me at a distance, not emotionally, but physically. Which was what was so confusing. We would grab dinner and have long talks. He listened to my dreams. He encouraged me to dream bigger. I found an honest and loving confidant in him. I told him I wanted to star in a Broadway show written expressly for me and win a Tony Award. I told him I wanted to be the male Whitney Houston. I told him I wanted to be a movie star. I even shared my "twilight years" dreams of becoming a director. I figured when I got too old to perform, I would go behind the scenes. Peter encouraged my desire to lead, said I had the power to do and be whatever I wanted. He told me not to let anything or anybody dim my light. At the time what he said was just words, but in due time I would come to need those words and their meaning to sustain me.

In the fall of 1990, Peter flew to Pittsburgh to see me in my farewell performance at CMU as Richie in *A Chorus Line*. He booked a room at the new hotel in Oakland, on Fifth Avenue. What I remember most about that crisp fall weekend was Peter's kindness. His compassion. His ability to create a safe place for me to land, when he himself was staring death in the face. He flew to Pittsburgh to see me, to see my show, to support my talent, my spirit, my humanity. He invited me to stay the night at the hotel with him. I was excited because I thought I was gonna finally get me some. But Peter gave me something far better than yet another transient sexual encounter. He held me instead. He stripped down to his boxers and I to my underwear . . . and he held me. He spooned me and held me. No one had ever just held me, with no reciprocal, sexual expectation. He held me all night with his face buried in the nape of my neck, his sweet breath finding a soothing rhythm. A continuous flow of breath that felt like safety. It felt like love.

It would be decades before I would feel that kind of love again. It would take me decades to even recognize what real love actually looks like. Peter was another angel; I understand that now. His light was then in the process of dimming, but I didn't know. Then again, I wasn't surprised. That's how it went in those days. Folk would just disappear, stop coming around to the parties, the benefits, the rallies, the marches, the clubs. And then after a certain period of collective denial, someone would have the courage to invoke the name of the missing and we would all have to deal with another person's mortality.

I visited Peter at St. Vincent's Hospital toward the end. He had disappeared for months, and I broke the silence and asked the question. I crawled into bed and spooned him, held as he once had held, trying to return the unconditional love I had been the beneficiary of some three short years before. In that moment I remembered how Peter would always close out his nightly sets with "That's All," a song about giving love and only love. "That's All" moved my soul to tears every single time he sang it. In St. Vincent's, I held him tight, trying to mirror back to him the kindness and love he had so effortlessly shared with me, and softly sang "That's All" into his ear.

Peter didn't sleep with me because he sensed I needed something deeper than sex. He was right. He gave me what I needed, not the carnality of what I thought I wanted. He chose to protect me even when I didn't know how to protect myself. His light burned out on December 11, 1993. He was thirty-seven years old.

* * *

Walking through the streets of Midtown is beyond eerie. Apocalyptic is what it is. It's June 5, 2020. It's the middle of the day, in the middle of the week, and no one is in the streets. No one. Businesses are boarded up for fear of damage and looting. The people have risen up. Protests over the murder of George Floyd got us our activism tool back. I'd been concerned. I'd watched how horrid images had been made commonplace, and I'd been afraid that we had been desensitized by the perpetual lack of humanity displayed through our devices—but George Floyd's death changed alla that. The American people are tired. The American people are galvanized. I find this newly invigorated energy to be comforting, inspiring if you will, but this pandemic shit is real and it's fuckin' with me. As of today there are approximately 108,000 dead. DEAD! Human beings are dying daily and the Orangina administration is fumbling the national response. The virus is disproportionally killing Black and Brown people. So, who cares, right?

The truth of the pandemic is hard to stomach. It's a tragic truth, and once again I find myself enveloped in death. My new therapy has brought the extent of my past trauma to the fore. Actual trauma therapy. Like, specific therapy with exercises and homework and shit. You know I'm an education type of bitch, so I'm truly up in it! I need a change. My coping mechanisms don't work no mo'. There's another person in the room now. My husband. Husband! There's responsibility that comes with marriage and the sanctity therein. I keep saying to Adam that because the world stopped, we have the space and time to heal our marriage. The whole world needs to heal. I'm trying to be present and open and mindful to all of these ideas and concepts. I want to heal. I can't keep going the way I've been going for most of my life with blinders on. Running. Muting. Compartmentalizing. Ignoring. Disassociating. And worst of all—numbing. Unconscious living, that's what I was doing, how I've been living for so long. Focused on the dream. Trying to get out. Trying to not be that statistic.

"The show must go on" is not going on. For the first time in history Broadway is closed. Shut down indefinitely. All the theaters are locked, the lights are out, the lifeblood of Manhattan, the culture, our world, my world, just gone. Evaporated.

The only reason I'm in the city today is because I have to get a bad tooth fixed. I'm in pain now. Can't hold out any longer. Doctors' offices are back open and working at 25 percent capacity, or something like that. We're renting a house on Long Island. By the water. With a backyard, and trees and birds and shit. Who knew that's what I needed? Space. Air. Quiet. Healing. My newfound television and film crossover success happened just in the nick of time. All of my Broadway friends are out of work. Many have had to move back home with their parents to ride this thing out—whatever this fucking this thing is! My dentist is covered in PPE gear when I arrive. Like, fully covered, with mask, goggles, shield, and hazmat suit. Well, I guess I feel safe—I guess?

* * *

I've been called on to participate in many, many benefits during this COVID time . . . times of need in general. The thing I hate the most in this life is injustice. Dr. King said, "Injustice anywhere is a threat to justice

126

everywhere." All I've ever known is injustice. From every side. The attack on my humanity started early and the gauntlet came down hard. Activism is second nature to me. Growing up first generation post–civil rights movement and then directly headlong into the AIDS crisis, I was uniquely poised to become a warrior in the fight. Lawyer? Preacher? Community organizer? Not my ministry. In the early nineties I didn't know where my place was in the fight. Who could I be? How could I show up? *I know, I'll do concerts!* A cabaret concert series to benefit Broadway Cares/Equity Fights AIDS. Kill two birds with one stone. Raise money for the cause while making sure the world knows my name.

My first show in the back room of Don't Tell Mama was sold out for four weeks in a row. One show a week for the month of July. Sunday nights. My day off from *Miss Saigon.* Full five-piece band with three backup singers. We blew the sound system out our first go-round. These cabaret rooms were used to more subtle musical situations. More organic. More acoustic. I was surprised to learn that all music rooms are not created equal. There was a snobby separation between "cabaret rooms" and "music industry" rooms. Music industry professionals did not see the value in Broadway. As a matter of fact, Broadway was considered corny. I was shook to find out that an entire industry had already decided I was valueless. I was from Broadway *and* I was a faggot. No place for either of those attributes in the nineties, mainstream, R&B/soul music business. None of these roadblocks were ever gonna stop me, though. I was armed with the voice. My savior. My weapon.

Just keep singin' as high as I can for as long as I can and the rest will work itself out, right? Clive Davis will discover me just like he discovered Whitney. I'm just as good as Mariah Carey; Tommy Mottola will see that, right? 'Cause I have the talent. I have the craft. I have that kind of gift. I know I do!

* * *

"Is it true that you have a connection to the producers of *Star Search*?" I asked Hinton Battle in his dressing room before a matinee.

"I sure do," he shot back, then cut his eyes at me with a scowl. "You wanna be on *Star Search*?"

I knew the show had lost some relevance, but the winner still received $100,000 in prize money, and I was trying to get a record deal. I figured the show could give me some visibility on that front. Hinton told me to get him a videotape ASAP and he'd get it to the producers.

Luckily, I had my July concerts at Don't Tell Mama recorded and filmed. I don't remember what I sent, but it was about fifteen minutes of performance. The producers immediately responded to my submission and sent for me. I was to be flown to Los Angeles to film the final weekend of the season. *If* I won those final four competitions, I would then advance to the semifinals to be filmed the following Friday. *If* I were to win the semifinals, I would then be advanced to the finals the very next day, with the prospect of taking the whole thing.

I took one week of the two weeks of vacation I had comin' to me from *Miss Saigon*, coupled with two personal days. I was flown out to Los Angeles on the first Friday of December in the year of our Lord 1991 and shuttled straight from the airport to the *Star Search* studio at Hollywood and Vine for rehearsal to shoot my first episode on Saturday. The entire experience was a whirlwind piece of manic showbiz swirl. It's hard to remember the details. I had to call upon my sister and my besties, Ron Pennywell, Joe Delien, and Walter McCready, to remind me of the songs I sang, which were, in order, "A Song for You" by Leon Russell (though I knew it from Donny Hathaway), "A Dream Out There with Your Name on It" by Jennifer Holliday, "One Song" by Tevin Campbell, and "Now That I Found You" by Michael Bolton.

Song choices were slim pickins so late in the season. No song could be repeated, and the popular song choices of the day had all been snatched up. Daddy needed to get creative! Thankfully, as a young artist who never fit into the status quo, I was already used to thinking out of the box. This task of finding obscure or something brand-spankin'-new was totally in my wheelhouse. I was shocked when "A Song for You," arguably one of the most significant soul classics of our time, was approved. I didn't ask no questions; I just said, "Thank you, Jesus," and kept that shit movin'. My second and third choices came from my love of new-music Tuesday in record stores.

Every Tuesday you could find me scouring the new-release CD section at Tower Records up on Seventy-Second and Broadway. That is where I found the new Jennifer Holliday and Tevin Campbell releases that supplied my second and third competition songs. The fourth tune, by Michael Bolton, was chosen because—who knows. I just knew that white man sang real high and real good and white audiences would probably know the song and I could sing the shit out of it, which would be a good thing for my advancement in the competition. In retrospect, I realize I was seeking visibility. My desire to be seen and heard in spaces where my humanity was consistently diminished or dismissed was my unconscious goal. This unnamed burning in my soul would turn out to become the engine that fuels my focus and my dreams to this very day.

I crept into that competition like a thief in the night, snatching wishes and dreams from all who found themselves in my path and, subsequently, my wake. To hear Ed McMahon utter the iconic, "Four stars!" as the tally from the judges for every one of my four performances on that first weekend was a euphoric experience. I advanced to the semifinals and finals, filming the following weekend. The rules were such that we final contestants could repeat one of our previous songs from earlier in the season. My repeat for the semifinals was "A Song for You."

"Four stars!"

The next day was the finals. I was facing the Male Vocalist Star of the first half of the season, a sexy, guitar-playing Latin man with a ponytail who oozed and caterwauled through his number with a sensual swagger that I'm sure left many a female viewer with her panties moist (maybe some men too). To be honest, he coulda got some if he wanted some. He had a *vibe* and that vibe was wholly masculine. I felt that familiar tinge of unworthiness waft over me as I watched him on the monitor from the green room. His vocals were fine, but his sex appeal was palpable.

I landed on heart. I had heart—and that's about all I had, too. I also had a tinge of an early-nineties fashion situation happening. I styled myself with a classic black pleated pant and black stretch cotton/rayon-blend mock turtleneck, paired with a vest with a rich paisley pattern and a chartreuse box-structured Yohji Yamamoto blazer (that Jonathan Pryce had gifted me). I was at what I fondly refer to as my *Juicy Billy* weight—with a face of Miss Piggy fullness and pre–dental reconstruction (my mouth was so cavernous that I didn't have enough teeth to fill it). I was serving you *Miss Saigon* contract hair, which meant standard US Army hair, a shapeless, cropped mini-Afro. The final touch was my silver cross necklace, worn 'cause I needed an accessory. I was styled to nineties R&B perfection.

When Ed McMahon, standing at the iconic *Star Search* podium, announced with his basso profondo, "From Pittsburgh, Pennsylvania, here is—Billy Porter!" I walked to the mic, standing dead center of a *star* on the floor of the stage. My body trembled involuntarily, like my mother's body trembled, but I opened my eyes and sang those children, what . . . ? Under the ground! Right in front of the judges, the audience, all the people, I gave it everything I had.

We were the first category to compete that night, which meant I had to sit in my feelings for an hour just waiting for the verdict. Would my talent obscure my abomination? Would my voice transcend my shame? Would my voice, my superpower, transcend the silent—actually not so silent, but deafening—phobias of our misguided, sometimey, hypocritical conservative American moral majority? Was I convincing? Did I pass? Was I masculine enough? Did they see my faggotry? Would I be judged fairly, for my talent, for my God-given gift? The seemingly endless hour finally passed and Ed McMahon announced, ". . . and the winner of one hundred thousand dollars and our champion: Billy Porter!"

I raised my arms to the sky, thanking my Lord and savior Jesus Christ for my win. I flew back to New York the next day and went directly back to performing my eight-shows-a-week ensemble track in *Miss Saigon*. My check came in the mail on January 3, 1992. After taxes I was left with $44,000. I did not know what to do with it. I didn't come from money. Nobody I knew came from money. Nobody around me stepped up with any financial advice. I didn't even know who to ask or what to ask for, so I got veneers on all my front teeth to close up those gaps and put the rest in the bank for a rainy day. My hope was that *Star Search* would give me some traction in my recording-artist quest; however, ten years in, *Star Search* wasn't so starry anymore. The show's reputation had declined through the years, and many broadcast markets didn't even carry the show, or relegated it to off-peak hours. In New York it aired at noon on Saturdays. My episodes aired in April 1992 to no fanfare or acclaim whatsoever. Most folk didn't even know the show was still on the air. So—onward and upward!

* * *

Anybody who works in the theater knows that every piece one works on is its own microcosm of the traditional family dynamic. *Miss Saigon* was my first extended Broadway family. The entire ensemble was housed in the basement of the theater, in bunkers of a sort. Lockers were erected side by side, creating two huge squares with a small opening for modesty, separating the men from the women. It was like a basement house party every day. Being an artist requires coming to work with an open heart, a present mind, and a sharing soul. This all-consuming emotional requirement can sometimes be tricky in terms of the artist's personal sanity, because while we are indeed "play-acting," our nervous systems don't know the difference. Comedies tend to be easier on the psyche. Dramas are different. The artist must stand in proxy as a vessel, allowing tragedy to flow through their body eight times a week. Sometimes twice a day. Many artists are oblivious to this cost, to this constant assault on our nervous systems, the perpetual chipping away of our sanity. Self-care would prove to be an elusive concept for me to embrace or even understand for decades to come; however, at the end of my first year on Broadway I was offered a vacation. A free one. Well, more like a *sing for your supper, quid pro quo* situation.

I met Rich Campbell through some of the Gaysians in the cast. You see, Rich was what we in the queer community at that time referred to as a "rice queen"—a non-Asian man who is mostly attracted to Asian men. Now, the past thirty years of politically correcting our discourse have deemed this once-very-common signifier a racist trope that is no longer appropriate. So, I'll just simply state the facts: By the time I met him outside the stage door, Rich had already dated a few of my very Asian *Saigon* castmates. Rich is a businessman who loves to travel, and he had an idea to create a business that would allow him to align his work with the activity that he loved most in the world. Atlantis Events is an internationally renowned gay travel company founded in 1991, whose founder was looking to create a unique place for the gay community to come together to fellowship. As we were all suffering from unimaginable daily loss due to the AIDS crisis, Rich was looking for a way to help heal our community through connection. Atlantis Events had held its first all-gay resort event with three hundred guests at a Club Med Resort in Playa Blanca, Mexico, in 1991. What started with the very simple idea of "a gay week on the beach with friends" has blossomed into a company producing all-gay cruise and resort vacations all over the world. Today, it is the largest company in the world dedicated to creating unique vacations for the gay and lesbian community. However, in the spring of 1992 Rich was looking for free entertainment for his guests. I was fresh off of my *Star Search* win and had never gone on a real vacation before. Rich offered me a gig that included a free vacation. Our handshake agreement was: I had to do my club act on one of the nights, and the rest of the vacay would be taken care of free of charge. All expenses covered for me and my musical director.

We flew to the all-inclusive resort "for families" in Playa Blanca. And here we were, all of us gay boys living our best fanciful vacation lives, free from the glare of homophobia and shame. Free to show public displays of affection anywhere on the property and anytime. Free to be as gay as we wanted to be without fearing for our lives.

My second vacation with Atlantis Events in Punta Cana, Mexico, a year later in 1993, would come to a cataclysmic end when, as our gaggle of three hundred gays was traveling back to our respective homes, a crane flew into the engine of our charter plane just as we were lifting off. Our huge 747 came crashing back to earth, just at the tail end of the truncated country airstrip. The plane hit the tarmac with a thud so violent it felt like a bomb went off. Luckily everyone was strapped in, so there were no injuries. The trauma came with the realization that had this happened ten seconds later, the plane would have been high enough in the air to crash and kill us all. This group of out, loud, and proud gay men who had just spent a bliss-filled, magical week were all together plummeted back to reality. Like, the real, unprotected reality that, while the Club Med organization found value in our commerce for a week, it seemed, based on what we experienced next, that we were *not* welcome when the next week of "traditional families" arrived. As we waited for a replacement jet to arrive, we were shunted to a room on the outskirts of the resort with no food, no drink. None of the superior hospitality we had previously received. We were told by the Club Med representative that the arriving families were not comfortable with our presence on the property. What did they think we were gonna do, have butt-sex in the pool? How dare we faggots have the audacity to think our humanity should be respected.

Nothing can describe the feeling of knowing that no matter what you do, how well you behave, or what you achieve in life that you will always be nuthin' but a stain on respectable society. We are family too. A chosen one. A necessary one. I found a corner and slept for the entirety of the malfeasance.

* * *

On the earlier, less distressful Playa Blanca trip in 1992, I met a man named Bill Butler. Bill was traveling with his then partner, Rich Bungarz. Bill was the younger, gregarious one of the couple. Rich was a bit more of the introvert. My concert was on the first night that we arrived, and word had gotten out that I was the *Star Search* champion, so I was a bit of a celebrity among the gays for the week. Bill came right up to me in the pool: "You're fierce, gurl!" And that was all she wrote. The three of us frolicked for the next six days together. Bill and Rich brought me into their friend group and we rolled deep with about eight of us altogether, spending our days and nights bonding. Vacationing without fear. Letting the terror of the plague go for just a breath. Learning how to construct a family, our very own chosen family, from the bottom up.

On our final day, while we were all wading in the pool for the very last time, I said, "Bill, I've never asked what you do for a living?"

"I'm an agent," he stated matter-of-factly.

"Oh, that's amazing. Where do you work?" I asked, not really prepared for his answer.

"The William Morris Agency."

Well, WERK!

CHAPTER ELEVEN

I found the number for the William Morris Agency in the Yellow Pages. Remember those? I straight-up called the switchboard. It had been a year since I had seen or spoken to Bill Butler after our Club Med adventure. He was an agent at William Morris, and I didn't want to seem thirsty. And besides, I had an agent from a very respectable firm. The year 1992 had been a forward-motion one for me. Cameron Mackintosh brought over yet another show from London. This time it was a Black show called *Five Guys Named Moe*, a musical with a book by the ever-regal Clarke Peters and lyrics and music by Louis Jordan and others. It originated in the UK and ran for four years in the West End. I had my eye on this show. I'm a preparation bitch, so Daddy did her research.

·I knew for a year it was coming. Every Black musical theater man in town knew. We were all planning and scheming, preparing for a very rare moment in Great White Way history, where the cast would be populated by six Black men. The audition process was grueling. The dance audition had me soaking in a bath of Epsom salts for hours.

So there's good news and there's not-so-good news. The good news is, I booked the gig! The not-so-good news is that I was hired as an understudy for three of the six roles: Little Moe, Four-Eyed Moe, and No Moe, played by Glenn Turner, Milton Craig Nealy, and Kevin Ramsey, respectively.

The rest of the cast was rounded out with Doug Eskew as Big Moe, Jeffery D. Sams as Eat Moe, and Jerry Dixon as Nomax. Michael-Leon Wooley and Phillip Gilmore were the other two actors I shared the distinction of "understudy" with.

For those who maybe don't know what an understudy is, I'll tell you. We're the artists who wait in the wings, literally eight shows a week, prepared and on call to step into any of our assigned roles at a moment's notice. Not my favorite position in the world, but I have to admit that, to this day, *Five Guys Named Moe* was hands-down one of the most enlightening and healing experiences I've ever had. For the first time in my life I was surrounded by Black men who were not disgusted by my presence. Black men who loved me and nurtured me. I was a twenty-two-year-old sass-a-frass whose only goal was world domination. These men taught me what to expect and how to navigate my way as a Black man in this business—and the world! They respected my artistry and buoyed my dreams.

My training and my craft had prepared me for the moment. I understood very quickly in the rehearsal room that *understudy* meant *backup*, and in the process of learning the show, we understudies were in the back. No one was attending to us. No one was checking to make sure we were getting all the information into our bodies. So I made a schedule for myself. We had four weeks of rehearsal before we moved into the theater for tech rehearsals, so I decided to focus on one role per week for the first three weeks and then in the fourth week amalgamate all of the information into a consolidated reference book, so that I would not be ass out if I found myself having to go on without a proper understudy rehearsal (which has been known to happen—a *lot!*). The focus is always on the main cast first. Understudies get no love from the creative team or management, but the unspoken requirement is that you better be ready—like you know my aunt Dorothy always told me, "Stay ready, so you don't have to get ready!"

I was not a morning person in my youth, and everybody in my life knew not to call me until "two digits," meaning after 10:00 A.M. It was Wednesday, April 29, and my phone started ringing at 9:00 A.M. I let the answering machine pick up. No message. The phone rang again. *Click-click.* No message. On the caller's third try I picked up and heard a muffled voice as I was trying to find some coherency. On the other end of the phone was the panicked voice of my stage manager, Marybeth Abel, calling to tell me that Kevin Ramsey, who played the character of No Moe, had injured himself the previous evening during the five tour-splits that punctuated the end of his tap solo. Apparently, he had woken up and couldn't even move his body out of bed. "You're on for the matinee," Marybeth dropped.

Now, let's talk a little bit about this *tour-split* situation for a minute. Let me give y'all a bit of a definitional context. *Sauté*: a simple jump in the vertical direction. *Tour*: turn of the body. *Tour en l'aire*: "Turns in the air." *Split*: Legs extended fully in opposing directions on the floor. So, combine the definitions of *tour en l'aire* and *splits* to understand the matter at hand. Needless to say, this particular dance move requires one's body to be extremely flexible, like stretchable rubber even. There were many, many men at the audition who could execute this challenging move. None of them were hired. Instead Kevin and I were hired without the required skill set anyway. Now, listen here—I told those bitches from the jump, at the audition, that tour-splits were not my ministry. Kevin told them too. We were both assured by the director/choreographer, Charles Augins, that "we'll work something out."

Turns out his definition of us "working something out" did not include changing the trick. And here we were, only in our fourth week of previews— hadn't even made it to opening night yet—and the whole experience felt like one big ball of toxic anxiety and crisis management. My matinee performance started without a hitch. The cast was gagged! Everyone at intermission was geeked! W. Ellis Porter had saved the day. (Oh, I forgot—I changed my stage name to W. Ellis Porter, because there was already somebody else in Actors' Equity who had the same name, and the rule at the time was that there could be no duplicate names. By the year 1994, a very kind man by the name of Stephen Spadaro who worked at the Actors' Equity main office would intervene on my behalf by calling the *other* Billy Porter, who was no longer working in the business, and getting permission for me to use my own name. *Like Tina Turner in divorce court with Ike: "All I want is my name!"*)

Adrenaline coursed through my veins as I launched into No Moe's solo tap number in the second act. The pristine *clickity-clack* clarity of every single tap rang through the theater. Kevin is a hoofer. You know, like Bill "Bojangles" Robinson, "Sandman" Sims, the Nicholas Brothers, Gregory Hines, or Savion Glover. Hoofing is an entire culture unto itself, with deep-seated roots in Black history stretching all the way back to the turn of the century, communicating our Black joys and traumas through the rhythms of life.

The sound is heavy, grounded in truth and Blackness. But I learned how to tap-dance from white people, how to articulate my sounds at a ballet bar. Think Gene Kelly, or Fred Astaire and Ginger Rogers. My tap skills were more aligned with the effortless, heavenly glide of the Golden Age movie musical than the more anguished, earthy expressive truth of the Black experience.

Nevertheless, I had heeded the advice of Aunt Dot. A bitch was ready! And as I pushed off the floor with all my strength to slide into the fifth of the tour-split situation, I heard and felt a *rip!* My hamstring! The pain was so intense the entire theater popped to a blood-curdling red through my eyes. I tried to get up from the floor, using the microphone stand to drag myself to my feet, but my left leg was like a strand of overcooked linguine. I tested to see if I could put any weight on the leg, but to no avail. I was officially injured. Down for the count. I hopped on my right leg into the wings and collapsed. The performance continued as I writhed on the floor in excruciating pain. I had about a ten-minute break and Roumel, the dance captain, kindly brought me some ice. I don't know how I did it, but I powered through and finished the show.

Mayday! Mayday! Two men down! No second cover. What's to be done? I literally crawled on my hands and knees up the stairs to my fourth-floor dressing room. Stage management came shortly thereafter to inform me that they were sending me to a chiropractor in between shows and that they would see me back at the theater at 7:00 P.M.

I shuddered. "Wait a minute, are you saying that I have to do the show tonight?"

"We have no other choice. Kevin can't even get out of his bed," the stage manager said, grasping for some semblance of compassion where there was none. I lost my shit!

"We both told y'all from the very beginning that we couldn't do that fucking trick and now we're *both* injured!"

Silence.

"Are you truly saying to me that I have to come in tonight and do this show on a leg I can barely put weight on at the moment?"

More silence.

Oh, I see how this goes now. And I got somethin' for yo' asses!

The three-hour break in between shows allowed for me to get some hasty healing work done on my leg by the company chiropractor, grab some food, and cab it home to my apartment on Forty-Fourth and Tenth. I iced my hamstring while I scarfed down my dinner. Then I decided to walk back to the theater around six-thirty. I figured that would give me some time to test my leg and see how I would need to alter my movements to accommodate the injury. There was an uncharacteristic, eerie silence in the city as I made my way up Ninth Avenue. Stores were closed. Many were boarded up, or folk were in the process of boarding up their property. *What the fuck is going on around here today!?* When I arrived at the theater, I was informed that a verdict had come in on the Rodney King trial. Four officers of the Los Angeles Police Department had been acquitted of the usage of excessive force in the arrest and beating of Rodney King, which had been videotaped and widely viewed in television broadcasts. In response to that shameful verdict, an uprising took place. Then it took a sharp turn, with widespread looting, assault, and arson. Entire swaths of Los Angeles were burning to the ground. The LAPD had difficulty controlling the scope of this reckoning, and the California National Guard, the US military, and several federal law enforcement agencies were deployed to assist in ending the violence and unrest. New York was on high alert. The NYPD was girding for the possibility of a civil unrest spillover three thousand miles away.

But the show must go on, Hennys! And go on it did. And I, too, went on that night, injured and weak in my body. My agent at the time—we'll refer to her as *Ms. Thing*—was in attendance. There was a restaurant space flush to the back of the theater, and Cameron blew out the back wall of the theater and put in two sets of double doors that opened directly into the bar, mainly for the purpose of the Act 1 finale's conga line, led by Milton

138

Craig Nealy (Four-Eyed Moe), weaving the exceedingly exuberant audience through the theater and directly into the bar for intermission. *Keep the children liquored up!*

I scarcely made it through the performance on my damaged leg, but I did it! I waited in my dressing room to greet my friends and agent, *Ms. Thing*, post-show. My friends showed up. *Ms. Thing* did not. Remember this was pre–cell phone, texting, and social media, so my friends and I waited for about a half hour before adjourning to the Tenth Avenue Lounge, a newly opened gypsy watering hole located on Tenth Avenue between Forty-Fifth and Forty-Sixth, right around the corner from my apartment. I thought it strange that my agent didn't come backstage to congratulate me. A tiny red flag went up when there was no message left for me with the stage doorman either, but I also took into account that my going on was a last-minute situation and, giving her the benefit of the doubt, chalked her absence up to probably having a prior engagement or something. All good! I was certain I'd hear from her the following day.

The next afternoon I was sitting on my sofa icing my leg and watching my stories, *The Young and the Restless*, when my phone rang.

"Hello," I answered with grace while nurturing my leg spasms.

"How dare you embarrass me in front of my colleagues!" *Ms. Thing* eviscerated me through the phone.

"Who *is* this?" I asked, befuddled.

"It's your agent! Who do you think it is?" She continued to assail me.

"I waited for you at Moe's Bar for over an hour with my friends and my colleagues that I brought to see you! And it is highly disrespectful and unprofessional to leave your representation hanging like that. Don't ever do that to me again!"

I tried to catch my breath. The inside of my body was aflame with revulsion. *Ms. Thing* had triggered what the old-timers used to call "gettin' my niggah up!" None of us cast ever hung out at Moe's Bar & Grill after the show. That shit was a tourist attraction. *Ms. Thing* would have known this had she simply come backstage post-show to congratulate me like every other agent I knew would, for not only saving the fucking day, but doing so with a gimp leg and no real support from upper management. There was an extended silence on my end of the phone as I tried to gather my thoughts. And then, without hesitation, I bristled, "Are you done?"

"Excuse me?" She *still* came out her face at me.

"I said are you done!" I barked back with my niggah fully up and 'bout to blow the back of my head off!

"Well, yes . . ." her tone of voice backtracking a bit.

"Because you're done!"

"What?"

"You're done. We're done here. *I'm* the client and I advise that you don't ever speak to a client like you've spoken to me today ever again. You're fired!"

* * *

And with that I hung up the phone and promptly reached for the Yellow Pages, feverishly thumbing through, looking for a number for the William Morris Agency.

Bill Butler. He liked me. He said I was fierce. We hung out for a week on vacation together. He felt more like a friend than an agent. It's been a year. I never reached out. I didn't want to seem thirsty. I didn't want him to think I wanted something from him. And now after a year of no contact I'm calling him because I need representation. I'm calling with something he needs. I have the goods. I'm inviting him to see me perform on Broadway. In a leading role. It's okay, this is business. If I make it through the gatekeepers at the switchboard and he actually comes to the phone—I'm in like Flynn!

The most pleasant of voices greeted me from the other end of the phone, and I said "Billy Porter for Bill Butler please," with as much authority and confidence as I could muster.

"One moment please." There was a click that signified the transference of the call. *Click-click . . .*

"Bill Butler's office," a direct, take-no-shit, female gatekeeping voice asserted.

If he comes to the phone, I'll be okay. If he comes to the phone, I'll be okay . . .

I stuttered a bit. "Hi, um . . . Billy . . . [clear throat] Billy Porter for Bill Butler."

"What is this call in reference to?"

Just tell the truth. That's all you can do. Ask for what you need. You are worth it. He needs you just as much as you need him . . .

"We met on vacation about a year ago. I'm currently an understudy in *Five Guys Named Moe* on Broadway, and I'm actually on for the next couple of days. I wanted to invite Bill to come and see me on the off chance that his schedule may permit, as I am currently looking for new representation. The tickets would be on me, of course."

"Hold please." Flop sweat streaked my face. And after what seemed an interminable wait . . .

"Billy! Oh my God, it is so good to hear from you! It's been too long! Rich and I wanted to invite you to our holiday party, but I misplaced your number. I'm so glad you reached out."

He came to the phone! I'm in!

Bill accepted my offer and came with his assistant, a no-nonsense, edgy Asian goddess, to see me perform in *Five Guys Named Moe*. They both loved me. Bill went rogue and took me on as a client, to be clear not as the William Morris Agency but personally, as what they used to call a *hip-pocket* client. To this day, Bill Butler has been my biggest fan and champion. For the better part of three decades, he has been with me through all the ups and downs of a career, and of life. Bill believes in nurturing talent. He sees beyond the surface. He's continued to believe in me and support me through the good times and the challenging times. He didn't drop me when the work dried up for over a decade. He didn't put me out to pasture when I was searching for my voice, trying to find my place in a world that doesn't give a fuck about me or my kind. Bill Butler has not only been my business partner for comin' up on thirty years now; Bill Butler is my family. I am so humbled and honored to have this man in my corner. When I cohosted *Dick Clark's New Year's Rockin' Eve* with Ryan Seacrest and Lucy Hale in Times Square going into 2021, Bill pulled me aside to show me the title he had given me, typed into his contact list, from the moment he met me all those decades ago: BILLY PORTER—SUPERSTAR!

Kevin and I were called to the stage management office. We both knew what it was about. We stood in solidarity with each other, deciding that neither one of us would be attempting that tour-split situation ever again, understanding a possible consequence could be our termination. My heart sank all the way down to my balls. You know, like how you feel when you get called to the principal's office in elementary school and you don't know why? That's exactly how it felt when we entered the office, where the director, Charles Augins, and associate director David Cameron were sitting on one side. One of the big-brass producers, Richard Jay-Alexander, was there as well, along with our stage manager, Marybeth Abel, and resident dance captain Roumel Reaux. I don't remember the specific conversation, but I do remember what felt like bullying. I do remember that these people used their power to try to push us both into doing their dangerous bidding. Our bodies were on the line. We were both still recovering from our injuries, and it felt as if our jobs, our livelihood, were being threatened.

There was a standoff. We were ordered to perform the tour-splits or else. Or else what? We both glared back at the men who held the strings of our survival. Kevin was a man of few words. "I'm not doin' it," he grunted. And then all eyes turned to me, the youngin'. Twenty-two years old and still wet behind the ears. Brand-new to Broadway and faced with a personal choice: Let them bully me into doing something that could harm my body, my facility, my money-making temple for good—or choose myself and my future and say no. And *no* is a complete sentence.

"This is a hard no. I won't being doing that trick ever again."

There was silence in the room. It was one thing for the grown man to buck the system, but they were not ready for this kid to know his worth. They were shocked that I had the audacity to push back. Who did I think I was? Of course, I should have just been honored to have been invited to the party. Fuck that!

"I told you at the audition that I couldn't do it and you hired me anyway. I plan to have a long, illustrious career post–waiting in the wings in *Five Guys Named Moe*. So please fire me. Please—I beg of you."

No such luck! Instead, the next phase of torture was the director calling for a complete overhaul of the tap sequence. Kevin and I were called in on a Thursday afternoon to learn the new choreography. This session was more like detention or a punishment of some sort. I guess they thought they could beat us into submission. Not such a great idea—for them!

Charles Augins, David Cameron, Marybeth Abel, Kevin, and myself were in attendance. It was three hours of nonstop madness, changing choreography for no reason, cracking the whip by making Kevin shuck and jive like he was a homeless man hoofing on the corner for somebody's loose change. I was forbidden to be onstage and learn the new choreography while it was being created. I was shunned to the back of the theater to take notes.

On our second break—about three hours in—Kevin went upstairs to his dressing room, used his telephone (dressing room land lines were a contractual perk in pre–cell phone days), called the stage management office just a floor below his, called out of the show for that night's performance, and left the theater! There was an hour left for rehearsal. I was called to the stage. The director left the theater, and the associate director, David Cameron, was charged with dragging me through my paces. And drag he did. Seeing as how I was not allowed to learn the new choreography while it was being set on Kevin, I was starting from scratch. David focused on how unhappy the creative team was with my tap dancing. Apparently the precision of my *clickety-clack*s was not enough for them. I was not "hoofing," and thereby was deemed not a "Black enough" tap dancer in their eyes.

The "not Black enough" trope was something I was used to hearing in my life. From the moment I started talking I spoke in complete and clear sentences, forgoing the normalization of Black slang, or what was commonly called *ebonics*. "You talk like a white boy," kids would bully. Damn, come to think of it, I even got that shit from adults. When I was just starting out in New York, film director Spike Lee made a point to call me out at an audition for his seminal masterpiece *Malcolm X*.

"Why you talkin' like that?" he irritably snarked at me with disdain.

"Talk like what?" I clapped back before I could even think about my tone.

"You talk like a white boy!"

And there you have it. I talk like I talk. I've always talked like this. Why do Black people hate me so much? Why do they associate my speaking the Queen's English with denying my blackness? When did intelligence become something to be mocked and shamed for? So now here I was again with a Black man clownin' me for not tap-dancing black enough. After about forty minutes of being berated for simply being myself. I took a breath. I looked around the theater. Everyone had gone. No director. No stage manager. No producer. No protection. So once again, I had to protect myself. "Listen, David. *I'm* performing tonight, so now is not the time to try and teach me how to hoof. If that's what y'all want, you need to rent a studio at a later date and have some hoofing sessions with me. But as for tonight—I'ma do what I know. Unless you would like to perform in my stead."

David was discombobulated by my decisive, cocksure response. I was *hot!* I continued my read for filth: "I'm a size forty-two. I'm sure my suit would fit you. You're welcome to use it tonight if that would make things better. Think about that and let me know. In the meantime, we're done here."

And with that, I went to my dressing room to prepare for that evening's performance. On my way out of the theater to grab some dinner, I yelled up to the stage management office from the ground floor with the vigilant fury of a lioness protecting her cubs, "AM I GOING ON TONIGHT OR ARE YOU, DAVID!" And I wonder why my low-key reputation in the business was that I was difficult to work with. Hmm—well, pardon me for respecting myself enough to not let bitches take advantage of me!

Another issue I was having at *Five Guys* was the keys that my songs were in. My tenorino, high-belting passaggio had always been at least a fourth or fifth higher than mere mortal tenor men. I belted like the ladies. I mixed like the ladies. My superpower was this fact. For a clearer understanding of what I mean, I offer this: I was a man who sang like a woman. Not just any kind of woman. I sang like a Black, female gospel soprano. Think Jennifer Holliday or Whitney Houston, Jennifer Hudson—you understand me?

When I sing the bullying stops. So keep singin' as loud as I can and as high as I can for as long as I can.

144

I learned early that I would need to enlist my college classmate Jeff Kubiatowicz and his skill to not only transpose all the traditional tenor audition repertoire up a fourth for me, but also hand-notate the music for me on oversized music paper with architectural precision. Once again, the creative team knew from the start that all the songs were in keys that were too low for my voice. They told me that we would "work it out." And now, a few months into my yearlong contract, I found myself once again having to take action for my own self.

So here I am one late night in Manhattan, minding my own Black business, euphoric after having just performed in *Five Guys Named Moe* in the role of . . . who knows, cain't remember, not important. Anyway, I float into my regular haunt, Don't Tell Mama, to get into my "mesmerize the bridge 'n' tunnels" with my dulcet, and sometimes histrionic tones. There was a gaggle of about five white women sitting at the table with playbills from my show. I went right in: "Oh lookie here, you ladies saw *Five Guys Named Moe*, how'd you like it?"

The ladies were "in their cups"—translation, "turnt up!" I could tell from their slurring southern accents that these ladies had taken advantage of the controversial decision Cameron Mackintosh had made to allow audience members to take their alcoholic drinks to their seats in the theater, during the performance. *How gauche! How irreverent!*

One of the ladies slurred, "The show was amazing! The cast was amazing! Although we saw an understudy whose voice was a little weak, but other than that—we had a good ole time."

First of all—these bitches don't even recognize me from thirty minutes ago?! There are only six of us onstage, WTF is that about!? I guess the theory is true: We all look alike to them.

Secondly, my voice is weak? My voice is WEAK?! That was my unfiltered review. After months of begging the music department to adjust the keys for my solos falling on deaf ears, I had a random southern woman roaming the earth telling the world that I had a "weak voice." No, ma'am. I'm not the one for that!

I was performing in the show on the next day as well, and I had a plan. I was on for No Moe—remember the tap dance, the tour-splits, the mayhem, the drama!? Right! It turns out that No Moe's vocal track was the lowest of my three. When it came time for my first solo, "Messy Bessy," I took the entire song up the octave, belting like a madwoman! The children gagged! The audience lost their minds! The musical director glared at me from the onstage bandstand. I was summoned to the stage management office at intermission. They railed, they scolded, they threatened.

I listened calmly and when they were finished simply stated, "I got an unfiltered review from an audience member after last night's performance who said, and I quote, 'The understudy's voice was weak.' That would be me. They would be talking about me! Saying that I, Billy Porter, have a weak voice! That's unacceptable. I deserve to be granted the respect to be able to put my best foot forward just like everyone else. That's not happening at the moment. I've begged for these keys to be dealt with for months. I will be singing everything up the octave until this issue is resolved."

"I wish I had balls like you when I was your age," my dressing roommate, fellow understudy, and adopted big brother Phillip Gilmore crowed when I recounted my story to him. Phillip took me under his wing. He was another one of my Fairy God Gays. Phillip was wise beyond his years. He had lived a full straight life, producing a son from his heterosexual experience.

By the time I met Phillip he was in a committed relationship with a man. He lived his life boldly, very often referring to his significant other as his "husband." He was way ahead of his time, for you see marriage equality would not become the law of the land for yet another twenty-three years! "The world's not ready for you yet, Billy. But they gettin' ready! Ain't nobody like you. You just gotta be patient. Never give up. It's gonna be hard on you, but know this—you are the head and not the tail, you are above and not beneath. The power of the divine is all over you. I can feel it." The room stood still. We were both caught off guard by his words, by his prophecy. Phillip spoke life into me when I didn't even know how to do that myself. I couldn't really receive his words at the time, but I would come to return to that dressing room moment in my mind for decades to come. Phillip's words would sustain me through years and years of homophobic dismissal and disenfranchisement. His words were a life raft for me as I navigated the stormy seas of living my truth as a Black queer man on this earth.

After a year my contract was up, and as a renegotiation deal point, I asked to have first refusal to replace any one of my three tracks if any of the original cast decided to leave the show. The producers came back with a hard no. They used the "he's too valuable" trope that I had peeped with other friends of mine who got stuck waiting in the wings because we could do multiple things. So, I quit! Yup—this twenty-three-year-old, uppity queen quit her high-paying Broadway gig to go sit on his sofa and live off of what was left of my *Star Search* winnings. They had to replace me and teach a whole new human three separate roles after all. And when Milton Craig Nealy fell ill a coupla months later, and they needed a quick replacement, guess who got the call? *Umm-hmm*—they called my happy ass right on up, and I stepped into the role of Four-Eyed Moe for six weeks. It could not have worked out better. These men had taught me lessons—a lesson about the business, yes, but most importantly they taught me lessons about life, about knowing my worth, about standing up for and protecting myself.

A little over a year later, on August 29, 1994, my big sis Phillip Gilmore succumbed to AIDS. He was thirty-eight years old.

CHAPTER TWELVE

I turned down the gig three times!
And now I sat in the historic room of Joe Allen restaurant. A Broadway institution, Joe Allen has been a staple for Broadway performers, creatives, and fans of the Great White Way for decades. Posters of Broadway flops line the cavernous brick walls. My heart was fluttering as I awaited my meeting with the director. *Fifteen minutes early is on time, on time is late, and late is unacceptable.* I can be a bit of a perfectionist, so I had gotten there *twenty-five* minutes early.

The director appeared, towering over my table like the Jolly Green Giant. Although Jeff Calhoun was far from green. He was actually blond, and stunningly beautiful. But that's beside the point. This man sat across from me, and I could barely get out a greeting before he dove right in.

"You must do our show!" he shouted with glee. "It's gonna make you a star! I'm gonna make you a star!"

Grease is the musical of which he spoke. And by 1994, while *Grease* had been successful both critically and commercially, becoming the highest-grossing musical film ever at the time and arguably the most culturally penetrative crossover musical in history, I simply cared not. I understood the appeal in theory, but there was nothing about the music, characters, or story line that spoke to me or my experience in any way. I found the ultimate message of the piece, which essentially is telling women to give in to peer pressure and dress like a hooker to be accepted by the popular kids, to be toxic and problematic at best.

I turned that shit down three times.

I tried to throw the audition. Mainly because my white counterparts were being called in for specific characters like Danny Zuko, Rizzo, Sandy Dumbrowski, Kenickie—archetypes that had been immortalized by the Caucasian likes of John Travolta, Stockard Channing, Olivia Newton-John, and Jeff Conaway, respectively, in the 1978 film version of *Grease*. I was just being called in to audition for . . . whatever? *Unacceptable!* "Audition for *what role*?" I barked at Bill Butler after the third time the casting director called to gauge my interest.

"They said you can audition for whatever role you want except for Danny Zuko. I truly do think this will be an amazing opportunity for you. Tommy Tune himself is overseeing the production. Rosie O'Donnell is already attached."

"Can Rosie O'Donnell even sing?"

No response.

I greased my overprocessed, dry-ass relaxed hair up into a fifties conch and prepared to audition for the role of Kenickie, singing the 1957 Jerry Lee Lewis hit "Great Balls of Fire." I figured, go big or go home! The request for a callback audition came swift. "They are asking that you come back in with an eye toward the roles of Roger or the Teen Angel."

Roger? Who the fuck is that?

Bill Butler, in all of his visionary acumen, suggested Teen Angel: "One song, in-out, stop the show and you're done. Very little work for lots of exposure."

I thought about it. I decided against his suggestion.

"If I'm gonna be in this bullshit, I wanna play a real person. I wanna play a three-dimensional human being!" As if that shit is even possible with . . . *Grease*?

In doing my research I discovered that Roger's character sings a song called "Mooning." I thought to myself, *How can I put a nail in this greased coffin once and for all? I know—since you bitches can't decide which role you wanna go "Black" with, I'ma show you the Blackity-Blackest version of this lily-white shit that y'all have ever seen.* I researched Black recording artists in the fifties and decided to rearrange Roger's song "Mooning" in the style of Otis Redding. *Cain't git no Blacker than that!*

I stomped into that callback with every intention of scaring the white people! I cooed and moaned, growled, riffed, and caterwauled my way through that audition like an old, defiant blues singer who brings all the pain and misery of being Black in America to light. I purposefully imbued my performance with what I thought to be ridiculous choices, over-the-top, bordering on absurd. Tommy Tune, Jeff Calhoun, and all the producers clearly did not agree. They all gave me a standing ovation in the audition room! Tommy Tune shrieked, "My God, Billy, that was a revelation! I want you to take that same visionary musical treatment and apply it to 'Beauty School Dropout'!" *Fuck! Bill was right!* By the time I had traversed the terrain between the Actors' Equity audition studios on Forty-Sixth and Seventh and my apartment on Forty-Fourth and Tenth, the official offer had already been made.

The director saw the skepticism wash over my face.

"This could be a big coming-out moment for you. Your version of 'Beauty School Dropout' will stop the show every night! And you will most definitely get a Tony nomination!"

What the fuck are you waiting for, you pompous, twenty-three-year-old, arrogant ass! These white people are begging you to be in their new Broadway show. Tommy fucking Tune! This is what you've been workin' for! This is the dream, right? Pull it together, bitch!

"Okay . . . ," I answered, with a pit in my stomach. "Okay, I'll do it."

* * *

Rehearsals started at the dilapidated Nederlander Theatre on Forty-First and Seventh on December 3, 1993 (three years later, this barely up-to-code theater would house one of the greatest contemporary musicals of the modern age: *Rent*). We were scheduled to go on the road for a pre-Broadway tryout before coming back into New York in late April, early May, right in time for the Tony nominations. The cast arrived on that wintry December morn all abuzz. Tommy Tune would go on to lead an ooga-booga, touchy-feely, hand-holding kumbaya warm-up for about thirty minutes every day before rehearsals began. After the warm-up, the entire cast and creative team gathered around for the sets and costume designer's presentations. That pit in my stomach started to gurgle with each moment. The set was Pepto Bismol pink. The costume renderings were all shades of primary neon colors. *I hate primary colors! I detest neon!* And then renowned, two-time Tony Award–winning costume designer Willa Kim unveiled her rendering for my Teen Angel costume. The subtle gurgle in my stomach became full-blown nausea. I thought I was going to vomit. The sketch unveiled had me wearing a futuristic white suit with giant shoulders, bare chested with a neon orange cummerbund, chunky white cha-cha heels, and an absurdist fourteen-inch neon-orange glittered pompadour headpiece, the reference being the mascot from the Bob's Big Boy restaurant franchise.

On our first break, I immediately ran to the pay phone outside of the theater and called Bill Butler. I wept. I pleaded. I beseeched him to get me out of my contract. *I knew this would happen. This is exactly why I turned this shit down three times in the first place. This is how they see me.*

"They're making me a clown! I don't know how I'll be able to come back from this, Bill! Frankie Avalon was just a regular person dressed in a white suit in the movie, with a normal fifties pompadour! But *this* is how they see the Black man doing it!? I'm not even human. They're turning me into a coon. A millennium fucking coon! I'll be a laughingstock!"

My musical arrangement matched the absurdity of the costume. Earlier that summer, I enlisted the help of my friends Kena Dorsey and the now Tony Award–winning beauty Renée Goldsberry, of *Hamilton* fame, to work out the arrangement. I'm not a piano player. I can read music, but I cannot notate. So we sat in Central Park one sunny afternoon and I sang what was in my head. We recorded it onto a tape recorder. Yes—a tape recorder. I then turned in the a cappella arrangement to the musical director John McDaniel, who would soon experience a kind of fifteen-minutes-of-fame situation of his own when he was hired by Rosie O'Donnell to be the musical director on her wildly popular morning talk show. I myself would become a regular on *The Rosie O'Donnell Show*, but not before the two of us had come to an understanding.

Let's face it. The behind-the-scenes popular opinion of Rosie O'Donnell was that early in her career she was a bit of a bully in her own right. And as a person who knows what it feels like to be forced to move through this life at a marginalized deficit, I have compassion and understanding for these realities. I know what it feels like to constantly have to beat the monkey of homophobia and oppression off my back. Rosie was no different. She is gay *and* a woman, thus our complicated and parallel journeys have ultimately bonded us together in solidarity, *for the culture*, for decades. However, in the first week of rehearsals this truth was not evident to us. She came into rehearsals kind but guarded—as well she should have been. There was a woman in the cast who she took a liking to. For the purposes of this story we'll refer to said woman as—*Ms. Gurl.*

Within the first week of rehearsals, Rosie and Ms. Gurl made a connection, if you will. I happened to be present when the "secret connection" was made. The producers had thrown the entire cast a congratulatory party at the tail end of our first week of rehearsals at a fifties-style soda shop called Ellen's Stardust Diner. The reality is, this connection brewing between the two ladies wasn't so secret. Matter fact, everybody in the cast saw the same shit I saw: Cupid circling. It was sweet to see, and no one was acknowledging their connection publicly. Unfortunately, however, I swiftly and without participation found myself dragged into drama surrounding this secret connection and the outing that could potentially derail a star show-biz career at that time. Ms. Gurl sheepishly approached me after our cast warm-up on the first day of our second week of rehearsals and, practically trembling, asked me to please "not say anything about us to anyone."

I took a pause. I looked Ms. Gurl in her eyes. I took her shoulders into my arms and assured her, "Under no circumstances would I ever do such a thing. You know me, I don't like mess. I steer way clear of that shit. You don't ever have to worry about me."

And that, I assumed, was that. Oh, but no! For on the following day, after Tommy Tune's cast warm-up, Rosie O'Donnell tried to drag me in front of the entire cast. We had barely finished taking our last downward-dog, sun-salutation breath before I heard her bark at me from across the room, "Yo, Billy, I heard you're running around tellin' everybody that I'm fucking Ms. Gurl. Well, when I start fucking her—I'll let you know!"

Umm . . . no! Right idea/wrong bitch!

I went full ghetto! Singling out both her and Ms. Gurl, with my right arm slashing through the air with pointed claw, "You and *you*—back of the theater! NOW!"

Once the three of us were alone in a private corner of the theater, I went *in*. Words were said. Gauntlets were thrown. Both ladies were stunned. I'm sure Rosie was not used to folks standing up to her at that time in her life. I walked away from that mess, and it was never spoken of again. I doubt if either Ms. Gurl or Rosie would even remember this altercation, but I do. *Please, children—do not mistake my kindness for weakness, people! You will get clocked!*

The real gag came when we presented the first pass of the absurdist staging of "Beauty School Dropout" for the cast. I realized by Rosie's response that she was the only person in the room who had not heard of me; she was the only person that didn't know my voice, my power, my weapon against the darkness. Bullies disdain weakness and recognize strength. They respect a formidable foe, if you will. And Rosie respects talent. She loves to support and spotlight extraordinary talent, and I was no exception. When Rosie heard me sing, I broke that bitch right on down. She quickly became one of my premier ardent supporters and cheerleaders. She would go on to have me as a guest on her talk show—I want to say seven or eight times in its six-year run. I like to say I was the Bette Midler to her Johnny Carson. Rosie's friendship and mentorship are things I cherish. There are no words to describe the influence she has had on my day-to-day business acumen, but most importantly—navigating my life in general. We were both faced with an existential crisis of choosing our humanity over our fame at the same time. She, already in the public eye, and me—kinda sorta on the precipice of a public-eye situation of my own. A crisis that was a direct threat to my career aspirations: *The Gay Thing.*

In the nineties, *The Gay Thing* was still very much an authentic truth that could destroy a person's livelihood. The shame alone was devouring us all from the inside out. The "Don't Ask/Don't Tell" policy of the Clinton administration. This policy was in direct correlation with the doctrinal rhetoric heaved upon me in my Christian upbringing. Having same-sex desires is not the point. You can be gay—just don't say anything about it. Don't act on it. Stay in the closet. Keep your faggoty-ass mouth shut and everything will be fine. Although it was not fine. Not fine at all. Because those of us in hiding were no longer comfortable in the darkness. Rosie, myself, and the queer community at large needed the light; we longed for the light of truth to shine down on us—to be seen. I don't think either one of us ever expected that we were the light that the world needed to receive.

* * *

Bill Butler called to check on me one day in early April when we were on tour.

"How's it going?" he asked with gleeful anticipation.

"Good! I'm going to be on *The Tonight Show with Jay Leno*," I stated with conflicted pride.

"What? When?"

"Today. We shoot this afternoon."

"Well, I'm in Los Angeles right now and I'm coming!"

The producers of *The Tonight Show* had come to scout our production by attending one of our performances at the Orange County Performing Arts Center in Costa Mesa, California. Much to the surprise and chagrin of many of my more famous castmates, the *Tonight Show* people chose me. They chose my number. Our producers pushed back, only to discover they had no power to dictate how this was gonna go. If they wanted the publicity of being on this highly rated late-night talk show—it would be *Ms. Porter* or nothing at all. The tricky part of this decision was that instead of the standard female backup contingency for the number, our version placed every male member of the cast, ensemble and principal cast members alike, in the absurdist space-alien Dairy Queen costume behind me. A couple of the principal cast members scoffed at the idea of backing me up on national television. They were overruled, and my performance went on as scheduled with all cast members present and accounted for.

A very supportive Rosie summoned me to her dressing room the night before the taping. "Take off the headpiece if Jay panels you," she advised. She knew my costume was some bullshit!

"What does 'panel' mean?" I asked, wide-eyed.

"The barometer for if Johnny Carson liked a new comedian or not was if he called them over to the couch post-performance. Jay has kept up that tradition with comedians and musical performances. Trust me, you're gonna get paneled. He's gonna call you to the couch. Take off that rubber albatross before you sit down on the couch."

Jay Leno did indeed call me to the couch. I took off the headpiece like Rosie told me to, and I'm glad I did. It's all a blur. The only reason I remember any of it is because I've been able to rewatch the entire performance and panel/couch situation on YouTube (go catch it while you can).

When the Tony nominations were announced in May 1994, the Best Featured Actor nominees were Jarrod Emick, *Damn Yankees*; Tom Aldredge, *Passion*; Gary Beach, *Beauty and the Beast*; and Jonathan Freeman, *She Loves Me*.

To say I was heartbroken would not even scratch the surface in describing what it felt like to be overlooked. *They promised I'd get a Tony nomination. They promised this would make me a star.* The production received three Tony nominations in total: Best Revival of a Musical, Best Choreography for Jeff Calhoun, and Best Featured Actress in a Musical, which went to the late, brilliant Marcia Lewis, who played the role of Miss Lynch. As devastated as I was in this moment, I was able to remember what my mother and grandmother would always tell me: "There's a lesson in every triumph, but more importantly, in every disappointment. Find the lesson."

Find the lesson?

What is the lesson?

As soon as I had a free day off, I took myself on a date one block down from the Eugene O'Neill Theatre, which sits on Forty-Ninth Street between Broadway and Eighth, to the Walter Kerr Theatre on Forty-Eighth Street, to see a play everyone was buzzing about: *Angels in America, Part One: Millennium Approaches*.

When the curtain fell, I sat weeping in my seat. The house manager had to peel me out and escort me to the street. I was so moved because, after watching the character of Belize (played by Jeffrey Wright with searing intelligence and without apology), I realized I had never seen an image of myself reflected at me in any way, in any positive form—ever. Belize was a Black gay man who was not the butt of a joke, or the reviled one, or the one to be pitied or killed. He was the voice of reason. He was the spiritual and moral compass guiding all the white folks to some sort of peace in the midst of the storm that was our plague. I thought: "This is me. And nobody knows . . ."

I was twenty-four and prancing around like a Little Richard automaton on crack in fourteen inches of clownish neon-orange rubber hair, a white high-collared space suit, cha-cha heels, glittered face—and singing as high and as loud as I could. I was blowing the roof off the joint, and stopping the show every night. But it wasn't enough.

Watching this artful masterpiece reminded me of my purpose, of the reason why I got into this business in the first place. *Do you want to be a star, or do you want to be an artist?* Being a star for fame's sake is ego-driven. Being an artist requires stripping away ego and grounding oneself in service.

My quest to align my art with my service started in earnest on that night. I didn't understand what my mentor Billy Wilson was talking about when he said, "You are the only one who's going to be able to hold yourself to a higher standard, because no one around you will know the difference."

Billy Wilson was right. Nobody around me knew the difference. Nobody understood who I was and what I aspired to be but me. I left *Grease* in September 1994 to play the role of Solanio in a production of *The Merchant of Venice* at the Public Theater, starring Ron Leibman as Shylock, straight from his Tony Award–winning performance as Roy Cohn in *Angels in America*. Nobody remembers that part because it was easier for the gatekeepers to keep me pigeonholed into the millennium coon show posture I had unknowingly created for myself, out of the need to simply work—so I could eat! I had come to New York with a mission: play the ace that was my extreme singing voice and then expand from there. It would take decades of hard work, rejection, and resilience to reach my ultimate personal goal, and I'm proud to say that day has finally come. However, in that moment, I understood the work that lay ahead of me and I dove in—headfirst.

CHAPTER THIRTEEN

I was sitting on my sofa minding my own Black, faggoty-ass business when my phone rang. It was my music manager, David Munk.

"What did you say to those ladies in the elevator?"

"Who . . . ?" I answered in a fog, having just returned home from the Hamptons very late the prior evening. It was Labor Day weekend.

I had taken the weekend off from performing in the hit Broadway musical *Smokey Joe's Cafe* in celebration of the completion of my first R&B album. The album was set to drop on September 21, 1996, my twenty-seventh birthday.

Before I dive into the music industry of it all, let me introduce you to some of the players:

David Munk, my music manager. David peeped me out on the cabaret concert circuit. My pursuit of a mainstream music career was building congruently with my Broadway career. I found myself wading in the waters of the New York cabaret scene, because those were the only spaces I knew. I was gaining a following. Building an audience. Selling out every concert I self-produced. I can't remember who introduced me to David, but he came into my life at just the right time and assisted in helping me cross the Broadway/music industry divide. I mean, let's face facts—the nineties R&B music scene was not looking toward Broadway to find its next megastar. As a matter of fact, I was told my Broadway affiliation would hurt my chances of being an R&B king. I was told explicitly to *not* speak of my Broadway career in any of my promotional interviews, because Broadway was corny. Yes, you heard me—by the time my first album dropped I had four Broadway shows to my career credit that I was forced to pretend never existed.

Ric Wake, head of DV8 Records. DV8 was distributed by the major-label conglomerate A&M Records—an American record label founded as an independent company by Herb Alpert and Jerry Moss in 1962. Polygram acquired the company and took over global distribution in 1989. A&M housed well-known acts such as Sting, Bryan Adams, Burt Bacharach, Liza Minnelli, the Carpenters, Quincy Jones, Janet Jackson, Carole King, CeCe Peniston, Shanice, and Sheryl Crow, to name a few. Prior to breaking out on his own, Ric had been a staff producer at Sony Music Entertainment, where he worked with vocalists such as Taylor Dayne, Mariah Carey, Celine Dion, and many more. He has won four Grammy Awards.

Peter Zizzo, in-house songwriter/producer/musician under the Ric Wake/DV8 umbrella. Peter has written hits for such artists as Celine Dion, Avril Lavigne, Donna Summer, Diana Ross, Jason Mraz, Vanessa Carlton, and many more. Peter was my number one at the label. He understood me as an artist *and* a musician more than anyone up until that time. David Munk found him, and they both championed me in every way that they could at the time. I loved working with Peter, because even though I didn't know how to play piano or guitar, he still had the utmost respect for my musicianship. Our work together on songs for my first album resulted in some of my favorites. Peter and I just clicked, and so we're clear—I didn't click with everyone on my team.

Tina Shafer, vocal coach. Tina is a multiplatinum singer/songwriter who cofounded the New York Songwriter's Circle, a long-running showcase for musical talent. The Songwriter's Circle still meets, showcasing artists monthly at the Bitter End. Tina has also penned songs for such artists as Celine Dion, Sheena Easton, Phoebe Snow, Vanessa Carlton, and many more. Tina was married to Peter during my tenure at DV8 Records.

Denise Rich, American socialite, philanthropist, and political fundraiser. Denise's love of music led her to be the lead investor in the DV8 universe. And as a songwriter, she has penned lyrics for songs recorded by Celine Dion, Mark Anthony, Natalie Cole, Patti LaBelle, Chaka Khan, and Diana Ross.

Now that you know the players, we can return to the drama.

So, David Munk calls me the Tuesday morning after Labor Day 1997.

"What did you say to those ladies in the elevator?" he hissed.

"What ladies are you talking about? What are you talking about?" I asked, befuddled.

"Ric called me this morning saying he got a call from one of the ladies you rode in the elevator with leaving Denise's party on Friday . . ."

I rewound my brain to try to figure out who he was talking about and what offense, if any, I had committed. At this point I was three to four years into R&B land, working on my debut recording project. I was slowly coming to terms with the fact that my sexuality was overshadowing the work. My voice usually squashed the blatant homophobia and sent those who sought to come for me scrambling underground. Unfortunately, this time my voice, my weapon, my savior was seemingly losing its power.

"Yes, okay—and what did this 'lady' say?"

"She told Ric that you should be careful what you say in public because people will know."

"PEOPLE WILL KNOW WHAT!?"

Silence.

I let my rage settle. And then I restated my question through clenched teeth.

"People. Will. Know. WHAT!?"

Silence.

This was it. This was the last straw. I had spent four-plus years being pushed back into a closet I never occupied to begin with. I realized in this moment that with every seemingly minor compromise I gave in to on my R&B crooner's journey, I had given away a piece of my soul. My debut album was about to be released in less than a month, and I found myself unrecognizable. I didn't want to be an R&B crooner; explicit sexualized romance was never really my thing musically. Coming from the church, I was more of a message music kind of guy. And had anybody on my team been paying attention, they would have known. Actually—they all fuckin' knew!

I steeled myself and spoke with measured precision. "I had pleasantries with those ladies in the elevator. I told them I had just finished my album and was taking the weekend off from my Broadway gig. I was with Bill Butler. I told them we were going to his house in the Hamptons to get some R&R."

"That's all . . . ?" David now asked, his tone shifting from savage to sheepish.

"That. Is. All."

Silence.

I felt a hole in my heart growing in the space where hope and dreams used to reside. I'd tried to appease everybody. I butched it up—and yes, I was butch. I have the receipts in the form of two music videos for my singles "Show Me" and "Borrowed Time" (Google a bitch!). I hid my Broadway credits from the press because that was way too gay. I embraced the shame-based don't ask/don't tell realness of the music industry by not flaunting my "lifestyle" in front of the people. I sang the love songs about girls that they chose for me. And I sang them fiercely. It still wasn't enough. I was not enough. And now, judging from this conversation with my soon-to-be former manager, my every move was under some sort of out-the-faggot surveillance as I was simply trying to move through my everyday life.

"So when Puff Daddy, P. Diddy, Puffy-Pouffy, or whatever he's calling himself these days spends time in the Hamptons he's an entrepreneur, but when I go I'm just a faggot!?"

Silence.

* * *

One of my unspoken duties as an artist under the DV8 Records umbrella was to sing demos for other artists/producers on the label. This was just an extension of my real life at the time. One of the ways I made a name for myself in the New York music scene was by singing everybody's demos. I mean, like, too many fifth-floor walk-up, home studio, vocal-booth-in-the-bathroom, singer/songwriter/producer type folks had my phone number. I actually enjoyed singing demos, because it gave me free time in "the studio" to hone my vocal recording skills. Now I was in the big time, so when Ric Wake asked if I would sing a demo for a new song that Celine Dion had recently passed on for her *Falling Into You* album, citing that they wanted a male voice on the tune to shop it around to male *and* female artists, it wasn't even a second thought.

"Love Is on the Way" is my song! I sang that shit first!

Actually—technically—I sang it second. Whoever sang the first demo they presented to the Celine Dion team, prior to my involvement, was first: identity unknown. With that said, the first time I heard the song I knew it was mine. Peter Zizzo, Tina Shafer, and Denise Rich cowrote the song, and it fulfilled every "male Whitney Houston" dream I ever imagined. It's a nineties power ballad of the highest order. Masterfully written. Emotionally manipulative, as nineties power ballads are, it's an ol'skool vocal showcase for any artist. It's the equivalent of the "mic drop." *If you don't know, now you know.*

The pushback from Ric was swift and uncompromising. We all knew that power ballads were reserved for women and Michael Bolton. To have this song on my album would essentially all but "out" me as the screaming, church-sissy qween that everyone around me was trying to hide.

So I just started singing the song everywhere I went. Every benefit, every Denise Rich party at her penthouse on Fifth Avenue next door to the Sherry Netherland, and then, most important and prominently, at my sold-out Christmas concert at Town Hall.

By 1995, I was deep in my hustle. I had become a fixture in the New York music club scene. The venues leaned more into cabaret rooms and small theaters, because of my Broadway connections. These concerts were almost always benefits for Broadway Cares/Equity Fights AIDS. We were in the middle of the worst of the crisis in '95, and my singing was my contribution to the cause. Over a five-year period, my Christmas concert became the most popular event of the season, with crowd attendance growing from the 150-seat Steve McGraw's cabaret space on the Upper West Side, to a

300-seat Off-Broadway theater on Forty-Second Street, to selling out the 1,500-seat Town Hall.

I was backed by an eight-piece band and the Broadway Inspiration Voices gospel choir, founded by one of my best buddies, Michael McElroy. Side note: Since the organization was formed in 1994, it has grown to become a staple in the community whose mission consists of providing HOPE to INSPIRE and TRANSFORM all in need through music and the arts. In 2019, Michael and the choir were awarded a Tony Honors for Excellence in the Theatre.

It was like a rock concert! The crowd response was insane. And when I introduced "Love Is on the Way" as a possible track for my forthcoming debut album, the song received a five-minute standing ovation. *I know what I'm talking about, bitches!*

As Ric Wake was coming to terms with the fact that his aversion to me recording the song for myself was wrong, we got another divine sign to our service. Denise Rich threw a fortieth-birthday party for my dear friend Jenifer Lewis, known now to many in the business and beyond as "The Black Mother of Hollywood." As per usual in this time in my life, I was trotted out as the crown jewel of DV8 Records to sing for my supper. And what did I sing? You guessed it! That packed penthouse went IN! Moments after I sang, Jenifer came and grabbed me by my arm mid-conversation: "Bitch, come with me, the Divine Miss M requires an audience with you!" Jenifer dragged me across the apartment into a different room that was a little quieter. And there was Ms. Bette Midler, the Divine Miss M herself, sitting on a sofa, just—chillin'. Now, I don't remember the bulk of the conversation with Miss M because, before I could snatch it back, my spirit completely left my body. What I *do* remember, when I was able to snap my happy ass back to earth, was this: "I'm making a film right now called *The First Wives Club* with Goldie Hawn and Diane Keaton. Your song is perfect!" And the rest, my friends—is history.

Peter Zizzo went into warp-speed production mode on the track. Ric Wake got into brokering a deal for the soundtrack rights. The plan was to partner with the ladies in the film and, for the first single, do a music video for my song in promotional support of the movie. It was commonplace at that time for major labels to launch a new artist through a collaboration with a popular film. Everything seemed to be going along swimmingly, and then one day I got word that Tommy Mottola, Ric's old boss, had swooped in with a higher bid and secured the soundtrack for Sony. Turns out he had a new artist by the name of Puff Johnson who he was trying to launch. And just like that—I was out and Puff Johnson was in.

The film was released in September 1996. One year before my album would be released, almost to the day. Johnson's single was called "Over and Over." From what I can recall, the new plan was to release her single first and then my "Love Is on the Way" would follow, as the film was anticipated to be a blockbuster hit! "Over and Over" dropped into the airways and tanked on the charts very quickly, and my "second single" moment never materialized. I also heard through the grapevine that the music moguls had ultimately decided that having a Black male R&B singer aligned with a film starring three middle-aged white women wasn't a good look.

Fast-forward to September 1997. The day my album dropped was my first day of jury duty! *Aw hell no!* I got selected to be a possible juror. In my interview before the judge, when she asked why I couldn't serve at that time, I told the truth.

"Your Honor, my debut album drops today, and I need to be free to promote it and celebrate. I brought a copy for you to listen to at your leisure." I passed an autographed copy of my debut album, *Billy Porter—Untitled*, to the judge.

She was a Black woman who clearly loved Black music, because when she read the song titles on the back of the CD, she actually recognized me.

"Oh, I know you. I've been seeing your music video for 'Show Me' on BET for weeks now."

I was excused from jury duty.

WERK!

There wasn't a huge push for my album from a marketing perspective. A&M didn't really invest much into the launch of my music career. I admit I didn't know a lot about marketing at the time, but I do know that I wasn't seeing my face in the windows of any record stores. There were no special, life-size cutouts of me. As a matter of fact, I found my album buried in the graveyards of the R&B sections of these stores, if at all. Many of my friends and family had similar reports from all over the country. My heart was broken. No *real* press. No *real* promotion. Not the kind that a multimillion-dollar major label would inject into an artist they actually believed in. The lackluster rollout confirmed what I already had the data to bear true: These people didn't care about me or my music career. It was like they threw me against the wall like an undercooked piece of pasta, thinking maybe it would stick, maybe not.

This next part of the story still guts me on every level. As I type these words safely in my brand-new home, with a thriving career that is beyond my wildest dreams, my nervous system still activates, my stomach bubbles with a bile that is over two decades old. But nevertheless, this tale must be told.

One day in October, not even a month after my album was released, I received a phone call from my dear friend Dan O'Leary, who, as fate would have it, was temping as an executive assistant for Tommy Mottola, who was the chairman and CEO of Sony Music Entertainment, which is the parent company of Columbia Records—home to such artists as Mariah Carey and Celine Dion. Dan's voice was tight.

"Hey, Billy, I'm calling with some perplexing information."

"Ahhhh, shit—what is it now? What did I do this time?"

"You haven't done anything but be your talented, fabulous self," he reassured.

"What is it, then?" I asked, with dread washing over me.

"The new Celine Dion record that is to be released next month just landed on my desk and 'Love Is on the Way' is on it."

"Well, that doesn't make any sense. That's my song. It couldn't possibly be the same song." I quaked, trying to hold on to some semblance of dignity.

"Billy, I listened to the track, and not only is it the same song—your team is credited as producers."

Water flew out of my tear ducts like a fire hydrant on a sweltering summer day. My heart began to race. My body began to tremble.

Dan went on to say that the song was in the same key (with the exception of a modulation in the final chorus), and that my every lick and riff sounded the same.

I drew the curtains and sat in the dark of my apartment for a week. Trying to justify in my mind why my team would betray me so. Why would Peter, my right hand, forsake me? This was it. The crossroads. My "come-to-Jesus" moment, if you will. I knew it was over. My dreams of being the male Whitney Houston had just evaporated into thin air. I decided it was necessary for me to take drastic action to change the trajectory of my life. It was time for me to take the reins. It was time for me to choose *me*! I called a meeting with Ric Wake. When I arrived at his office, I found him sitting behind his grand desk—chipper.

"What can I do you for, Mr. Porter?"

"Y'all gave my song to Celine Dion?" The sprightly air was sucked out of the room. Ric was clearly caught off guard by my confrontational posture.

"How do you know that?" he asked with a slight cower.

"That's all you got for me? How do I know that? What in the actual fuck is going on! Did you honestly think I wouldn't find out?"

He had no explanation for me. My body felt as if it was about to detonate from the bowels of my soul, leaving macerated chunks of my being splayed all across his office walls. But why would I do *that*? Why would I destroy myself? Why had I allowed the cancer that is other people's fears to control my life? *Fuck this! I'm not goin' out like that! Everything is on the line, Miss Gurl. Your existence, your dignity, your basic human presence on the planet.* I took a deep grounding breath and began the journey of choosing myself, my truth!

"Here's how this is gonna go. Since y'all have made the executive decision to turn me into a demo singer for Celine Dion—we're done here!"

"Wait, what?"

"We're. Done. Here. Thee end!"

"Well, what are you gonna do?" Ric blustered.

"Whatever I do, I won't be doing it here!"

* * *

And with that—it was all over. I walked away from my dream in honor of myself. I languished in the haze of failure for months—actually, for years to follow. In the immediate months afterward, I found myself scrambling for work to make ends meet. I took a business theater job, commonly called an "industrial," for a pharmaceutical company to make some coins. I was away from my apartment for about a month. Upon my return I entered my apartment to a putrid stench engulfing every nook and crevice. Turns out, a basket of fruit and other like sundries had been delivered while I was gone. The card read:

"Thank you for your inspiration. Love, Celine Dion."

Now, I'm not tryin' to drag Celine Dion, y'all. I love her. She sings her ass off and what transpired was not her fault. She's like the female Elvis to me. She single-handedly revived the Vegas Strip with her legendary residency at Caesar's Palace, paving the way for a renaissance of other modern-day musical acts like Janet Jackson, Britney Spears, and J-Lo to make the Vegas thing cool again. I own *most* of her albums and listen to them occasionally. We've never met in person. I doubt she would even remember our connection.

And I will never know exactly what went on in meetings behind closed doors about me and my humanity during my first try at being a recording artist. I felt maligned by the gatekeepers of the industry. It felt personal. I felt dismissed. Put out, once again, just like the church, just like everything. Invisible. But the difference was, this time my voice didn't save me. My weapon, my savior. Fear of "the other," the silencing of my natural human impulses, my open heart, the dismissal of my humanity, became my kryptonite. I languished for the next two years feeling *some kinda way*, floating emotionally, alone at sea.

The implosion of my recording career was a huge blow to my ego. Up until this point my voice had made me feel safe, feel protected. All of that was gone and I was lost, without a clue as to which path to take.

I am more than just my singing voice.

I gotta find out what that means.

I was wandering in Midtown one night and had a panic attack. I sat on the back stairs of the Imperial Theatre on Forty-Sixth Street between

Broadway and Eighth. I called my mother for comfort. I never played this hand very often. I saved mother for the big stuff. This was some big stuff. I wailed and railed. Mommy listened with loving intention, as she always had. And just like clockwork she prayed for me at the end of my rant. *Prayer changes things, right?*

CHAPTER FOURTEEN

A week later I received a letter from my mother.

"Dear Billy, It's 7 o'clock in the morning. I've been praying and thinking. You have always been a special child and now a young man."

But, she wrote, "The Lord does not want anyone living in sin and being gay is a sin. I know that you told me that you have always been like this, however, you must resist Satan and he will have to flee . . . The Lord can turn your life around if you want him to. I love you so much and I want to do all that I can to help you."

Emotion washed through me like acid through a clogged carburetor. Thirty years of emotional grit and grime had built up in my heart.

I didn't even know where to begin, how to respond. My mother's letter sent old memories rushing back—being called a faggot when I didn't even know what the word meant, fear emanating from the women in my life that something was wrong with me, something that needed to be fixed, the man lessons. I thought that he was my remedy. I thought that if I did everything he said to do, my sickness would disappear. I couldn't remember a time when I felt anything other than gay. But I heard hate and condemnation from every direction. It was a sin I was born with. Everyone hated the gays. We brought "the Plague" into the world; very Sodom and Gomorrah. I heard this on television. I heard it in church. I heard it in my own home. Silence fosters fear. Fear fosters hate. Hate leads to violence. Silence = Death. Why me?

I had to come out to my mother three times! Once is scary enough, but three times over a decade is simply absurd. The first time was when the memory of my sexual abuse at the hands of her second husband flooded my senses while I was on a break from performing in the shows at Kennywood park. The second time was when I brought my first bona fide boyfriend home to meet her, sometime in the summer of 1989. I actually said the word *boyfriend*. Went right over her head. I let it be. What's the point? Let her grow at her own pace, right? And then the letter. That was like a dagger through my heart. The rejection. The dismissal. The feeling of being cast out. Here I was, almost thirty years old and still paralyzed by other people's convictions, *other* people's belief structures. In my mommy's defense, the Bible is all she knew. I know what I'm about to say is gonna be controversial. Some may even say heretical—but this Bible situation is problematic. It's been weaponized by the oppressor to prop up hypocrisy and to justify hate. *Hate the sin but not the sinner? Y'all can miss me wit dat!*

I wrote a long letter in response to my mother's obligatory churchy "gays are an abomination and you need to be fixed" letter. I wrote to her about traumatic memories, about shame, about how "I prayed for God to fix me," but that "I wanted something different, and I set out on my own two feet to find it." After blame, and denial, I wrote to her about how I found theater, how it had saved my life, how it was the only place I could go where I didn't feel I was being judged. And it provided an emotional and spiritual connection unlike any I'd ever known, so important because her religion, her church, used religious beliefs to justify hatred of me.

"I don't say these things to be disrespectful of the bible, or what you believe," I wrote at the end of the letter. "I don't say these things to shock you. I'm just trying to help you understand my truth. I have faced it. I can't protect you from it anymore. I don't have any answers; nor will I waste another minute of my life hiding in religion and acting as if I do. I live with the spirit of God in my heart, and with him I'm experiencing a full, happy, and peaceful life. A life firmly planted in truth. I pray you have the same joy I have come to know. I love you more than anything I've ever known. I will always love you. I know now your love for me is true. I release you to strive for your higher and greater good. I ask you to reciprocate that same spirit to me. Someday maybe our spiritual paths will align, but until then—this is my truth. God Bless You."

Upon going back and reading my response to my mother all these years later, I marvel at how I was able to speak life into myself without any idea of how I was gonna achieve real peace, real joy. I stand in amazement at the opportunities the universe has provided me on my journey toward healing. It's been long, it's been challenging, and I'm grateful to have lived long enough to experience the shimmers of light from the other side of the darkness.

* * *

Dr. Fauci said the fall would be worse, and he was right. The number of cases just keeps climbing. Over three thousand people a day. WTF—that's more than the number of people who perished in the 9/11 terrorist attack, and this fucking bitch is saying he won the election by a landslide. Lying! And the GOP is right there lying to the American people with him. The election was the safest it's ever been. When they win, the elections are fair, when they don't win . . . ? Who's the snowflakes now? It's been weeks and Orangina has still not conceded. He's continuing to perpetrate the fraud that the election was stolen from him, and there are one hundred and forty-seven enablers in Congress who are cosigning on these lies. And they just keep getting away with it. They are lying, playing with fire. They know it's a lie. But it's over, y'all, and history has its eyes on you. We won. Joe Biden and Kamala Harris are the new president and vice president elect. There will be a transition of power come January 20, 2021, whether that bitch likes it or not! Will it be peaceful? Well . . . we'll see . . .

* * *

Adam and I moved into our new home out on Long Island during Labor Day weekend. We've been out here since fleeing Manhattan and

CORO-NO-SHE-BETTA-DON'T back in March 2020 and haven't missed it one bit. First we rented a house, thinking the pandemic would be over in a few weeks tops, and then we would return to our Harlem apartment and resume our normal lives. Quickly and tragically it became clear that nobody was going anywhere anytime soon, and we decided it would be better to stay put, in quarantine, safely on Long Island. I've loved having time to just *be* with my husband—and myself! I've never had the luxury of even thinking about the concepts of self-care, balance, or boundaries. This dreadful time has at least given us that, and I'm grateful. I'm grateful to finally be working on healing my trauma, which can be a Sisyphean task at times. It's time to leave my past behind. My trauma has been my engine for my entire life, and I don't want to be defined by my past anymore. It's time to tell a different story. A story of healing. My therapist says in order to do this I have to find a way to metabolize my grief. What does that mean, you ask? It means I gotta go and *feel* shit now. And *talk* about shit. And learn how to have some *compassion* for myself.

* * *

What is family? Most would say family means a group of people closely related by blood or marriage, as parents, children, uncles, aunts, and cousins. This is family of the biological kind. By the same token, I've learned in my life experience that family can also be of the chosen kind. As queer people, we very often find that our chosen families are the ones who love us unconditionally and pick up the slack in support of our personal truths and humanity when our biological family members don't have the tools.

My mother just simply did not have the tools at the time to understand a gay child. Her letter to me arrived in a very specific moment of deep despair. I wish I could say it was unexpected, but it wasn't. Still, it was devastating.

I wrote a long letter back to her, and kept a copy. I wasn't sure why I decided to save both her letter and my response for all these years. Now I know why. To look back at those words and realize how far we've come overwhelms me. "Fake it till you make it" is a concept that I've believed in for years. *We are what we say we are. Speak life into yourself. Law of attraction, blah, blah, blah.*

My mother was actively encouraged by her church family and society at large *not* to love me unconditionally. They convinced her that my sexuality was a deal breaker and if I didn't pursue deliverance for my sinful ways, she should abandon me. So I drew a line in the sand, not only for my relationship with my mother, but also for my relationship with myself. This was the beginning of the evolution of the man I am today. I chose my truth. I chose myself, and subsequently chose a different kind of family.

My chosen family are the ones who have sustained me for my entire life. I'm alive and still halfway sane because of them—my lifers, my ride or dies: Ron Pennywell, Walter McCready, Kena Dorsey, Joe Delien (Greg Galick), Vanita Harbour, Virginia Woodruff, Rema Webb, Ty Taylor, Michael McElroy, Natalie Belcon, Renée Goldsberry, Eric Woodall, Matt Zarley, Ron Kellum, Nathan Lee Graham, Bill Butler, Wilson Cruz, Chris Belcher, Dennis Stowe, John-Eric Parker, Suzi and Lenny Beer, Sheryl Kaller, James Sampliner, Tracie Thoms, Bryan Terrell Clark, Leslie Odom Jr., Patina Miller, Tim Smith, Larry Poston, Kali Evans, Aaron and Andrew, Sean, AC . . . and the list goes on and on and on. If I forgot your name in this list, please charge it to my head and not my heart.

As for my biological family, my absolute and unequivocal extraction from the dangers of their lack of understanding of me and thereby their inability to love me unconditionally was my only path to survival. The Bible had become the breaking point, and I was no longer interested in believing in something that didn't believe in me. Sorrowfully, with much pain and sacrifice, I cut organized religion out of my life. And when I say I drew a line in the sand, I mean—fo' real, fo' real. I stopped going home to Pittsburgh for holidays. Hell, I stopped going home to visit, period! I had already had one foot out the door for a decade, but I held on to the hope that my community would choose love over fear. Most didn't have the tools. So I bounced. I have discovered in recent years that there was a lot of collateral damage in the wake of my decision. At the same time, I have observed how many of my family members and extended members of the community have evolved. I never even gave some of them a chance. I just cut them out. I'm sorry for that now.

My sister, M&M, has been the conduit for healing the fractures of decades of separation. My cousins Stephanie and Chris and Alicia have always made their love known. Grandma and Aunt Dorothy died before the "elephant in the room" conversation even came up (with the exception of that time when they found out I was sharing an apartment, "living in sin," with my sista schoolmate Natalie Belcon in Squirrel Hill sophomore year of college. Mommy was horrified. Grandma said, "Well, at least he's livin' with a woman!" *Oh, the shade . . . the shade of it all!*). Other extended family members have stepped up, mostly in the form of social media, and come to my defense when folk try to drag me for the way I live my life out loud and proud. One of my preacher cousins called me to apologize for the way the church has treated me and the LGBTQ+ community.

"I have an LGBTQ-plus ministry at my church because of you. I've lost some members as a result and I don't care, because God is love and love is God. I'm sorry for how we did you dirty like that. You deserved better. And now I know better, so I'm dedicated to doing better."

Well . . . WERK!

I couldn't wait for my sister to grow old enough so that we could be best friends. She's ten years younger than me, so at the time I booked my first Broadway show and left Pittsburgh for good, she was only eleven. Her father, my stepfather, the provider, the predator, had died when she was nine. I felt horrible leaving her in what I knew to be ultimately a questionable environment, but on the day of my departure I held her sweet face in my hands and promised, "I have to go now so that I can prepare a place for you. I gotta go make something of my life so that I can take you with me! I promise I'm comin' back to get you—real soon!"

I held fast to my promise, and within a year, starting when she was twelve, I was sending for her in the summer. I started keeping her for two weeks, then a month at a time. By the time she was sixteen I was keeping her in New York for the entire summer with me, purposefully exposing her to a world beyond our limited upbringing. I came out to her when she was sixteen. I remember sitting on the sofa in my apartment at 449 West

Forty-Fourth Street, weeping, with a fear of rejection. But it never came. She held *me*! She comforted *me* by simply stating, "I love you, brother. With all my heart. Nothing will ever change that." M&M resides in Manhattan today, and beyond anyone and anything else in the world, I am proud to say our sibling love for each other has sustained me through the best and the worst of times. Mommy always cries when she sees our love for one another.

It was at this time in my life that I erected an immovable wall around my heart. I would come to pay a price, but I felt I had no other choice. My trauma was my life's engine. My trauma activated me to desire greatness, the hope being, if I were to be considered great, my trauma would dissipate. What I didn't understand was how deeply infected my nervous system was. What I didn't understand fully, even after decades of personal therapy, was that I subconsciously was suspect of the idea of unconditional love. I didn't trust it. Especially the romantic kind.

I met a handsome man in 2009. I was uncharacteristically flirtatious and forward. We ended up going home together that same night, which is the way things go for the gays—most of us anyway. When we were gettin' busy under the sheets he stopped for a moment, looked me dead in my—most likely *dead*—eyes, and challenged, "I think we should keep it PG-13 tonight." I knew this man was special. But I didn't know he was the one. How could I? Up until this point, our love was considered by society to be perverted. Abomination and shame were all we gay folk knew. So to be transient in our romantic interactions was baked into our psyches. Adam and I never called it a relationship. We never owned what we both knew felt different about our connection. So the non-relationship/relationship imploded.

"I think that was love, and it just walked out the door," I said to my therapist when he broke up with me.

She buoyed my spirit. "Well, now you know what love looks like for the next time it shows up!"

* * *

The last couple of years before the turn of the century were filled with confusion. I was working here and there. Making my way, if you will. And

I still felt disjointed. Something wasn't right in my spirit. Turns out the world was, indeed, not ready for me. But I soldiered on.

I begged to get an audition to play the MC in the 1998 revival of *Cabaret*. Word came back, and I quote, "That's not the story we're telling." *Oh, so* Cabaret *is not about oppression and discrimination and the rise of the Nazis? Okay din.* Shortly after this dismissal, I stumbled across a book at Barnes & Noble called *Destined to Witness: Growing Up Black in Nazi Germany* by Hans Massaquoi. I bought ten copies and sent them to the Roundabout Theatre Company's artistic director and the entire creative team of the production, with a message inscribed that read, WE WERE THERE! Of course I never heard back.

There was also the time when I personally approached director/choreographer Kathleen Marshall about auditioning for the role of Hines in her upcoming Broadway production of *The Pajama Game* for the very same Roundabout Theatre Company. I had a unique connection to this show, because it was the second production I had ever done way back in middle school in Reizenstein Musical Theater. I got a hard no. Her justification: I was too young for the role. Hines is the manager of the pajama factory, and it wouldn't be believable that I, a thirty-five-year-old man at the time, could be the manager of Harry Connick Jr. and Kelli O'Hara, *because no one has experienced being managed by someone younger than them in the workplace . . . ? Okay din.*

In the Year of our Lord 1999 I was finally cast as John in *Miss Saigon*. I had spent a decade making a name for myself in the Broadway community and building a solid reputation, mainly for my unique and specific singing style. My mother always says, "You may have left the church, but every time you open your mouth to sing it ain't nuthin' but JESUS!" So when the musical supervisor for all of Cameron Mackintosh's shows, David Caddick, gave me free rein to ad-lib in the final, gospel-ish, chorus of the second-act opener, "Bui-Doi," I was pleasantly surprised. I had learned swiftly and in no uncertain terms that when white theater composers write "ad-lib" in their music, what they are looking for has nothing to do with personal self-expression in the least—all they truly want is for me to sing it like the white man from London sang it on the record originally. Their attempts at an authentic "Black/gospel" sound are derivative and cultural appropriation at best. Caddick knew the difference. He looked at me in my put-in rehearsal and said, "You're a gospel singer. Do your gospel thing! I trust that whatever you sing in the ad-lib section will always be connected to truth."

I would proceed to have nine months of bliss on Broadway. I was playing a leading role, a character, not a clown or a magical Negro, but a real person. A real three-dimensional human being. I was carving out my niche. I felt seen and heard. It was 1999 and I felt progress. I, Billy Porter, cast as a soldier, one of the lead soldiers, was proving to the world that I could be macho. Masculine. I could act well enough to convince the world that I was a straight man. And not just any old straight man, but a soldier . . . a marine! *And* Lea Salonga had come back to the show to reprise her Tony Award–winning performance in the role of Kim. This was a full gag!

To say that it felt like the entire Cameron Mackintosh era, across the board, was fraught with toxic work environment situations is to literally say—*the sky is blue*. And with the surprise arrival of the show's composer, Claude-Michel Schönberg, during the week of Thanksgiving 1999, we all knew some shit was 'bout ta go down . . . at least I knew. Claude-Michel secretly watched the show on a Monday night and called a full-cast, all-day, mandatory music clean-up rehearsal for the following day—the Tuesday before Thanksgiving! *Rude!*

The full cast arrived at a rehearsal studio in Midtown Manhattan with the room set up to intimidate. So there we were: the creatives sitting lined up behind a table, with the cast facing them, knowing our doom was imminent. Rehearsal began and we sang through Act 1 with barely any hiccups. We were all pleasantly surprised. We took a ten-minute break and all reassembled to sing through Act 2, which opens with a big, rousing gospel-lite number led by the character of John, yours truly. Instead of launching right into singing, Claude-Michel offered us, in particular me, a lesson in what it means to embody a gospel preacher. Yes, you heard right. This white man, from France, stood flat-footed in all of his European glory, literally trying to explain to me what gospel preaching is. I was confused. I didn't understand what he was talking about at first, and he was talking, and talking and talking. After about five minutes of his yakking, it became clear to me that Mr. Schönberg thought it was appropriate for him to school me on what it means to be a gospel preacher, so I stopped him with a raised hand.

"I'm sorry, Claude-Michel, but I must stop you."

You could feel the air in the room get tight. Nobody spoke truth to power during the Mackintosh era, for fear of retaliation. I knew my worth and I wasn't scared, so I let him have it.

"I gonna respectfully ask you to skip this part of the conversation and get to the note you need to give me . . ."

I had waited for anybody on the creative team to step in and take up for me. David Caddick gave me permission. The resident director had exclaimed at my audition that it was the best he'd ever heard it sung and acted. But they all just sat there, wordless. Dead-eyed. So I did it myself. I protected myself.

"I will do my best to adjust my performance to whatever you need. That's my job and I will do that. However, what I don't ever need is a lesson in gospel preaching from you. I'm good with that one. Thanks."

Oh, shit. Did I just say that out loud. From the look on everyone's faces . . . that would be an affirmative. Well, may as well go big or go home.

". . . and my contract is up in three weeks, so you won't ever have to hear it with me again."

* * *

Around this time I was also cast in two movies back-to-back: *Intern* was a film about the machinations of the fashion industry, with a cast of celebrities and fashion cameos that would make your head spin. Think the low-budget, indie version of *The Devil Wears Prada*. Less Meryl Streep and Anne Hathaway, more Joan Rivers and Kathy Griffin. I also booked one of the very first gay rom-coms to go mainstream, *The Broken Hearts Club*. An up-and-coming young writer/director by the name of Greg Berlanti had written the script. One of the first of its kind in the queer cinema space.

The story focuses on a gaggle of gay friends in West Hollywood and all of the dramas, struggles, joys, and triumphs that come with being out, loud, and proud at the turn of the century. Bill Butler was slipped the script through the casting director and one of his dear friends, Joseph Middleton, and while every character was assumed to be white (which was the way in those days), Bill heard my voice in the character of Taylor: the resident, fabulous drama queen. I read the script. It was a very good script. But I noticed that, while whiteness was implied for every character, Taylor was specifically described as white and blond!

"Now, how's *this* one gonna work?" I side-eyed Bill.

"You're gonna go in and change their fucking minds!" he declared.

Well . . . WERK!

My audition was in a hotel suite on a Sunday evening around 7:30 P.M. Weird. I walked into the room and immediately proclaimed, "I hope y'all don't think this is gonna be no casting couch shit!" Miss Ice was *broken* and I read my scenes with Greg. He was young like me. He was truly open to a different interpretation of Taylor from the one that sprang forth from his mind. I am thankful for this fact. 'Cause a bitch got the part!

We shot the entire film in twenty-two days. This was some full-on indie guerrilla filmmaking, and I had a ball. The cast bonded immediately in a very profound way. We all knew how special this piece could be. And with Greg at the helm directing for the first time, we understood that we were in the presence of greatness. Greg Berlanti has gone on to become one of the most prolific auteurs in the business, with a slate of eighteen television shows on the air in the 2020 network season. His advocacy and activism populate his art, as he is a champion for centering queer stories in the mainstream. His work has truly moved the needle of respect and understanding in our favor. This is God's work. His most recent film, *Love Simon*, is the queer, teen coming-of-age movie the world didn't know it needed. I can't imagine how much freer I would have been moving through my youth knowing, through representation in the media, that I was not alone.

Both *Intern* and *The Broken Hearts Club* were accepted into the Sundance Film Festival in 2000. *Hearts* was selected for the coveted spot of "premiering" and not competing, as we already had Sony's Screen Gems as our distributor. The cast was populated with some star folk, like Dean Cain of television's *Lois & Clark* fame, as well as Mary McCormack, Nia Long (one of my favorite Blacktresses), and the scene-stealing comedienne

Jennifer Coolidge, with whom I would be reunited decades later playing besties in 2020 in Paramount Pictures' *Like a Boss*, starring Tiffany Haddish, Rose Byrne, and Salma Hayek. The rest of our cast was filled out with up-and-comers like me, Timothy Olyphant, Zach Braff, Justin Theroux, Matt McGrath, Andrew Keegan, and Ben Weber, many of whom have gone on to have the most illustrious of careers.

Sundance is very, very *that!* She posh. She star-studded. She full-time fancy. An over-the-top, wintry fashionista, ski-ish situation for mainly the white and overprivileged. Gina Prince-Bythewood's *Love & Basketball*, starring Sanaa Lathan and Omar Epps, premiered in the same "noncompetitive/premiere" theater on a different night, so thankfully I wasn't the only chocolate chip in the snowy Utah-elien hills.

* * *

I started traditional therapy in earnest in 1995. I was scared that I was way too damaged by my trauma to have a real intimate relationship with somebody. It had been since the summer of '89 when I had dabbled last, and that three-month teenage dream went up in smoke when I found out my man was secretly creepin' with a close friend of mine. Forgiveness for both parties was swift and necessary—for my own sanity. But I had not found the space or trust to try again until I met Matthew Anderson sometime in 1998.

My memory surrounding how we met is blurry; however, I do remember how sweet he was to me. And funny. He worked in the news department at MTV at the time and had his finger on the pulse of American pop culture. He was then and remains to this day a mainstream cultural purveyor of anything pop!

By the time 1999 rolled around my record career had imploded, my Broadway career was deleterious, and I had just kept myself out of jail by not bashing that French bitch in the face, *call himself tryin' to school me on how to be a gospel preacher.* I found myself spiraling out one late-fall night between Thanksgiving and Christmas. That was the night I had that panic attack and called Mommy from the back stairs of the Imperial Theatre . . . And we know how well *that* went—*Whew . . . chile!*

Winning roles in two films in the same year, both films premiering at the Sundance Film Festival, made me feel courageous about taking a leap, the possibility of a change, like a move-to-Los-Angeles kinda change. Matt's seventeen-year run at MTV News was coming to an end, and it just felt right. So we loaded up the truck and we moved to, well, not quite Beverly Hills, but maybe Beverly Hills adjacent?

We moved into the ground floor of a duplex house at 1073 South Ogden Drive, where my bestie Ron Kellum already resided.

I wanted to play three-dimensional human beings. I made this desire clear to all in the industry who would listen. The work on both coasts dried right on up! A year went by in LA. No auditions. Okay, maybe two or three, but always the same feedback: "too flamboyant." *But the description in the character breakdown describes him as flamboyant! WTF!* The gay roles I was auditioning for—and let's be real, they were *all* gay roles—went to straight men. *So, I'm locked out of playing straight roles because I'm too flamboyant. And when I'm supposed to be flamboyant, I'm too much? And the self-hating white gayt-keepers go and hire straight white men to play the roles anyway! It's a vicious cycle; can't get the gay movie made without a star, but the gayt-keepers won't let any of us gay boys through the gayts! So what is one to do but take matters into one's own hands?*

I called my film producer friend Bruce Cohen, who had just won the Academy Award for Best Picture for *American Beauty*. We met for lunch at California Canteen on Cahuenga Boulevard, that stretch of highway just over the hill where Hollywood meets the Valley. I asked him what I was doing wrong in Hollywood, and he came back to me with the same ol' line I'd come to dread over the years: "You're such a singular talent, Billy. Nobody knows what to do with you!" *And there it is again—the smoke up my ass, and it's giving me IBS! Singular talent without a gig don't pay the bills, and a bitch needs to eat!* However, this particular conversation took a different turn when Bruce asked, "Do you write?"

I rolled back in my mind to one of the days when I was shooting on the film *Intern*. I was standing on the sidelines watching the filming of a scene that wasn't going so well. I was marveling, out loud, as to how this film was getting made. It was written by two unknown female fashion industry interns who magically pulled a rabbit out of a hat simply by the fact that this film was getting made. "How on earth is this happening?" I muttered without realizing I could be heard. The first AD turned to me.

"They wrote it!" he answered, maintaining his deadpan focus on the scene being filmed.

"What?"

"You asked how on earth is this happening and I'm telling you—they wrote it. You have something to say, get to sayin' it."

He's so matter of fact. Like . . . no irony or nuthin'. Like he knows something about me that I don't know about myself. Maybe I should try my hand at it!

I spoke, trying to gather my thoughts. "I wouldn't even know where to begin. Like how to format stuff. I don't even own a computer."

"Well, first of all, it's 1999, computers are mandatory in life—period! Secondly, there's a writing program called Final Draft. It formats the shit for you. They even have example templates of some of your favorite television shows, so now what would be your excuse?"

I gagged. I barely knew this man, and I don't remember his name, but I thank him all the same. The next day I went out and bought myself my very first computer. It was a Sony VAIO. Then I searched the world over Manhattan to find this Final Draft situation the wise 1st AD spoke of. I found the computer program at the Drama Book Shop. As soon as I got home, I set up my computer, with an AOL email account and everything, and loaded Final Draft onto my computer forthwith!

The 1st AD was right! The Final Draft program included a template for *Will & Grace*, one of my favorite shows of the era. My instincts told me to start this new writing thing with something familiar, so I dove into writing an episode of *Will & Grace* with a Black person in it. Unfortunately, racial diversity was largely absent from the casting on *Will & Grace*, with the exception of Gregory Hines as Grace's boyfriend for a time (oh, the irony! the one consistent Black character on this gay juggernaut of a show was *straight*!).

Anyway, I wrote myself into the narrative. I wrote a storyline for *Just Jack* where Karen hires a new Black director for Jack's show, based on my mentor Billy Wilson, who comes in and swirls *Just Jack* into a major Off-Broadway sensation! I wrote in private. I wrote in secret. I wrote for myself and myself alone. When I found myself at Sundance chillin' with my old pal from back in the Broadway revival of *Grease*, Megan Mullally (Ms. Karen herself), I slipped her a copy. She read it overnight and the next day emboldened me: "Honey, this is really good! You really captured our voices. You're a great writer!"

I held her words close to my heart as I embarked upon tackling *Sex and the City*, one of my other favorite shows from that era. I was gonna write an episode where all the women fucked Black men, but in the process of outlining the episode I decided, in my yet-uncharted trajectory of finding my voice, to create a brand-new series, in the spirit of *Sex and the City* but with a cast of all Black gay men!

I called the series *The Ladies Who Lunch*. I finished two episodes and decided to "come out" as a writer. I called some of my actor friends over, and we had a reading of the two scripts in our living room, so when Bruce Cohen suggested that I should take matters into my own hands and create a space for myself by writing, I was already one step ahead.

"You're gonna have to show the world who you are. They don't understand you yet," Bruce said.

I told him of my secret, burgeoning writer-realness and how I came to this particular craft. I explained that while I was having some success just jumping off the proverbial writer's ledge, I had no real skill, no craft—and y'all know I'm an education bitch! I likes to know the rules so I can choose to *break* the rules. Don't git it twisted, this shit ain't no accident!

I asked Bruce if he knew of a writing course that I could take somewhere, and he suggested the Professional Program in Screenwriting at UCLA. "It's just the writing class without all the graduate-degree required classes." I sped home and got online to check the UCLA website for information on when the class was offered. The application deadline had been the day before. I picked up the phone and called the switchboard, Hennys, and just so happened to get the lady in charge of applications on the phone. I told her that I had just heard about the class through a friend and begged her to accept my application. "Do you have writing samples?" she inquired. "Yes, as a matter of fact I do!" She offered that if I could deliver my writing samples to her that same day, my work would be considered. The very next morning I got a call from the Application Lady. I got in!

CHAPTER FIFTEEN

---

*R*ing ... *ring* ... *ring* ... *ring* ...
   The answering machine picks up in the back office.

Stirring in my California king–size bed, I cover my head with the pillow to drown out the cue for the beginning of the day, my reintegration into life as I left it ...

"Hi, you've reached Matt and Billy. Please leave a message after the tone and we'll get back to you as soon as possible."

Click/click—dial tone.

... Or the beginning of a whole new life. Who could have known or predicted what was to come.

Half a second later.

Ring ... ring ... ring ... ring ...

Answering machine.

Click/click—dial tone.

WTF time is it for bitches to be calling me!

5:46 A.M.

The Qweens know not to ever call me before double-digits except in case of emergency!!!

Matt was serving narcolepsy-realness beside me. A piece of bedrock. Unconscious. Immovable. And sawing logs for your nerves!

Matt only snored when he was exhausted. And the trip back from our legendary gay cruise of the Mediterranean was fraught with flight delays, lost luggage—and COACH!

It was an exquisite trip to places I had never been. Places I'd never even dreamed of going to. Didn't even know how to dream of those places, to dream that big. Barcelona was where we started. Gaudí! Are you kidding me with this? From the Casa Batlló Barcelona Gaudí, to that church the divas have been building since water was created, to the actual museum that feels like Disney threw up all over it, in a good way. Then there was Rome—the Colosseum, the Trevi Fountain, St. Peter's Basilica, the Sistine Chapel and Vatican City—

Ring . . . ring . . . ring . . . ring . . .

The phone breaks me out of my dreams.

I guess this may be an emergency. I'm not ready for emergencies this early; what time is it . . . ?

"Hi, you've reached Matt and Billy . . .

"Billy! Matt! Wake up! Get up! Pick up! Wake the fuck up and pick up the phone! Right now. You gotta pick up! Comeoncomeoncomeoncomecomeon! A fucking 767 just—"

"Hey, hey, hey, I'm here. What's up? What's going on?"

Aaron could barely produce words.

"You gotta wake up and turn on your television. A plane just crashed into the World Trade Center. They think it might be a terrorist attack."

The walls seemed to be caving and twisting in on me simultaneously. Wringing the tears from my eye sockets as I tried to make my way to the living room. The tears were void of emotion. Just raw, visceral, terrifying— attached to something unfathomable, yet currently unknown.

What does a terrorist attack even mean?

Breathe.

Calm.

Just get to that fucking clicker and turn on the television.

It can't be all that bad, right . . . ? Let's not be so hyperbolic as to cry wolf over nothing, right . . . ?

Of course, it was worse than I thought. September 11 was, to this day

185

and most likely till the day I die, the single most defining moment of my life. And I'm sure I'm not the only one. I would venture to say it was the day that the entire world changed forever. Simply. Just. Changed. The kind of change that's evident and illusive and manic and empowering. A change that has no definition, no words to describe it. For the lucky, sane ones (and I would blessedly count myself in that number), perhaps a shift in consciousness. A higher level of connection. And for others, less fortunate in the sanity department, just an excuse to vilify "the other" and declare wars that never end.

That morning I sat comatose on the floor in that position that we sat in as kids, cross-legged, directly in front of the screen. Mesmerized. Hypnotized. Nose-to-nose with the human forms behind the tempered glass. I couldn't pry my eyes from the devastation. There was this clip that CNN kept running over and over. A pedestrian on the street, some blocks away. A surreal vantage point. Then in slow motion, this huge mass of migratory metal slowly eclipsed the blazing September sun—engines roaring and rumbling out of control, the moment just before detonation—savage, monstrously alien, like in some sort of Spielbergian science-fiction/disaster movie. Like a movie, everyone says. But it wasn't a movie. It was real. I started to choke—a visceral reaction. I was gasping for air.

When I came to, I found my bleary eyes swollen almost shut from the tears, from the fear. A strange feeling of nothingness washed over my being. The savage imagery of the moment and the immediacy with which this . . . this . . . unfathomable information was accosting my senses caused my emotional hard drive to shut down. There were tears. There was emotion. I just couldn't seem to marry the two energies together. My psyche was trying to wrap her mind around the idea that the debris, the shrapnel spewing forth from the mouth of floating fire in the sky, was not simply steel and glass and fire and computers and desks and chairs and sinks and briefcases and pocketbooks and toilets and fluorescent lights and asbestos—cell phones, family photos, cement—but could be . . . human— human beings . . . ? Heads? Leg? Arms? Entrails? JESUS!

The desolating realization that somebody's mother, brother, lover, husband, homey, sister-friend had just been blown to smithereens, evaporated in the blink, left me feeling disabled, impotent. Jihad. A Holy War. In God's name? That very same God who is rumored to love us? I just can't imagine what it must have been like to stare death square in the nose of a 767. I don't know that I could bear that kind of hell.

* * *

BOOM!!!

6:03 a.m.

A second Boeing 767 detonates the South Tower of the World Trade Center. I'm blasted back into reality and realize that Matt is still sound asleep in our bed. No doubt my sweet boyfriend is still dreaming of cruising through Santorini, the little town built on the side of a mountain, or Monte Carlo, where we were banned from shopping because we were wearing shorts, or the white sand beaches of Mykonos.

"Boo, you gotta get up." I shook him gently. No luck.

"Babe—wake up. You gotta wake up. The world is on fire!" I was screaming at this point.

"Stop yelling at me!" Matt mumbled. "I'm up."

"No, you're not up. You still asleep. And I'ma need you to pull it together pronto and come with me!"

I almost yanked his arm out of the socket dragging him to the living room. We both resumed that cross-legged position directly in front of the television. I'm not sure why. Maybe we needed to feel close to the action, as twisted as that may sound, because we weren't there. We both came out to LA with a hope and a dream. It was the turn of the century and we had both recently turned thirty. Y2K felt like just as good as any time to make a change.

Matt and I had brought in the new century in the heart of all the festivities. The lobby of the Minskoff Theatre overlooked Times Square, and there was a big, swanky party being thrown by the theater owners, the Nederlander Organization. The world was all aflutter with concerns about whether or not the computer grid would shut down. Everyone was preparing for elevators to plummet and planes to fall out of the sky. None of us could have predicted this!

All I could think of as I watched the world blow up before me was how suddenly traitorous I felt for leaving New York. When the shit got real I cut and ran. I deserted my friends, my family, my art, my dreams, in an attempt to . . . what? Find myself?

Yeah, somehow now that all seemed frivolous. I searched my soul to find justification for my betrayal but all I felt was a hostile emptiness, the kind of vacancy that makes a bitch just want to check out. Like—for *real* for real. I had moved to LA with Matt because I was feeling disenchanted, so I needed to displace myself. I needed to step back and reassess what I wanted for my career, for my life, for my survival on this planet.

A sense of dreadful reflection washed over me. I questioned everything. Every decision I had made up until this point had been based on either fear or a manic need for approval and acceptance. It was time to try something new. Time to take myself out of the masculinity race—actually, I took myself out of all the races. My goal became to relinquish the need for validation outside of myself. It was time to choose myself. It was time to no longer need the idea of acceptance or tolerance from anything or anybody else. My demand became respect! Respect me—respect my humanity and we'll all be just fine. It's hard to teach an old dog new tricks, and this life transition took some time to fully take hold—*and* bitch still needed to eat!

And then it hit me. *FUCK! What about* Into the Woods? *That shit ain't never gonna happen now.*

* * *

In early 2001, I had heard through the grapevine that Stephen Sondheim's *Into the Woods*—one of my favorite musicals by one of my favorite writers—was being revived. I called my agent immediately to get an audition. Word came back to me that the casting director was dragging his feet as to whether he thought I was "right" for the project or not. Being not "right" was code for "not white." And I knew this. Race was always an unspoken roadblock, one of which I was very aware. I was also very aware of the pigeonholed box I'd been placed in by the gatekeepers of the industry. To them I was an extremely gifted singer. Nobody thought I could act, so I was not surprised by this casting director's response.

However, I know for certain with my history in this business over the prior decade that my talents had proven me worthy of my five minutes in the room: ". . . and you tell those bitches that if they don't give me an audition appointment, I will just crash that shit down there at that Mark Taper Forum and show my belligerent Black ass until they acquiesce . . . *and I've worked with James Lapine!*" I bristled. James Lapine, the book writer/director of the original production of *Into the Woods*, was returning to the directorial position for this revival that was set to open in the spring of 2002. Needless to say, I got my five minutes.

The audition was in Downtown Los Angeles at the famed Center Theatre Group. I auditioned for the role of the Baker. In this audition I tried something new: I sang the ink. Remember *Grease?* That way of presenting myself became my normal. It was expected. People enjoyed it. I never fit into any traditional box and I needed to be heard, so this was my way.

But for this particular audition I had a different goal. I needed to actually *not* blow the roof off the joint. I needed to be regular. I need to show them that I could simply fit into the box the gatekeepers constructed. So I sang the ink—the notes on the page, and nothing more. I sang the song in the original key, which was so low for me my vocal cords could barely phonate to produce sound. The goal was to remove my extreme singing—my gift—from the equation, thereby opening up a space for the people to experience my acting ability. That was always the rationalization for not casting me in roles that required dimension. My work was not experienced as three-dimensional. As grounded. As human. I was considered an amazing singer with the ability to stop a show, yes. But I was nothing more than a clown to them in that moment in time. I respectfully refer to this time in my life as the *Millennium Coon Show* era. My goal with the *Into the Woods* audition was to dispel the myth that I couldn't act, once and for all. So, I stood flat-footed and, with galvanized intention and focus, sang with a quiet, transparent stillness.

When I was done there was a lingering silence that was finally broken when James Lapine spoke. "You are an extraordinary actor—I had no idea." And there it was; there was my proof. The knowledge of perception is key to success. One must know how one is being perceived from the outside.

Now, my mama used to always tell me to not concern myself with what other people say or think about me: "That's not your problem, son." And this is a good way to live most of the time. But in this particular situation, the change could only come with the knowing. One must know how one is perceived by the folks who can give one the job.

My good friends and colleagues would dismiss my complaints of not being regarded as a person with acting chops as being silly, or overreacting. But I always knew the truth. My friends weren't in the audition rooms with me. I accepted the truth and therefore was armed in the proper way to create a space for myself in this world. I knew—and I proceeded with knowledge. 'Cause knowledge is power!

In my mind I had already won. The fact that James Lapine had just commented on my acting instead of my voice was the goal. I knew that I was not the correct type for the role of the Baker as it was originally conceived. I knew that it would take a very specific kind of miracle to be in a world where I would be cast in a Broadway revival of yet another lily-white show. *The Great White Way, indeed!*

I thanked James as I gathered my things to leave the room.

"Where are you going?" Mr. Lapine asked.

I was tingling at this point. I had scaled the first wall. Lapine's interest was piqued. I saw a light bulb go off in his brain.

"So, I don't think you're the right type to play the Baker. You have way too much pizzazz for that . . ."

"Pizzazz" . . . ? That's code, bitch. Don't think I don't know what chu tryin' to say.

". . . however, I do think you're a perfect fit for the Witch."

Biiiish—don't play with me! That's my dream. I been dreaming about playing this role since I saw Phylicia Rashad replace Bernadette Peters on Broadway.

The nontraditional casting struggle is real up in these streets! But there is a caveat: If one is famous, one can do things that other lay-minorities cannot do—i.e., if you are famous enough to sell tickets and you just happen to be Black, it's all good. So my goal is, get famous enough to be a bankable entity, and then I'll get to transcend race. Otherwise—stay in your Black-ass place!

I was speechless that the idea came from the middle-aged white man himself. The author. The director. It wasn't me muscling my way in and demanding a place at the table, which I had done in every aspect of my existence up until this point. It wasn't me doing the work for them and showing a possible new way to interpret the material so as to possibly carve out some sort of niche for myself. I showed up at that audition with every intention of just fitting in. See me like you see all the other white boys you hire for every gig in town. All of my contemporaries seem to be able to keep a job. However, I found myself waffling between the changing winds of possibility and obscurity. It seems absurd, but I'll tell you the truth. As sure as I breathe air, the work dried up the minute I demanded my humanity—and that's the God's honest truth. Turns out my perception of how I was being perceived was not off the mark after all. I finally gathered myself to answer.

"I would . . . I mean, it's always been a dream of mine to play the Witch, so please don't tease me," I pizzazzed.

"I'm not teasing. I'm very serious. I've been looking for a fresh way to approach this material, and I was ruminating privately just yesterday about the possibility of a male witch. I mean, it's already a fractured relationship between a mother and daughter. That could just as well very easily translate to father and daughter." He talked himself into a creative orgasm. "Why not! And I wrote it, so what I say goes." *Famous last words . . .*

"So why don't you take this material home and come back in a couple of days, let's see what you do with it."

"I don't need to." I smirked.

"I'm sorry . . . ?"

"I don't need to take the material away, I can do it right now," I said, foaming at the mouth.

"But I need you to sing the Witch's material."

"I know. I know it." My brain was on overdrive.

Stay ready, then you don't have to git ready!

Success is when opportunity meets preparation; dat's what Oprah said!

"I just need a couple of minutes to read over the sides and I'll be ready."

To say I slayed the children would be an understatement. I acted and sang that man into the ground! As I've stated before, the audition room is my favorite space in the world. It's the place where I get to lay it all on the line. Strut my stuff. Hawk my wares. They flew me to New York for my first callback. Lapine greeted me at the door with a huge smile and a hug. Warm. Open. Dare I say welcoming—in that kind of way when you can feel that the winds of subjectivity have blown in your favor.

"I would like to start with what we refer to as the Witch's rap. It's in the opening sequence. Are you familiar with it?"

"I think I've heard of it." I played coy.

"Well, come over to the piano and let's read through it."

I feigned ignorance as I pretended to sight-read the rap over the accompanist's shoulder. Then took my eyes off from the page as I began to spit rhymes, from memory, like it was some hip-hop freestyle rap battle.

There was a silent space in the air when I finished the stanza. Lapine hung on my every word like a ghetto-fabulous diamond hoop earring on Beyoncé's earlobe. I kept going, going full gansta rap on those bitches.

Lapine asked me to sing "Stay with Me" next, and when I finished he got up from his chair and paced for a bit. It felt like he was fighting to keep a lid on his excitement. His poker face was melting away as I saw him see something in me that made him smile. Lapine is not a big smiler. His creative juices were flowing, and I truly felt like I was a part of making that river flow. You get enough *nos* in this business to know when a *yes* is possible. And I knew for a fact that Lapine loved me. Be that as it may, he knew how persnickety Mr. Sondheim could be in relation to the interpretation of his work. He was notorious for shutting the children down! So a work session was scheduled for me with Mr. Sondheim's longtime musical director Paul Gemignani.

Three months later I was flown back to New York for my work session with Gemignani and my final callback with the man himself. The final candidates for the role of the Witch were Jennifer Holliday, Vanessa Williams, and . . . herself, yours truly. I finished singing my first song for Gemignani and he was thoughtful . . . in silence. After a spell he simply asked me for the next song. After I was finished, he looked up from the keys and said, "Just do it like that."

I was already moist with nerves when I took to the stage for my final callback at the Westside Theatre on Forty-Third Street between Ninth and Tenth Avenues. I summoned the god of all things fantastical to enter the building. I focused in on the spell that needed be to cast. It wasn't nuthin' but the spirit of Jesus that possessed my body on that oppressively muggy July morning. I finished performing the audition packet, and Mr. Sondheim quizzed me in disbelief at what he had just witnessed.

"Wow! Can you do that eight times a week?"

Without skipping a beat I blurted out with fearlessness: "You bet your ass I can!"

* * *

By mid-August 2001, I hadn't heard anything from the *Into the Woods* folks, and I had started to get antsy. I asked my agent to inquire about my status on the project. Was I still in the running? Was I not? Word came back that all the creatives were on the Billy Porter train, but the producers had concerns. To this day I still can't figure out what they were concerned about. If the creators of the piece thought I was the one, if James Lapine and Stephen Sondheim themselves thought I was the right one, then I was the one, right?

I took it upon myself to be proactive and write a letter to Mr. Lapine. I told him I was overwhelmed by the artistic freedom he gave me, just by allowing me to be myself. He had said to me, "The Witch doesn't fit in. You don't fit in, Billy," and I told him how profoundly his words had resonated with me, just as Sondheim's had from my days of riding the school bus in Pittsburgh, listening to *Sunday in the Park with George* on my Walkman. And I told him I wanted the job, that we had the chance to change theater together, to not be elitist or irrelevant, but to bring in the new and make the bold choices that would help American theater survive into the twenty-first century.

On September 10, 2001, there was a message on my answering machine when Matt and I returned from our Mediterranean cruise.

"Hi, Billy. It's James Lapine. Just calling to let you know that I received your beautiful letter. We've been navigating some pushback in our creative ideas regarding *Into the Woods*, but never fear, we're working them out. Rehearsals start December 13. Don't take any other work . . ."

* * *

Sitting cross-legged on the floor in front of my TV in Los Angeles, watching the aftermath of the terrorist attack in New York, I knew my dream of playing the Witch was gone. If the show could even go on, there was an excuse now. The producers now had a bottom-line reason for not taking the risk. A need for fiscal responsibility. The artistic choice, the fearless choice, the choice that included me, once again would have to wait.

I stood over my answering machine in a trance. Pressing repeat on that message over and over until I had heard it enough. I needed to make sure that what I was hearing was real. I needed to hear the hope in his tone as I mourned the loss of yet another "almost." In my heart I knew that Mr. Lapine had promised something to me that the universe would not allow him to fulfill.

I pressed the delete button on my answering machine. I couldn't bear listening any longer. I never heard from Mr. Lapine, or anyone involved with that *Into the Woods* revival, ever again.

CHAPTER SIXTEEN

*T*his is a fucking lynching! A modern-day public fucking lynching. 9:29 . . . this coward knelt on this man's neck for 9:29. Cell phone cameras rolling, capturing the execution. It's terrorizing to know that at any moment I, a Black man in America, can easily and systematically be killed at the hands of the precise institution that is supposed to serve and protect all citizens.

This week has been rough on Black people. In an attempt to threaten and weaponize the police against a Black man, some white lady, breaking the law by walking her dog in Central Park without a leash, called the police on a bird-watching Black man who simply asked her to adhere to the leash law. So she called 911, her voice trembling, saying she was being threatened.

This not-so-micro-aggression shit happens every day. Just days ago, I was shooting the cover of Essence magazine—the first Black gay man to grace the cover, for the institution's fiftieth anniversary—and this bitch across the street from our rental house on Long Island called the cops on me.

This cover photo shoot was my first gig back during the pandemic. I was excited. This was major for me, seeing as how I've consistently felt dismissed by the Black community. My queerness has always been a bone of contention, my masculinity always cited as a reason to erase my humanity and existence. The all-Black creative team was fired up for this shoot, sure that it could help to crack open the conversation that needs to happen between homophobic Black folks and the LGBTQ+ community. Dripping in Thom Browne couture, on the streets of a desolate cul de sac, we commenced making some COVID-protocoled, socially distanced, gender-smashing, rejection of toxic masculinity, fashion magic ovahness.

Now the truth is, we were feeling so effervescent and grateful to be working that we may have overreached by setting up a shot in front of our across-the-street neighbor's sprawling driveway. I immediately felt responsible for our gaffe as I heard the rustle of a car behind me creeping over the impeccably manicured white gravel. As the car inched haltingly in our direction, a sense of urgent racial backlash bubbled within us all. The older white woman who occupied the car glared at me. Window rolled completely down, as if an invitation for clarification.

"Hi there! How are you doing today?" I offered the most respectful tone to deescalate a possible tricky interaction.

Instead of responding to my overture with the respect I deserved, that we all deserved in the moment, this woman chose to glare at me, roll her window up, and proceed to the corner of the block, where she waited in neutral for the next five minutes. Unmoved and unbothered, my team and I continued our work. But when the local police pulled up five minutes later, we all knew what had happened. Just like always, that woman played her white-woman-in-distress card and told the authorities that she was confused by "people on my street in masks and costumes."

Now, let me break this down for y'all: first and foremost, we're in the middle of a pandemic, and the CDC's recommendation is that everyone wear a mask. Secondly, I was standing in the middle of the street in full-on, unapologetic Thom Browne couture, resplendent in a pink, corseted eighteenth-century number commonly known as Mantua or court dress. My head was adorned with a white hat with an overlay of lace that extended at least a foot off of my head, shaped like a heart, with a six-foot white-laced train affixed to the top.

So, this was yet another common case of #[insert any activity here]-whileblack. But to add insult to injury, I found out shortly after this kerfuffle that this bitch's family business was in fashion. The fucked-up reality is, if she'd had the capacity to see me as a human being and actually talk to me when I offered a connection, all of this mess could have been circumvented.

The horrifying images of Minneapolis white police officer Derek Chauvin pressing his knee on George Floyd's neck for 8:46 has been running on a loop nonstop on my television screen and in my mind for days now. I'm tired. I've had enough. We've all had enough of this. Four hundred years of the same shit. Every day of my life I live in fear for it. EVERY DAY of my life my humanity has been up for legislation. And we're supposed to just sit down and shut up. We are at a tipping point, and Orangina 45 and his cronies know exactly what they are doing. Create dissent. Create division. Create chaos and watch it all burn and then blame Black people for having a response. We are tired. We are enraged. I'm so mad I don't know what to say. I'm so enraged that I have a hard time speaking because all I want to do is scream. All I want to do is rage. All I want to do is burn it all down. Dismantle the entire system and let the chips fall where they may. I don't know how else to do it. They have pushed us, once again, to the brink of insanity. Every day of my life I have to make myself smaller so white folks will feel more comfortable. I'm done doing that.

The whole world watched as that smug bastard lynched George Floyd, comfortable that there would be no accountability. He knew he could murder this handcuffed Black man with impunity. The sound of George Floyd's voice crying out to his deceased mother as he lay pinned to the asphalt, begging for his life, haunts me every day. That could have been me. I am George Floyd. I am Breonna Taylor. I am twelve-year-old Tamir Rice, I am Philando Castile, Freddie Gray, Eric Garner, Michael Brown, Ahmaud Arbery, Rayshard Brooks . . . the list is endless. The stark reality is traumatizing. The silver lining, if that can even be a thing in this instance, is watching the world wake the fuck up. This tragedy has sparked a flame inside of our souls. The children have taken to the streets in protest, and not just in Minneapolis, but the entire world! Enough is enough, and we the people are rising up once again to get up in these streets and get into some "good trouble."

* * *

I woke up on September 12, 2001, with no voice.

Could not speak.

Could not sing.

Could not produce sound in any way.

My vocal cords were not phonating.

I went to my voice doctor.

Severe acid reflux.

Brought on by stress!

My savior. My weapon.

GONE.

For real.

No sound at all.

Kryptonite got me.

I am more than my voice!

I been screaming that from the mountaintops.

I asked the universe to be seen.

I prayed to God for guidance. For courage.

This feels like forced courage.

But courage nonetheless, I suppose.

After many months, many doctors . . .

An endoscopy appointment bore no reason.

Stress.

Just like in the seventh grade.

The nodules on my vocal cords.

Vocal rest for six months to get it back.

The affair . . .

Sorry—the abuse.

It was not an affair; my therapist corrected me.

I was sexually abused, but I'm the abomination.

Nobody helped me. Nobody protected me.

But I'm the abomination.

I *am* more than my voice.

And . . . without it, who am I?

What am I?

How do I breathe?

How will I live?

Here I stand on the precipice of obscurity.

For a reason.

For a healing.

Necessary . . . and profound.

Okay, God—I see you . . .

* * *

I met Black Dr. McDreamy at a party in Los Angeles. July 2001. I saw him from across the room. We locked eyes. He took my breath away. We were both attendees at a fabulous Black, gay soirée on the border of Baldwin Hills, commonly referred to as "the Black Beverly Hills." All the divas were present and in full effect. I came in an Abercrombie & Fitch ensemble. Not really my style, but 'twas all I could afford in the moment. The party was in full swing when I arrived. It was a cookout. You know Black folks love a cookout. I attended alone because my boyfriend, Matt, was out of town on business. I hadn't planned on stayin' long. I was just gonna pop by and show my face for about thirty minutes and then leave. I got a drink. I got a plate. Ribs, collard greens, potato salad—you know the drill. I found a corner in the dining room to sit my plate upon while I fed my face. There was a tap on my shoulder. It was *Black Dr. McDreamy.*

"Hey there—I saw you when you came in, and I just wanted to come over and say hi. You're Billy Porter, right?"

"Yes, I am!" I gulped. Tingling all over as this fine-ass Black man engaged me in conversation.

"I just wanted to let you know that your album got me through medical school."

"Oh my God. That's so sweet. You're one of the ten people who bought it!"

He took a pause, and then: "That don't matter. If you only touch just one—that's all that counts, right?"

And that was it. We were engaged in conversation for the next three hours in the corner of that dining room. We talked politics. We talked the semantics between "gay" and "same-gender-loving" individuality. We talked purpose and mission and calling and ministry. For you see, *Black Dr. McDreamy* was called to be a healer. Based in Atlanta, with his medical focus on HIV in the Black community, it felt like he was sent to me for a reason. A divine purpose. I couldn't put my finger on the why of it all; all I know is, I sat in my car and cried for an hour before even being able to drive. I looked at myself in the rearview mirror and realized in that moment how much my early trauma had influenced who and what I was attracted to as an adult. I realized in that moment that, up until that point, I had never allowed myself to even *think* about being attracted to a Black man. Black men were a danger to me. It was a Black man who abused me. Black men hated the sissy, thereby hating me. Black rap artists made money off of their hatred of gay people, even the conscious, pro-Black acts like Brand Nubian ("fuck up a faggot / don't understand their ways, I ain't down with the gays") and Goodie Mob ("the world would be a better place to live, if it was less queers"). And Black comedians were worse. The genius Eddie Murphy went all in on *the faggots* in his stand-up comedy special *Delirious*, saying, "When I do my stand-up . . . *faggots* aren't allowed to look at my ass while I'm onstage," and going on and on about gay sex, gay panic, and AIDS.

I was thirteen years old when *Delirious* came out, and I remember sneaking down to the living room late one night at Grandma's house to watch, and registering how unabashedly the audience howled, roared, and whooped at Miss Murphy's degradation of what I knew deep down would become my personal authentic humanity. In this moment it became even more clear that the world at large was laughing at us, at me. There's no safety in that. No protection for the faggots.

I will say this: In the decades that have followed, I have watched many former, notorious homophobes evolve. Common once had homophobic lyrics but disavowed them; even Eddie Murphy called his old jokes ignorant. I'm grateful for their public evolutions; I'm grateful for their allyship. Bravo! And after I met Eddie in person at the 2020 Golden Globes ceremony, he reached out to my team to say he was a fan of my work and my commitment to my own authenticity, and has a project he would like to collaborate with me on. Progress, Bitches! *WERK!* So looking forward to what transformative art we will create together.

* * *

I couldn't stop weeping. I couldn't run anymore. Unconscious or otherwise, I had to face my reality. I was afraid of Black men. I didn't know how to love a Black man intimately, because at my roots, my personal-experience roots, Black men were not a safe space for me. And unfortunately, the gag is, if I have issues with the Black man, then I have issues with myself. If, indeed, I'm afraid of the Black man, then I'm afraid of myself. Dare I say, if I hate the Black man—I hate myself. Not good! I'm a Black man first! That's what the world sees first!

How could I not have seen this sooner? I was so embarrassed. If I'm being honest, almost a decade prior, I felt this coming. I knew I needed to address my feelings of completely unaddressed self-hate. In the mid-nineties I joined a Black gay book club to get more in touch with my Black gayness. I built relationships with Black gay men outside of my intimate circle of chosen family friends, most of whom are Black. I made real connections with Black men who were not in show business. I never ended up dating any of the men, never got to the sex of it all, but I *did* make enduring, loving, brotherly relationships that I cherish to this day.

Black Dr. McDreamy and I stayed in contact through the following year. And while I kept our association to myself, never speaking of him to my partner at the time, I'm proud to say there was never any cheating. I never stepped out on my relationship.

By the spring of 2002, post-9/11, I knew I needed to make some changes—the biggest change being breaking it off with my partner of four years. He didn't see it coming. He was blindsided. My friends were blindsided. Nobody knew how I felt. I never spoke about my feelings, where I was emotionally in the relationship. I kept it all to myself. That was wrong of me, and I paid a severe price for it. My ex-partner shut me out. Completely. However, he aggressively remained connected to every single one of *my* friends whom I'd introduced him to, while refusing to even talk to me. This went on for almost a decade. Some folks took sides. I let them. I moved on. I felt betrayed by some, mocked by others, misunderstood by all.

In the process of my torturous breakup I was presented with an opportunity to create and direct a Broadway-style musical revue based on Stevie Wonder's musical catalog, called *Signed, Sealed, Delivered*. The project was set to debut at the Venetian hotel in Las Vegas. I worked with brilliant musical director and close friend Stephen Oremus on crafting the arrangements. Stephen would go on to musical-supervise Broadway hits such as *Avenue Q, Wicked, The Book of Mormon, Kinky Boots, Frozen*, and many, many more.

My first directorial experience turned out to be a wash of trauma. Firstly, I was embroiled in the middle of a desolating breakup. Secondly, the shifty producer found himself embroiled in some legal trouble, of his own making, and disappeared three days before rehearsals were set to begin. Thirdly, we were blessed to have the incomparable Chaka Khan to headline the production. Maddeningly, though, the Venetian had no incentive to support our efforts, so there was no promotional support for our production, and therefore our show fizzled and shuttered in just shy of three months.

Black Dr. McDreamy and I engaged in a torrid affair during the months between *Signed, Sealed, Delivered* closing and my moving back to New York to start rehearsals for the Broadway-bound production of *Little Shop of Horrors*. That experience didn't turn out so well. But it's all good. Things are werkin' out!

The intensity of our love affair came to an abrupt end when, after flying to San Francisco to finally consummate the relationship we had been fostering long-distance for at least a year, Black Dr. McDreamy informed me, postcoital by-the-by, that he had met someone else and intended to move forward with the other fella. Needless to say, I was out on the next thing smokin'. *I guess my trauma was too much? Too hard to navigate? Too much to hold space for? Not Black enough? I don't know, at least that shit was quick!*

We had no contact after the breakup, if we can even call it that, for about a year, and then—a rapprochement. He apologized to me for being an asshole. He owned up to how shady the situation was, and we remain very dear friends to this day. Black Dr. McDreamy has dedicated his life and career to addressing the systemic racial disparities in America's health care system. He's changing lives one Black, plundered body at a time. I'm proud of my friend.

* * *

Do you believe in relationships? Is a committed, monogamous relationship between two men even possible? Why is it's about sex. S.E.X.!!! Sex inside the confines of a relationship, or more accurately, the lack thereof. The more I fall the less I can connect. To sex . . . I mean, I guess it's not a new issue or dilemma. My therapist tells me I'm not the only one with this problem.

I . . . I . . . I am having a problem. A problem connecting, a problem closing the chasm, that hole in my heart, that hole that exists between sex and intimacy.

Where I come from, being gay is not an option. The last taboo. The ultimate sin. An abomination. My people would rather I be a serial killer than a faggot.

Some people . . . most people aren't strong enough to overcome the rejection, the abject alienation, so they—so WE—burrow underground. I tried to bury my instincts. I tried to squash the impulse, replace the pain, replace the shame. Pray it away?

Our Father

Who art in heaven

Hallowed be thy name . . .

The desire comes in waves. I call it the Entity, the Other, the splitting off of personalities. Compartmentalize. Disassociate.

Bernie is in my bedroom, AIDS is in my bedroom, always.

Have a drink, drop an X, do some blow, block out the noise, mute the shame, if only for a moment. I don't know how . . . I don't know how to connect.

AIDS is in the room, Bernie is in the room. Cumulonimbus clouds of shame. Always.

It's like a demon possessing, trauma engulfing my mind, tryin' to turn my mind reprobate. Like the Bible says, Romans 1:28, fools who don't acknowledge God will lose their minds. Where are you, God? Am I losing my mind?

Every minute of every day, feeding the bastard of shame, bound by her fiery talons. I can't catch my breath. I can't feel my soul. I'm fucking to remember. I'm fucking to forget. I'm fucking away the shame. I'm fucking my way through the pain. I'm fucking for my freedom. I'm fucking to feel something—anything . . .

Or is it to numb, anesthetize. Coming of age, experimentation.

Silence = Death

Sex = Death

Trollin' the streets, after Pegasus—da' club. Hoe strollin' around "Dithridge" in the middle of the night. Picking up trade at "The Fruit Loop" up in Schenely Park, blue collar blow-jobs in pickup trucks, dusty boots from venturing into woods, into the shadows. Always in the dark, always in secret, under the shame of night. When contempt and oppression, stigma and shame are all you know . . .

I can't dream much anymore—really . . . but I'm haunted. Not a day goes by that I don't think about it. Every choice, every decision, every relationship, every fucking breath I take . . .

Then he died! The motherfucker died! Before resolution, before closure, forever traumatized . . .

I hate him for that. I hate him for robbing me of my childhood, my innocence. He dumped his shit on me and then disappeared. Now it's my shit. And I have to live with it, pay for it, the Sins of the Father. My fath—my *stepfather* . . .

Our Father

Who art in heaven

Hallowed be thy name . . .

The hate consumes me with a power that paralyzes. I'm better sometimes. I have really great days. I have really bad ones, trying to sort the shit out. But he's not here. He's not physically here.

I thought Mommy knew. I thought it was all a part of the plan. PLEASURE turned to SHAME turned to RAGE. I need it to go away. I need to heal. I need peace . . . I understand now how people lose their minds. I understand the addict who needs a fix. 'Cause she just wants the pain to go away, or to subside at the very least. And just when I think it's over, that pain, that fury . . . Every time I feel like I've made progress, forgiving him, forgiving myself, forgiving God, the universe, or WHATEVER . . . The shit comes back . . . the Entity, the Other, morphing into yet another terrifying monster, coming for me bigger and stronger than the time before, laughing at me.

Just laughing . . .

CHAPTER SEVENTEEN

*I*t's a novel virus. And a novel virus is one that has not previously been recorded. It's new, a new threat, a new killer. Scientists are scrambling. Orangina 45 lied to us all. He said it was just like the flu, said it would go away by Easter. Gotta get the economy back up and runnin'. While dead bodies are being stacked up on top of each other in overflowing hospitals. Nursing homes all over the country have patients dropping dead by the hundreds. He says it will disappear by summer—like magic. And proceeds to not engage. No national plan, no protection. Every man for himself. Every local government can figure it out on y'all's own. And ain't no PPE for those frontline workers either. Ain't enough, and what's actually available will go to the highest bidder, each state left to compete for the medical supplies that will save lives. Fuck 'em.

"It is what it is . . ." That's how the leader of the free world responds to a global pandemic.

Wearing masks would be of great use in bringing down the spread of this virus. Orangina don't care. None of his cronies care. The GOP is still actively trying to dismantle Obamacare, Medicare, and Medicaid. During a pandemic . . .

It's been the long game for decades. One of the long games. The other is the courts.

Doesn't matter who the president is, or what party controls Congress, if all the courts are conservative. Ruth Bader Ginsberg has died. Of course the GOP is rushing to fill the seat with a female conservative who has been against anything and everything that we've spent the last century-plus fighting for. The hypocrisy! The bullshit!

Actually, the entire system is bullshit. It's not broken. It's working exactly how it was set up and intended to work. To keep us Negroes in our place! James Baldwin wrote, "To be a Negro in this country and to be relatively conscious is to be in a rage almost all the time."

It's all a game to them, and we got played. The Democrats got played because we still naively believe Michelle's "When they go low, we go high." It's time to redefine what "going high" means. It's time to play the game that we're in and stop taking a bag of popcorn to a gunfight.

We got played. For years. For decades. For centuries.

During the 2016 election, when Orangina entered the race and everybody thought it was a joke, I fucking knew he was gonna win. 'Cause we were asleep at the wheel. We had a Black president and we was all like, "Kumbaya, bitches—racism is over!" In December 2015, GOP senator Lindsey Graham said Orangina was "a race-baiting, xenophobic, religious bigot," but as soon as the choice came down to denouncing Orangina or the loss of his power, sycophantish #LadyGraham fell right in line.

I can't breathe. I literally cannot breathe right now as I live inside of this terror that is America.

* * *

Back in 1992, I kept hearing about this new show called *Jelly's Last Jam*, based on the life of Jelly Roll Morton, the self-proclaimed inventor of jazz. At the time, I was in rehearsals at 890 Broadway for *Five Guys Named Moe*, and I would run into the cast in the elevators. I was excited to see this new Black Broadway show that I had not even been considered for, had no idea it was even happening. I treated myself to a preview during the first week of performances. It was not good. It was four hours long and mostly incoherent, a disaster to my young, pretentious, Carnegie Mellon–ass, twenty-two-year-old self.

Four weeks later *Jelly's Last Jam* opened to rave reviews and went on to garner eleven Tony nominations. In his effusive review in the *New York Times*, Frank Rich called George C. Wolfe, who wrote the book, "a visionary talent," and the show "a sophisticated attempt to tell the story of the birth of jazz in general and, through that story, the edgy drama of being black in the tumultuous modern America that percolated to jazz's beat."

He didn't see the same show I saw. I don't know what they talkin' 'bout. I'ma have to go see that shit again.

I didn't know much about Wolfe. His rise was meteoric, as far as I could see. He had seemed to come out of nowhere to me, when in, like, a three-year period, he became the it man of American theater. I knew a little of him because my drama teacher in high school hooked me up with one of his first plays, *The Colored Museum*: a series of eleven "exhibits" (sketches) that explore prominent themes of African-American culture and identity. I performed the searing Miss Roj monologue from *The Colored Museum* to audition for Carnegie Mellon, but had not truly paid attention to the name of the playwright at the time. I was young; please forgive me.

Being that I was a standby in *Five Guys Named Moe* a few blocks south at the Eugene O'Neill Theatre, it took me some time to steal a moment away and take myself back to the see *Jelly's Last Jam* again. By the time I got back there, it was post–Tony Awards, where *Jelly's* took home a total of three: Best Lead Actor in a Musical for Gregory Hines (God rest his fine-ass legendary soul), Best Featured Actress in a Musical for Tonya Pinkins (who, come to find out, is a CMU Drama Department alum who also left the program early, to make her Broadway debut in the ensemble of Stephen Sondheim's *Merrily We Roll Along*), and Best Lighting Design for a Musical for Jules Fisher. *Five Guys* was nominated for two Tonys: Best Musical and Best Book of a Musical. We lost both.

Jelly's Last Jam was revelatory. Astonishing. A masterpiece. Period! This is the moment I learned what the "preview period" in the theater is truly meant for. You see, the last scene partner we have in making theater is the audience. The audience will always tell you if yo' shit is working or not. Previews are the time when a show can go from good to great! That means that there is work happening during the daytime. Book changes, musical changes, new full dance numbers, and the like. Previews are ostensibly a "work-in-progress" situation. At this point I was on my second Broadway show, and both pieces had transferred from London, so by the time these shows came to America the preview "fixing work" had already been done. My preview period for both *Miss Saigon* and *Five Guys Named Moe* was merely performing a show that had already been "frozen" years prior.

Ticket prices for previews also used to be cheaper back in the day. Like, 30 percent less, sometimes only half the price of a normal ticket. This practice really gave the magical theater makers time to perfect their work without disgruntled audiences leaving the theater and talkin' shit about a piece of art that's not finished. Sorta like what I was doing.

When I saw *Jelly's* again, I marveled at the way the artists found the space to use tap dancing as an emotional language, as a life force that is needed to propel the narrative forward. Not just shuckin' and jivin' and coonin' for white folks' entertainment pleasure. This was the first piece of theater I had ever experienced that asked the mainly white audiences of Broadway to consider the cost. What do racism and white supremacy and alla that cost us spiritually, emotionally? What toll do they take on one's psyche? Gregory Hines, a young Savion Glover, George C. Wolfe, and the entire cast of exquisite artists managed to redefine and reclaim the meaning of our African-American heritage, which in this particular piece is found in the rhythms. From the drums of Africa to the tap, tap, tapping of our feet to the rhythm of life, we search for our history, for our collective healing— our rhythm is our life!

I would spend the next decade trying to get in a room with the genius whom I fondly refer to as "GCW." But to no avail. Like . . . nuthin', no love whatsoever. After a number of years of literally feeling invisible to this man I adored from afar, I gave up. Moved on. It almost felt personal.

* * *

In 2002, my two-year-and-nine-month Los Angeles exploration had come to an end. I can count on one hand how many film and television auditions I had in almost three years. I had blown through my savings attending the Professional Program in Screenwriting at UCLA. I had broken it off with my boyfriend of four years, Matthew Anderson. So I jumped at the opportunity to move back to Manhattan with a gig on Broadway. I was poised to make about $300,000 to sit backstage in a sound booth and voice a man-eating plant—playing Audrey II in a revival of *Little Shop of Horrors*.

And then along came *Radiant Baby*, a new musical based on the life of Keith Haring. I had participated in several readings of this piece at the behest of the writers, Stuart Ross and Debra Barsha. And when an exuberant Debra came to me with the news that George C. Wolfe had taken a liking to the piece and was announcing a fully realized production for the 2002–2003 Season at the Public Theater, and that *the man himself* was going to direct it, I told her that Mr. Wolfe would probably not want me.

Debra scoffed, "That's ridiculous! Who wouldn't want Billy Porter in their show?"

Turns out—a lot of people. A lot of people didn't want me in their shows. "Listen, I would love to be a part of this project, I'm just letting you know, based on my history with George, he won't want me."

So, the myth goes like this: George knew I had been involved with the project. They started casting. They saw the entire world. I was broke— excuse me, *financially challenged* at the time and doing a play in New Haven, Connecticut, called *Going Native*. The Long Wharf Theatre Company was housing me, but the play was closing in a couple of weeks and I was waiting on George to say yea or nay. My friend Jordan Thaler was (and still is) the in-house casting director for the Public Theater, so I called him personally. "George has till midnight tonight to make a decision. I've been waiting long enough, and I have another offer on the table that I need to take if this ain't happenin'. A bitch needs medical insurance!"

Jordan called me at 11:30 P.M. It was a Friday night. "So . . . Debra Barsha went off!"

"Really, what did she say?"

"She tore into George!"

"For real?"

"She screamed, 'Billy told me a year ago that you would stonewall him, but I didn't believe him. What is your problem? If Billy Porter wants to be in my show—I want him in my show!'"

"So . . . what he say?"

"George threw up his hands and said, okay."

It wasn't even a real part. It was a bunch of little moments strung together. What we in the theater call a "utility character," an actor who slips in and out of different identities throughout a given piece, one who moves through space very often as a cultural generalization, whose character name in the program is usually denoted as "Man 1," "Woman 2," "Disco Soloist," "news reporter," etc. But that didn't matter to me. I wanted to be in the room with GCW. I needed to be in that room. I knew the artist's life I longed for and aspired to harness was in that room. So, it wasn't about my ego. It wasn't about the role. It was—and always is—about the work.

Well . . . WERK!

At the opening night party on March 3, 2003, George took me aside and offered an apology. "In my experience, people with the kind of singular talent you have are crazy. I assumed you were crazy, and I never felt like a had a big-enough role for you to deal with my assumption of your crazy. Thank you for being a leader for these kids. Your presence and professionalism truly enhanced this process." Or something like that.

Wow! This was the wish, the dream come true. Just basking in the presence of the divine is all I ever wanted. George became, like, the artistic father figure I never really had.

Then in the summer of 2003, I found out I had been fired from *Little Shop of Horrors* (still three weeks shy of closing in the out-of-town tryout at some random, nonunion theater in Coral Gables, Florida), and with a formal announcement on Playbill.com naming my old *Five Guys Named Moe* standby friend Michael Leon Wooley as The Voice of Audrey II. Instead of $300,000, my payout for being let go was $15K. I was spinning out, trying to figure out how to make ends meet, relying on the kindness of friends for sofas and guest rooms to lay my head. *3 Suitcases, 22 Boxes & a Chaise: A Life in a Decade* was what I named this complicated era of my life.

I was grasping.

George offered me a lifeline.

"Oh, please. Fuck them. You don't need to be singin' in an off-stage booth nohow. Come back to the city and just come on down to the theater. I'll give you a desk somewhere in the building and you can do a residency here. I know you want to write and direct and create your own shit, so come on!"

During my residency at the Public Theater from 2003 till around 2006, I rose to the next level of my artistry under the tutelage of my hero and mentor George C. Wolfe. I was in the room soaking up all the gems of information I could when he was creating *Caroline, or Change*, written by Jeanine Tesori and Tony Kushner. I shared a hotel room with him in London when he went over to remount Suzan-Lori Parks's Pulitzer Prize–winning play *Topdog/Underdog* in partnership with the Royal Court Theatre, starring Jeffrey Wright and Mos Def.

I pitched GCW on an all-Black-cast Sondheim show, and he barked at me, "Sondheim is overrated!" in his flippant GCW way. So I burrowed into my own original work. Telling my own story, since nobody else was interested. Be the change.

I developed my autobiographical one-person show *Ghetto Superstar* during this time, and George made sure to produce it in the 2004–2005 season in partnership with Tracy Brigden and City Theatre in my hometown of Pittsburgh. There were very few people on earth whom I imbued with the kind of supreme creative control over my own thoughts and ideas. My trust and admiration in George's genius was and still is one of the greatest loves of my life. So imagine how terrifying it was to have to respectfully deny his direction. Go against the master.

I was in previews for *Ghetto Superstar* at Joe's Pub, where the venue had been transformed into a proper jewel-box theater. The small stage was expanded. The lighting elements were upgraded, and my one-man show was the first of its kind: an actual musical/play performed on the Joe's Pub stage. The second number in my piece was an original tune I wrote with my writing partner, James Sampliner, called "Sissywhippers." A title that, to my ear, is self-explanatory. To George's ear, not so much.

"I don't understand it. I don't know what *sissywhippers* means," he snarked.

I was like, "What's not to understand? It means exactly what it says. sissywhippers—people who whip on sissies."

George was not the director of my show. He was my producer. He was the artistic director of the Public Theater. The Black gay man was runnin' shit! George was the HNIC, Henny! There was an almighty omnipotence to George's creative ideas, and generally we all bowed down to his wisdom and expertise. I wanted George to direct my show. He didn't want to. That's cool. So, I hired Brad Rouse to direct. He came from a recommendation through Tracy Brigden, the artistic director of City Theatre Company in Pittsburgh, our producing partner. We kept getting notes from "on high" from George (his office was on the second or third floor of the theater complex), essentially telling us, telling *me*, that "Sissywhippers" wasn't working and I needed to cut the number. Here's the tricky part: Everybody on my creative team—director, band, Black-up singers, lighting designer, sound designer, hell, even the ushers and the bartenders—was in agreement that "Sissywhippers" was one of the best original songs in the show!

I avoided George for two weeks of previews. I was the artist. I was performing the show every night. I know what works. I knew the song worked. However, I didn't know how to address this conflict. Finally, after the third or fourth admonishment from on high, I decided to try cutting "Sissywhippers" from the show. The cast and band were confused. I assured them, "We're in previews. This is precisely the time to try shit out. If it don't work, 'Sissywhippers' will go back into the show tomorrow night!"

It didn't work. "Sissywhippers" went back into the show the following night. George had a fit from on high. I let him have his fit. I tried his idea and my show suffered. I suffered. The song was the second number in the show, the first two numbers being my own original songs. The "Sissy-whippers" cut left me with about twenty minutes of jabbering between the opening number and the next piece of music. It was not a good look. It did not work. I had scalding, gooey egg on my face. I made an executive decision. I broke rank and file and now awaited the guillotine. But the guillotine never came. I heard word that George was furious and fuming. I let him fume. I trusted my instincts. I chose myself—and it worked! And at the opening-night party George cornered me, while deep in his cups, and yapped, "You were right. 'Sissywhippers' works!" And he trotted off to enjoy the rest of the party. He wrote me a sweet note on opening night that I still have framed and hung on a wall in my living room:

> Billy—See what you can accomplish when you stay out of the bars and clubs! Your work is amazing. It's been a joy watching you rise to the occasion, and not just rising—but taking flight and soaring. Love, George

George had offered me a lifeline. Not financial, but artistic. Artistic and thereby spiritual, allowing me to hold on to some semblance of faith, hope, grace, gratitude, sanity, and self-respect. So when George dismissed my Sondheim idea, I didn't have the fortitude to press further. I simply moved on and never thought twice about it again.

* * *

Suzi Dietz kept pushing. She emailed me at least once a month, but I had a new account and wasn't checking the old one that often. When I did, there were three years of emails, checking on me, asking about my Sondheim idea. It was something I had briefly mentioned to her in passing at our first meeting, and she had pursued me. For three years. I almost missed my blessing.

I thought, *Why is the white lady from LA, who claims to be a Broadway producer, bothering me about Sondheim?*

I was kind, answering Suzi's emails with polite detachment. I thought, surely it would be the Black, gay, HNIC God of Theater who would usher me into my rebirth. I couldn't wrap my mind around even fathoming a white Jewish lady, whom I barely knew, wanting to produce an idea that I had about an all-Black Sondheim show. I had only just started writing, just started directing, just started to find my voice.

And anyway—GCW said it was a bad idea.

Three days after opening night of *Ghetto Superstar*, Suzi Dietz flew in from Los Angeles with her producing partner, Paula Holt, to attend my show. They took me out to dinner at the now-shuttered Noho Star, right down the street on Lafayette, for a post-show repast.

"So what's your next project, Billy?" was the first sentence Suzi uttered.

"Umm . . . not really thinking about that right now? You see what I just did, right? I mean—three years of development from the page to the stage. The back of my head is about to blow off!" *These are the jokes, kids.*

That got a laugh. But then something different happened, something I had not experienced before in my career. This woman who I barely knew showed up for me, believed in something inside of me that I was only at the beginning of discovering for myself. Suzi opened her purse, pulled out a folded check, and conspiratorially slid it across the table, like those art-of-the-deal-makers we see in the movies and shit! $7,500?! I tried not to cry.

"Well, I guess I'ma be working on an all-Black Sondheim show next!"

Suzi Dietz saved my life! Like y'all know I always speak of the angels in my life. Suzi swooped in and literally saved me. First and foremost, she believed in me and my art beyond what came before; she saw the artist I could become. Suzi and her husband, Lenny, became my patrons. Lenny Beer is the founder of *Hits* magazine, the music industry insider's most accurate singles and album charts, a supplement to the more widely pub-licized *Billboard* charts. Lenny is also a music manager and a fierce busi-nessman. Here I was, in the middle of my "in the valley" moment of life. Just about to throw in the towel and move on back home to Pittsburgh to teach full-time, but the universe had different plans. The universe was teaching me something. Something I couldn't quite put my finger on in the moment, but I tried to stay present. I tried my best to be open. I learned there's no shame in needing help in this life, and checking one's ego at the door in order to find the vulnerability to ask for it.

Patrons of the arts were something I had only known from history books. I never predicted that I would be in need of somebody's help. I never had the luxury to depend on anybody but myself for anything. "Folks do exactly what they want to do and nothing more," my mother would muse. And as glib as she may have sounded, I found my disabled mother's plaintive introspections to be more than a notion, and to only illuminate the state of truth. "Don't nobody owe you nuthin'," she would often say, trying to prepare me for the rigors of life. "Ain't nuthin' comin' to you fo' free!" So, when Suzi and Lenny showed up in my life to help, I was suspect.

Suzi and Lenny allowed me to lay my head at their Manhattan apartment when I was serving homeless-realness. They gave me the run of their Laguna Beach house to focus on my writing (I finished my first full-length play, *While I Yet Live*, there). Suzi cut a check for the full payment of nine months of rent for me in 2007. That same year she followed through and produced that all-Black Sondheim show I had been threatening to create. She pushed me. She believed in me, probably—no, definitely—more than I, believe it or not, believed in myself.

So here I was, hanging out with this older Jewish couple in Laguna Beach, wondering how I landed here. Why did these wealthy white people like me so much? Why did they take me in? Who was I to deserve this? When was the other shoe going to drop?

And I had never experienced, in such close proximity, a relationship like theirs. Suzi and Lenny have been together for over forty years. They have two children. Multiple grandchildren. A solid, loving, evolving, trusting partnership. With Grandma and Aunt Dorothy, they both had married names, and yet I can't recall either one of them ever uttering the names of their long-forgotten husbands. My mother and my other aunts never spoke on it either. I had extracted myself from my inherited-by-birth confusion and traumatized childhood some twenty years hence, and the separation, the disassociation, had gone unchecked for decades. So simply being in the presence of love, graceful love, mature love, truly cracked open a space in my heart and led me to dream that maybe, just maybe—I could know a love like that one day too.

* * *

I reached for a gourmet Harry & David pear from the fridge. It was in a gift basket they had received for the holidays. It was the sweetest, juiciest pear I had ever tasted. Soon, a tooth on the bottom right side of my mouth began to tingle. Within thirty minutes the pain transitioned to throbbing, a pain so intense it had me contracted into myself in a fetal position on the bed. It was late on a Friday night and there was no emergency dentist to go to, so Suzi and Lenny offered up the liquid Vicodin they had in the fridge left over from a procedure one of them had had in the past. I took a swig, and within an hour I was puking it all back up. My body was in rejection mode, trying to push an infection out of my body that had already gone systemic (we would come to find out this fact early the next morning, when Suzi arranged an emergency appointment with her dentist).

I had no medical insurance at the time and was totally stressed about how this bill was going to get paid. But there was never a bill. Suzi and Lenny took care of it all. The dentist diagnosed me with an abscessed tooth. Infection already systemic throughout my entire body. The dentist prescribed two different strains of the most intense antibiotics on the market, and I flew back home the next day to start rehearsals for *Langston in Harlem*.

But back in New York, I didn't get better. One morning I woke up and realized I was just getting sicker and sicker. The past three weeks had been hell on wheels. I was losing weight, like twenty-five pounds. I was weak, fatigued, thirsty all the time. I had gone to see *Jerry Springer: The Opera* the night before, and my vision was blurry. I couldn't really make out the faces. I blamed it on the antibiotics, but M&M said it sounded like I had a touch of the sugar. But how . . . ? I'm the bitch who eats broccoli for breakfast!

Diabetes runs in the family, though. Grandma and Dot had to prick themselves before every meal. They had to carry around a chilled pouch with them everywhere they went. Never really paid much attention beyond that. It's the antibiotics! Gots ta be!

I went back to the dentist after the first antibiotics cycle, and the infection wasn't gone. I had to take more—more poison ingested into my body. Ingesting poison to kill the poison?

Sumthin' ain't right, sumthin' ain't right with me.

M&M said I needed to go to the doctor.

"With what insurance? What money am I usin' to pay? I'll put some Neosporin on it. I'll be fine."

That morning I dragged myself out of bed and into the bathroom. Then I caught a glimpse of my face in the mirror. Gaunt. Skin ashen. Cheeks sunken in. Cheeks turning black. Wasting, wasting, wasting away.

I left, walked, to the subway, just blocks away.

IgottapeeIgottapeeI'mapeemypantsIgottapee . . .

The transfer in Times Square. The walk to the theater, the Public down on Lafayette. Exhausted, don't know if I'ma make it today.

Igottapeeigottapeei'mapeemypantsigottapee . . .

Cain't stop crying. Folk must think I'm crazy. The presentation. In front of an audience. *Langston in Harlem.* I told the director, Kent Gash, I'd do it. I pulled myself outta every ensemble number. Just my two solos. I can handle that, right? I do what I say I'm gonna do. Don't wanna let nobody down. Two solos. Two presentations. Back to bed. Only thing that feels good is the cold, and I hate winter. But this cold today, the freezing February cold, feels good.

Igottapeeigottapeei'mapeemypantsigottapee . . .

I make my entrance. The audience gasps! Collectively audible. I finish my two numbers. I tell Kent I can't do the second show—gotta go to the doctor. I don't have any medical insurance. I can't pay for this. Put some Neosporin on it . . . I walk from Lafayette and Eighth Street to Twenty-First and Fifth. I walk into the doctor's office; he takes one look at me and says: "You're diabetic. Go to the emergency room now!"

Igottapeeigottapeei'mapeemypantsigottapee . . .

I walk alone to St. Vincent's on Seventh and Greenwich. Ground Zero. Emergency room . . . waiting . . . two hours gone by. My cell phone rings. It's Stephen Oremus, musical director extraordinaire, a dear friend. He's calling to say hi, check to see if I liked his show—*Jerry Springer: The Opera*—the one where my vision was foggy.

"Where u at . . ."

"I'm in the emergency room at St. Vincent's—waiting."

"What's wrong?"

"I don't know. Don't feel good. Haven't felt good in weeks."

Neosporin ain't werkin' this time . . .

"We need to call Doctor Dan? He's the head physician."

"Do I know Doctor Dan?"

"You've met him a million times with me and Vincent . . ."

I don't have the energy to talk, but I keep tryin'.

IgottapeeIgottapeeI'mapeemypantsIgottapee . . .

"Let me call you back," Stephen says. "I'm gonna call Doctor Dan!"

Within minutes a set of previously locked double doors swings open to reveal the angelic silhouette of . . .

Doctor Dan!

"Billy! What are you doing here?"

I looked up, almost blinded by the celestial glow that washed over him.

"I don't know. A doctor told me I have diabetes."

"Come with me!"

And, as if Moses were parting the Red Sea, the majestic double doors part, making way for my infirm body. The walls are cream white. The carpet feels like walking on clouds. The doors close behind us, and there's peace. Like noise-canceling headphones on a 747.

Doctor Dan ushers me into a bed. Draws the curtains. Takes my vitals. Measures my blood levels. He's gone for about thirty minutes. He returns, clipboard in hand. The face, his face, has sympathy in it. I don't need sympathy. I don't want anybody feeling sorry for me.

I'm not a fucking charity case! Or—am I? The voices in my head blare with remembrance of the curse.

"So . . . good news or bad news first?" Doctor Dan asks.

"The bad. Give it to me."

"Well, your sugar levels are at seven hundred fifty."

"Okay—what should they normally be?"

"Between eighty and one twenty, one thirty tops."

"So, I'm diabetic."

"Yes. Now, do you want the good news?"

How the fuck did this happen? This wasn't supposed to happen. I eat broccoli for breakfast!

"The good news—no, the great news—is, you're healthy!"

"I am?"

"Like, healthy as an ox. Usually vital organs start shutting down around four hundred fifty. You've managed to be walking around this earth for the past three weeks virtually dead."

"Oh my God!"

The tears come. They flow like rivers. "How did this happen? What did I do?"

"Nothing. It seems as if the abscess infection triggered an internal predisposition. Do you have diabetes in your family?"

"Yeah—my grandmother, great-aunt, father, my aunts on both my mother's and father's sides, if I remember correctly . . ."

"And there you have it!"

"Okay, so now what?"

"You're gonna have to stay put for a while. We gotta get these sugars under control."

Fuck! Fuck! Fuck! I don't have medical insurance.

"I . . . I . . . don't have medical insura—"

"Don't worry about any of that right now. We just have to focus on getting you well so that I can come see you perform again. You're one of my faves!"

An orderly wheels me to a private room. I doze off . . .

The hospital phone rings.

"Hello?"

"Hi, Mr. Porter. I'm calling from the hospital billing office."

"Okay . . . ?"

"I'm calling to ask who your insurance provider is."

"I don't have insurance."

"And how do you plan to pay for your treatment?"

The nerve of these muthafuckas. I haven't even been in the room for ten minutes and they callin' me asking for money!

"Ask George W. Bush! See what that bitch says and get back to me!"

Click.

I spent ten days in the hospital. More than I've ever spent in a hospital. The public understanding about type 2 diabetes always seems to blame the victim. Every single one of my friends who visited me asked me what I did. I explained it was hereditary, but still got the side-eye from a lot of folks.

Doctors sent me home with lots of medicine, and within a week of taking insulin, my blood sugar was plummeting to the depths on the daily. Turned out, once my blood sugar was under control, I no longer needed the insulin. The benefits of living a relatively healthy life.

I stepped myself down from the medication slowly and maintained my blood sugar through diet and exercise, without medication, for almost four years.

Then my body gave up. Blood sugar levels skyrocketed for no reason.

"There is a reason, and it's called a hereditary predisposition," my doctor assuaged. "It's not your fault. Stay off WebMD and take your meds!"

* * *

I went to the lawyer's office to sign the papers. I gave up all my credit cards. I turned in all my debt. Twenty thousand dollars had ballooned to one hundred thousand in just five years of trying to pay my minimums on time and keep a good credit score. I was always pretty good with credit cards, considering they are set up to prey on the financially undereducated, which, incidentally, most of us are. I don't know nuthin' about money. Ain't never had none. Learned how to live hand-to-mouth from jump, so being a "starving artist" never felt much different from anything else I had experienced in my childhood.

I was proud of myself that I had left home at seventeen, and for the first twenty years of my adult life I was handling my finances pretty well, considering I had no guidance. No financial mentorship. When I won *Star Search*, nobody told me I should have taken that money and invested in real estate (I shoulda bought a studio in Hell's Kitchen before Disney moved into Midtown and all the property in the surrounding area tripled, sometimes quadrupled). Who knew? Not I, sir. That money just sat in the bank, and I lived off it till it was gone. Turns out after taxes, $100K ain't that much.

I took a risk in pursuing my dream. I jumped off the ledge with no net and here I was, seven years later, still free-falling. I never imagined that walking away from the insulting, Black, magical Negro, fairy clown roles of Broadway I was being offered would render me uncastable. After a decade of being in the business, I saw my future and didn't like what I saw. No shade, but I didn't see much growth or depth on the path I was headed down, so I shifted gears and took the road less traveled. None of this was easy. I lost high-profile roles I knew I could have gotten, and the paychecks that went with them. Homelessness and bankruptcy were part of this journey as well. There were many nights when I cried myself to sleep on someone's sofa, where I had overstayed my welcome. And here I was, seven years into my step-out-on-faith realness moment, and I was signing . . . I'm so embarrassed . . . I was signing bankruptcy papers. Bankruptcy! I was officially bankrupt! WTF!

When I charged my screenwriting class at UCLA, I never imagined I wouldn't be working for a decade. My trajectory up until that point had been positive. I had worked all through my twenties. Five Broadway shows. Lots of amazing developmental work. An R&B record contract. I was turning it! I was making a name for myself. Making a mark. I never imagined the work would go away. Dry up completely. So here, at thirty-seven years old, on the brink of obscurity—I signed the bankruptcy papers.

* * *

I've managed to stay COVID free. Been sequestered out here on Long Island. Found this sweet little haven for me and the hubby just by chance. We lost Nashom on March 23. It was a shock. He was my age. Big and strong as an ox. Found dead in his bed. Terrence McNally passed the next day. Adam freaked out, demanded we get the fuck outta Dodge. I'm glad he did. I was in a daze. The terror in his eyes, my heart, my breath. Where could we go? I've never done such a thing as rent a house before. Never had the means. Now I have the means. I remembered my friend John, who moved his family out to Long Island. I texted and asked if he knew of any other houses for rent. He hooked me up with his real estate agent, and within two hours we had rented a home for three months. We moved in that Sunday, March 29. We booked only through the end of June, mainly because the house was already booked for July and August, and who woulda thunk that America would be forced to shut down indefinitely. Who could have predicted our government would completely ignore a pandemic and turn America into what looks like a Third World country. But when I think about it honestly, when it comes down to America and who and what the white people in power choose to care about—it ain't neva been me, or anybody who looks like me.

* * *

It was the spring of 2007. It started as a little pimple on my right butt cheek. Just a smidge above the seat. For three weeks it grew. It grew to the size of a quarter. And hardened. There was no continuing to ignore the bump. It became sensitive to the touch and so it was hard to sit. I was secretly favoring my left butt cheek. I didn't have medical insurance at the time. So, you know, it was like my childhood all over again. We didn't go to the hospital unless your eyeball had popped out the socket. Put some Neosporin on it. I did! I had been putting Neosporin on the pimple, the bump, the cyst.

I decided to head down to the Callen-Lorde Community Health Center, a primary-care center located in Chelsea, on Eighteenth Street. Callen-Lorde is dedicated to providing medical health care to the city's LGBTQ population without regard to ability to pay. It is named in honor of Michael Callen and Audre Lorde. I strode into Callen-Lorde on an enchanted spring day. You know, the kind where you feel for certain that the weather has broken for good. No more dipping down to below freezing in a snap. The queen at the check-in counter was fun and flirty. I told him I was there to get a pimple on my butt drained, and he asked if I wanted an HIV test too. "They're only ten dollars," he offered.

"You know what, it's actually past my usual six months, so yes!"

The doctor was kind. He checked all my vitals. He checked out my pimple. He administered the HIV test and then disappeared for about twenty minutes.

When the doctor returned to the exam room, his energy had shifted. He was solemn. Pensive. I don't remember much after the word "positive" fell from his mouth. Everything constricted. I stopped breathing. I could see the doctor's mouth moving. I caught snatches of sentences:

"It's not the death sentence it used to be."

"Do you have a GP to follow up with?"

"Everything's gonna be all right."

But would it be? Would everything be all right? Nothing has ever been all right. My whole life I been runnin'. Runnin' from my family. Runnin' from the church. Runnin' from my circumstance. Runnin' from the inevitable. Runnin' from statistical data that said I would be just another Black faggot who would die destitute and penniless, because that's all that faggots deserve. The lady told me from the pulpit all those years ago that I would never be blessed if I didn't stay on the "straight and narrow" path that God had designed for me. Forever the cursed, all I could hear in my head was what I always heard: "AIDS is God's punishment!" I chose to be a faggot and now I was paying the ultimate price. So here I was on this magical spring afternoon: diabetic, bankrupt, and now HIV+. All the things that society said I would be. Here I was—the statistic. The embodiment of that statistic the entire world predicted I'd be. As hard as I tried, hard as I prayed, I couldn't outrun it. The obvious. The common. The inevitable.

CHAPTER EIGHTEEN

In 2010, I was in tech rehearsals for my return to the American stage, starring as Belize in the Off-Broadway revival of *Angels in America* at the Signature Theatre Company, when I got a call from Jerry Mitchell to come and participate in an informal table reading for a new musical he was working on, an adaptation of the British-American comedy film *Kinky Boots*. Jerry had been set to lead the creative team as director/choreographer, with book by four-time Tony Award winner Harvey Fierstein and music by two-time Grammy Award winner Cyndi Lauper.

Based on a true story, *Kinky Boots* tells of the straitlaced Charlie Price, who inherits the family business, a struggling British shoe factory, after the sudden death of his father. In a ploy to save the family business, Charlie forms an unlikely partnership with Lola, a Black drag queen, and develops a plan to produce custom footwear for drag queens, rather than the men's classic English-brogue dress shoes that his firm is known for, alienating many in the process.

When the original film was released back in 2005, I carried my happy ass alone to the movie theater to see it. I didn't know anything about it, but the poster art intrigued me. There was a Black man standing with a white man and woman, with a sparkling red stiletto-spiked thigh-high boot in the foreground. The film stars Joel Edgerton and Chiwetel Ejiofor in the leading roles as the owner of the shoe company and his drag queen muse, respectively. I was bowled over by the film. The movie made me feel like, with a little more push, my natural gifts could indeed make room for me. The role of Lola, the drag queen, the star, the moral heart of the piece, was played by a Black man. A Black man from England, but a Black man nonetheless. I literally said to myself, out loud, that if I had lived in London and had access to audition for the role of Lola, Chiwetel Ejiofor would have been out of a job. No shade. Just fact. Chewy, as I have heard friends refer to him, was wonderful in the role. Fierce even, as the qweens would say. However, I simply knew that given the opportunity to show my stuff with a role like Miss Lola, I would be able to not only inject my career with some staying power, but also transform the world.

Straight men prancing around in dresses to entertain the masses has been a respected art form since the beginning of time. Men played female roles in ancient Greek theater, just as they did two thousand years later in Shakespeare's time—in fact, women weren't allowed to even *be* actors. And it continues in modern times, from Tony Curtis and Jack Lemmon in the hilarious and classic *Some Like It Hot*, to Dustin Hoffman in *Tootsie* (one of my favorite films of all time), to Robin Williams in *Mrs. Doubtfire*, to Flip Wilson's Geraldine, to Eddie Murphy's countless portrayals of buxom, zaftig Black matriarchs in the *Nutty Professor* films, to Wesley Snipes as Noxeema Jackson in *To Wong Foo*, to Martin Lawrence's side-splitting ghetto diva Sheneneh on his hit television sitcom *Martin*, to Tyler Perry's Madea—Hallelujer! Society's capacity to receive these heterosexual men, in full drag, without any pushback, was the norm. Even in *Kinky Boots*, the intention was clearly the illusion of straightness. "Cross-dressing," if you will. "They" cut their dicks off and the world ate that shit up like bees to honey—for centuries.

When I heard about *Kinky Boots: The Musical*, I saw an opportunity with the character of Lola to reframe the narrative. Defy expectations and create a three-dimensional human being, not simply a fabulously flamboyant clown for the world to laugh at. I wanted the world to laugh and cry and grow and transform *with* me. I wanted my Lola to be sexy, sassy, grounded, and most importantly—gay! Because while straight men in drag had always been considered part of the art form, gay men in drag (at least before the explosion of and world domination by *RuPaul's Drag Race*) were very often vilified by mainstream society as perverted and predatory. This trope is particularly dangerous and damaging when the direct line of messaging lives inside the idea that if I'm a gay man choosing to be a drag queen, or wearing a dress simply because I like it, that somehow I'm/we're coming to molest your children. *STOP THAT SHIT!* I don't even *like* children. Predators come in all shapes, size, races, and sexes. Whether one is wearing a dress or not while engaged in predatory sexual misconduct has absolutely nothing to do with it.

Much to my dismay, the creators were going along with tradition. The casting breakdown described the role as *a Black, cross-dressing boxer. Must be able to do a British dialect.* "Cross-dressing"—translation: heterosexual. Once again, I was confronted with the "masculinity" conversation. Here's a character, and an archetype, that had never been seen before on a Broadway stage. A Black drag queen at the center and heart of the story. Not the butt of the joke. Not the person who's being vilified for his humanity. Not the side character with the obligatory gospelian number bringing the house down. No! Finally I had a real shot at bringing to life a groundbreaking actual, real, authentic human being. There was just one snag—I had to book the gig first!

I got a phone call from Jerry Mitchell on a Monday to come in and participate in an informal table reading of *Kinky Boots*. The moment was set up to simply sit around a table with a few actors and read the script that Harvey Fierstein was adapting from the screenplay. They also wanted me to learn one song.

I had been waiting for this call for over two years. I had heard that table readings were happening sporadically with a different actor. In a previous call I had made to Jerry, letting him know my interest in the project, he reassured me that I was at the top of his list. Unfortunately, my history (remember that *Into the Woods* revival) had proven to me that just because you're at the top of somebody's list does not necessarily mean the job is yours. I knew I would have to fight for it, and trust—I was armed with all the ammunition required.

I arrived early the following morning to go over the song Stephen Oremus had sent me the day before, "Not My Father's Son." I was so moved by the lyric. The melody. The intention. The song felt like it was written for me, for *me*—Billy. Not just the character. The song is about a man coming to terms with his father, with not being "the image of what he dreamed of," but realizing "that I could just be me." It spoke to the source within all of us for activating forgiveness. Love is an action. Forgiveness is active and ultimately healing for the one being forgiven, but *most* importantly for the forgiver.

The hoops of fire that I was required to jump through to book this gig were some of the most scorching I've ever encountered in my thirty-plus-year career. Having suffered through almost a decade of severe acid-reflux agony, I still found my instrument in the void of inconsistency. Sometimes my voice was fine, and other times the reflux would flare up and I would be ass-out! The goddess voice guru Joan Lader, known the world over for her extensive therapeutic knowledge of the vocal cords and how to heal voice injuries, showed and showed out for me. I literally had to relearn how to sing. Stress was always the determining factor for my flare-ups, and the stress of knowing I was not *everybody's* first choice took its toll.

Many people in the industry assume that I was a no-brainer for the role of Lola. And history shows that fact is indeed true. However, to be clear—I was *not* offered the role straight out. I had to audition just like every other Black musical theater actor alive at the time. I endured months and months of friends, and potential Lolas, calling me and asking why they were even having auditions. Raging to me that the powers that be should just be giving me the role. I felt the same way but also understood that I needed to check myself, check my ego at the altar, and go to that audition and do what I know how to do best—slay!

They didn't make me come in until the final callbacks. My reflux was flaring up, but even on my worst day I was confident I could call on my decades of voice lessons and attention to my craft and pull the rabbit out. Upon returning to Suzi Dietz's apartment, where I had been bunking— for I had no home of my own—I received word from my manager that the musical director wanted to have a vocal work session with me. *Wait!*

Stephen Oremus wants to have a work session with me on my singing?! Are you fucking kidding me?! My dear friend with whom I've created arrangements for productions of Jesus Christ Superstar *set in South Africa in 1998, and* Signed, Sealed, Delivered: The Music of Stevie Wonder *in Las Vegas— the artist who claims me as a mentor and calls me his muva, wants a work session to see if I can, what . . . handle the material? Something ain't right.* I continued to check my ego at the altar and went on ahead to that there werk session.

"Just belt everything." Stephen threw up his hands and rolled his eyes all the way to the back of his head.

"What the fuck, Stephen?" I spewed.

"Everyone thinks that your scene work is by far the best. However, some people are concerned that you don't have the stamina for eight shows a week." I took a deep breath, chuckled at the irony.

"Okay. I'll belt it all. It's a pop music show, so we all know that makes no sense. But whatever. I'll come *back* in tomorrow and serve those muthafuckas Patti LuPone realness for ya nerves! Are we done here?"

By the time I got home and ate a bowl of soup for dinner, my mild acid-reflux situation had flared up and went postal in my throat. My cords would not phonate. I could not make any sound whatsoever. It was like September 12, 2001, on steroids. I had lost my entire voice the day after 9/11. I had about fifteen hours to pull myself together—and find a voice! I called my mother to pray with me.

"Mom, I need you to call on Jesus for me. I have this final, *final* callback for *Kinky Boots* tomorrow, and my throat ain't cooperating. This is it for me, Mommy. This is my true first and last shot. I gotta be able to belt out some tones by tomorrow at noon."

My mother prayed for me. It felt like the laying on of hands through the phone ethers. I took a white-lady pill and passed out. I needed rest. I awakened around 7:30 A.M. and began my Joan Lader vocal warm-up therapy to get my cords phonating. It took a full four hours for my cords to relax, clear enough to produce a sound sufficient for the lead of a Broadway musical.

I belted the music full-out! *WERK!* I served them full High *British* Mighty White Woman realness (remember I got an A+ for my high British accent in dialects class at CMU). *Shablam!* I gathered my shit and washed my hands of it all. By the time I got outside, my voice had vanished again.

I received a call from Bill Butler, my manager, that Jerry wanted me to come to his penthouse apartment for coffee. I called my friend personally. I was tight.

"Jerry, is this good coffee, or bad coffee? 'Cause I don't need to come to your house for bad coffee, I can receive bad coffee over the phone!"

"Billy! Shut up and just come over now!"

I walked trepidatiously up Ninth Avenue from Forty-Second Street, crossed over on Fifty-Fourth Street to Jerry's apartment between Seventh and Broadway. *Is this really happening? Am I about to create a role in a Broadway musical? Is the original dream finally coming true—for real?*

By the time I reached Jerry's penthouse I was drenched in flop sweat. He opened the door with two glasses of champagne in his hands. He pulled me into an embrace and squoze me real, real tight and whispered in my ear, "It's you. It's always been you. It's never been anyone else. And I'm sorry they made me put you through that."

I took a breath. I was so moved that my buddy, my friend of twenty-one years, remembered me. He reached back and pulled a brother up. I bring light to this fact because many people, when they get in positions of power, *don't!* Jerry did and changed my life forever.

I recently received some insider information about my journey to Miss Lola. As I have stated, *some* folks, actually some producer or producers, did not want me. One went so far as to bring an agent from CAA to the backers' presentation to see if there was anyone, "a star," on their roster who they could replace me with. Blessedly that agent was Joe Machota. And blessedly he schooled said producer that I, in fact, was the only star they needed, and if she couldn't see that, her show would never be a hit. Which is why I am now represented by Joe Machota. *WERK!*

* * *

The production schedule for *Kinky Boots* was officially set. July 2012: four-week workshop. September–November 2012: Chicago out-of-town tryout.

February 2013: Rehearsals begin for Broadway production. April 4, 2013: Opening night on Broadway.

Stark Sands, Annaleigh Ashford, and myself were officially cast as the headliners. An astonishing cast of virtuosity was compiled, and we set out to make some theater magic and hopefully change the world by changing some minds.

During the audition process I didn't focus at all on my uneasiness surrounding the idea that the creative team was writing Lola to be a straight boxer. Matter of fact, I said nothing about it until the last week of the workshop, after our backers' presentations. I called a meeting with Jerry, Cyndi, Harvey, Stephen, and the lead producers, Hal Luftig and Daryl Roth.

"Okay—now that you all have seen *my* interpretation and creation of Lola, can you honestly say that anyone on the planet would believe I was a straight man?"

The answer was a resounding NO, and everyone moved on. Except for that press junket day in the Al Hirschfeld Theatre where infamous New York journalist Michael Musto blindsided me with the "Lola-is-a-straight-boxer" insider information. I played it off and cheekily said that Harvey and I were still in a girl-fight over it. I told him that after having a heart-to-heart conversation, where Harvey spoke to me about how "we've seen and I've written the character of Lola before," I informed him that the archetype he had traversed in as a writer for so many decades never included *me*. A Black man. "When has Zaza in *La Cage aux Folles* ever been a Black man in a first-rate Broadway production?" The answer is—never! Believe me, I've tried! And for what it's worth, I believe, first and foremost, the brilliance of the story, Harvey's writing, Cyndi's lyrics, and the themes in general transcend our humanly flawed, perplexing sexuality and gender conflicts. As "Raise You Up/Just Be," the triumphant final song of the show, says, "Never let 'em tell you who you ought to be / Just be. With dignity. / Celebrate your life triumphantly." That's it! It's just that simple! Love yourself, and have the courage to love thy neighbor as you love yourself. We changed many a mind during the Obama-bliss/pre-Trumpian, Blacklash regime. I received many messages in many forms from many people all over the world who had been transformed by the message of *Kinky Boots*, our little show that could.

And not for nuthin', Wayne Brady, a very straight man, with a very heteronormative interpretation of Lola, replaced me on Broadway—and it werked! Same message. Different vessel!

So the scene is set: Chicago, September 2012, Bank of America Theatre, the first day of tech rehearsals. We sailed through the opening sequence, titled "The Most Beautiful Thing in the World," with the greatest of ease and aplomb. Then came my entrance. Miss Lola—in an extravagant Gregg Barnes creation that was designed to represent the sun. A skimpy, one shoulder–strapped, bedazzled-shimmering, sunburst, total high-fashion couture gag of a dress with tentacle fringe dangling from my coochie-pop. The wig was the color of a sweet merlot, if that's even a thing. The creations for my girls, "Lola's Angels," aka drag performers, were meant to conjure the spirit of flowers, the likes of an Alexander McQueen haute couture runway extravaganza of the highest order.

The staging of my entrance was a rather grand one. Echoing in the shadows, mysterious—a lady, of sorts, in a leather trench coat, scurries, being pursued, preyed upon by menacing bullies. The enigmatic life force reaches into her purse to retrieve a thigh-high stiletto boot. She weaponizes the boot as she raises it above her head to strike her assailants, somehow missing them completely and knocking out an anonymous kind man who has crept into the encounter, trying to come to her aid.

BAM! (The kind man is knocked out stone-cold.) A musical glissando springs forth, and we hear voices in three-part harmony herald the arrival of the qween herself, "Lola / Looola."

Spotlight pops to reveal Miss Lola in full, couture sunburst-realness effect. She proceeds to invite the audience into her embrace with her seductive prowess—she purrs that "he's not the first man to fall for me," and that by the response she's seeing, "he won't be the last." And with that she. Is. Off.

I'd made it through three and a half sultry stanzas when . . .

"*HOLD!*" Jerry yelled over the God-mic, and production came to a screeching halt.

"Everybody go to lunch!" Work lights popped on. The house lights were brought up full, and from the stage I could see the entire creative team huddled in the back of the theater in deep, concentrated, analytic problem-solving mode. The director in me wondered what were the goings-on. What was the problem to be solved?

"You're too pretty," Jerry declared with glee from the doorway of my dressing room. "You all are just simply too gorgeous for words."

"Well, isn't that the point?" I smirked. "I mean, a reviewer from the *Pittsburgh Post-Gazette did* describe me as being reminiscent of a young Diahann Carroll back in '89 when I played the role of Mary Sunshine in Kander and Ebb's *Chicago* at the Pittsburgh Playhouse!"

"Well, they didn't lie. I mean, I knew you were going to be pretty, but I didn't realize how striking the Angels would be as well, and the power of all that beauty *will* be too much for our audiences at the start of our story. We have to draw them in. Make them feel safe."

"So what does this mean, then?" this creative problem solver inquired.

"Not sure yet. I'm discussing our options with Gregg over lunch. I'll have some answer for you then."

Well . . . WERK! For the first time in my life, I feel beautiful. Can it be? Is the original dream actually, finally coming true? I've waited decades to be given access to such greatness, to my responsibility in such a time as this. I've spent too much time running from my queerness, my faggotry, my femininity. All these qualities were my liability in this business, just like everybody said they would be. "They" were right (whoever "they" actually are). They were right. But now I think "they" are all 'bout ta be wrong! Cause I'm gittin' ready to eat dis shit right on up!

"*This* is gonna make the white folks feel safe?" I stood apoplectic, holding a strapless, black-lace bra and panties up to my newly snatched body.

"This is just a placeholder for the time being as I design something new for this opening-look undergarment. You will be exposed for a moment as you're changing onstage into the Black Widow frock," costume designer Gregg Barnes said, trying to console. "The sunflower idea, as well as the undergarment support structure, isn't really working."

"Yeah, turns out that original Playboy Bunny undergarment idea feels dated and is not flattering to your body at all, " Jerry chimed in from my dressing room sofa, peering at my body through the mirror. His brain actively downloading how to solve the problem that lay before him.

Within the two-hour dinner break, Gregg Barnes had shopped an entirely new idea. The back-to-the-drawing-board goal was to make the visual impact of Miss Lola and her Angels one of invitation. A welcoming of sorts, into what, for many, will be a brave new world. Miss Lola and her Angels are an inherently subversive construct. Even today, in 2021, even with an entire world intoxicated and mesmerized by the art form of drag, which has been elevated and immortalized by the genius that is RuPaul Charles and her cottage industry of *Drag Race* qweens—back in 2013, making the breeders feel comfortable was our only way in, our only way to change the status quo and begin a new conversation with the world, our way of getting the masses to laugh *with* us not *at* us, all the while wielding *love* as our weapon of healing.

I carefully combine the words *weapon* and *healing* for a purpose. Because sometimes love is tough. Sometimes to love is to be uncomfortable. The 2013 Macy's Thanksgiving Day Parade fallout was precisely one of those moments. We hadn't even finished our number before we were backlashed with hate and homophobia. Headlines were popping off all over the country. Conservatives formed a militia of panic and hate rhetoric meant to subvert the *Kinky Boots* message of love, tolerance, acceptance, and inclusion by turning the simple act of a celebratory performance on a television show into the "gay agenda" to come and seduce and rape their children. *Here we are once again . . . STOP IT! Never mind that* Matilda: The Musical, *which performed directly before us, presented the world with a man in full-on drag as the wickedly evil headmistress Miss Trunchbull.*

I'm just gonna say it out loud for all the world to hear: The character of Miss Trunchbull is ugly. Inside and out. Borderlining on grotesque—actually, I take that back: fully grotesque. On purpose! The kind of feminine form that goes unnoticed by mainstream culture. The kind of ugly that straight men ignore, thereby rendering their existence on this planet invisible. A woman with the kind of looks that y'all's ex-president would proffer, "She's not my type!" as defense-proof that the sexual assault allegations coming from the likes of E. Jean Carroll must be untrue. Suffice to say, Miss Trunchbull didn't give middle American house-husbands boners during Thanksgiving Day breakfast. *Why y'all mad, Million Moms?*

Don't hate. Just appreciate the beauty, the legendary realness that is never going away!

Much respect must go to the Macy's organization. They stepped up and supported our message of inclusion, equality, and love by hosting me and my costar Stark Sands the day after the kerfuffle. As a direct response to *the haters*, we stomped and shopped in our finale costumes, me in full drag, him in a blazer, long tie, boxer shorts, and identical candy-apple-red thigh-high kinky boots. Harvey Fierstein accompanied us on our Black Friday shopping spree and released a statement to the press: "I'm so proud that the cast of *Kinky Boots* brought their message of tolerance and acceptance to America's parade. Ten years ago I was humbled to ride a float dressed as Mrs. Claus and it was the thrill of a lifetime. Congratulations to Macy's, on leading the world, not only with your salesmanship, but also your humanity."

* * *

By the time we'd made it to our first preview, on October 2, 2012, in Chicago, the outside air had already sharpened its claws and teeth to a dull but present roar. I was wrapped in full protect-the-gift, overly cautious, borderline-hypochondriacal outerwear: oversized cashmere coat, winter beanie, multiple scarves—looking like somebody's bag-lady auntie! However, indoors these bitches had me clickin' and poppin' around in that black-lace bra and panties number. They *did* add a little mini lace skirt to the panties, and by *little* I'm talking itsy-bitsy. Just enough to cover my . . . well . . . you know . . . *cock!* Yes, I said COCK! And I said *cock* from the stage at a quarter to midnight when dat bitch Jerry yelled over the God mic, "You look fierce! We gotta do something about that bulge, but—"

To which I cut him off, with hands on hips, fully exposed and vulnerable in a way I'd never been before: "I cain't help that! I have a huge cock!" There was a beat . . . another beat . . . and another beat . . .

And then Jerry growled into the God mic, making sure it would reverberate throughout the entire theater, "BITCH! WE ALL DO!" And that was a wrap. The day was done. We all laughed for hours about that moment. That story is still the stuff of *Kinky Boots* legend.

I had not been in or associated with a Broadway show since *Miss Saigon* in 1999, and we all know how that ended. So here I was twelve years later, exiting the stage door of a Broadway-equivalent theater in Chicago, looking like one who had been rehearsing all day and performing all night would—crusty and busted. There were fans waiting. Just a few. Photos were taken, as they are—if we're lucky—and I carried my tired, happy ass home. Only to discover a mere eight hours later, after my morning constitution and ablutions, that my *bag lady realness-chic* lewk had been forever immortalized on this new online situation called social media, specifically in this instance—*Facebook*. I looked just awful. I wanted to crawl under the theater! *This means I have to start now. I have to start dressing up now. I was already planning on serving the children Geek-Chic Realness for press events, but now I have to rethink my entire fashion takeover plan. I have to dress for success every day! Aunt Dorothy always said, "Dress for the job you want, not the one you have!" And the job I ultimately want is to be the HBIC (Head Bitch In Charge).*

We opened in Chicago to very strong reviews. They were encouraging. They were relatively fair and constructive, which is very rarely the case. One review by Michael Roberts in *Showbiz Chicago* said, "*Kinky Boots* has something unique going for it that will add to its success; that is Billy Porter . . . I would venture to say that *Kinky Boots* will do for Mr. Porter what *Hello, Dolly* did for Carol Channing, *Funny Girl* for Streisand; *Phantom* for Michael Crawford and *Evita* for Patti LuPone. This is a show and role that will be forever synonymous with Mr. Porter, and rightfully so." Wow! I'm not a review bitch, but come on—that is extraordinary.

Bill Butler told me later that producer Hal Luftig had cornered him at the opening night party in Chi-Town and told him, "We are so lucky that Billy has no ego and didn't walk away from this project with what we put him through during the audition process. If we didn't have him—we'd be fucked!"

Good on you, Hal! Thank you for acknowledging the truth.

* * *

The cast had a couple of months off for the holidays between closing in Chicago and beginning rehearsals for the Broadway production. I needed to find a place to live. I had not had a lease in my own name for over a decade. Couch surfing and subletting was my way of life. Filing for bankruptcy in 2007 meant that I had "bad credit" for a decade. Translation—I couldn't get a lease in my own name without a cosigner. Enter Suzi Dietz. When I found the apartment I wanted, in Harlem on the corner of 127th St. and Adam Clayton Powell Jr. Blvd., Suzi traveled uptown on the A train with me to go get it. This is when we found out that the rules of engagement had changed, and cosignatories were no longer a thing. Suzi would be required to sign onto the lease as my roommate in order to transmute my bankruptcy situation. This next moment is the *full* gag . . .

So I fill out the apartment application and it gets to the part where one is supposed to share one's yearly income. I share my new projected *Kinky Boots* approximated coin and then I pass the application to Suzi. She fills out the entire form, but leaves the income question blank. Not knowing this fact, I turn the application in to the real estate agent. He goes into another room to process said application. After a spell, the real estate agent returns, perplexed.

"Excuse me, ma'am, you left the yearly income question blank."

"I know. Just run the name," she politely and dismissively said.

"But I need your yearly income to run the application," he politely pushed back.

"No you don't. Just run my name."

Bay-bee . . . when I tell you, the back of my head almost blew off when that bitch came back to us with awwwlll the copies of the applications, with awwwlll the dotted lines X'ed and highlit, and awwwlll the ink pens for signage, no more questions asked, no more yearly income concerns spoken of—I gagged! *Now that's some High Mighty White Woman shit right there! I know she's Jewish, but she a full-time fancy regular ol' white woman today!*

Previews on Broadway brought with them some strange behaviors from folks in attendance. Several people, who shall remain nameless, on several occasions came backstage, post my undeniable slayage, holding their throats and sayin' shit to me like, "Are you okay? Is your voice holdin' up? You better be careful, what you're doing out there is unsustainable."

Unsustainable for whom? I know what the fuck I'm doing. What are these muthafuckas talking about, and why are they trying to come for me?

My initial instinct was to bash these basic bitches' heads in and worry 'bout heaven later, but I took the more observatory and inquisitive road. I knew in my spirit what was happening. As my mother would always say, "Not today, Satan!" This same faction of folks were also the types of people with whom after I methodically got my body, mind, and spirit back in shape for the eight-show-a-week realness reality of Broadway, through my work with the wacky and ingeniously targeted *Mark Fisher Fitness: Snatched* program, would screech with incredulity when they saw me on the street, "Oh, my God! You lost a whole person!"

Really, bitches?! Really? I know I ain't neva been nobody's sex symbol, nor the object of anyone's affection in the marketplace—but a whole person? Fuck y'all! I lost twenty-five pounds. I got in better shape, yes—as folk do when preparing for the role of a lifetime. Quiet as it's kept, I wasn't in that bad of shape to begin with. At my heaviest, I was five foot ten, weighing in at 180 pounds. No, I wasn't Calvin Klein, Marky Mark billboard, underwear-model material—but I also was not walkin' around here like the Klumps either! The fucking nerve!

I needed an outside eye to tell me I wasn't crazy in thinking that the motives of *the faction* were to get in my head, infiltrate my spirit with doubt. Their endgame was to throw me off *my* game. *My* game in *the* game, where the majority of gatekeepers and players alike had written me off, a decade prior, because of what were perceived to be my inherent handicaps and liabilities.

I was chillin' with three-time Tony Award–winning, and seven times more nominated, director Jack O'Brien at a soirée honoring Jerry Mitchell during the spring 2013 Tony season. *Kinky Boots* had been nominated for a record thirteen Tony Awards that year, a definite upset over *Matilda: The Musical*, which the *New York Times* described as the "unalloyed critical hit" of the season. *Matilda: The Musical* had annoyingly been anointed as "the most satisfying and subversive musical ever to come out of Britain."

In addition to its critical success, *Matilda* had won the Drama Desk Award for outstanding musical and had set a record by winning the most Olivier Awards in history. The *New York Times* and the entire theater community at large had already made the decision, before our show had even begun rehearsals, that *Matilda* should and *would* sweep awwwlll of the awards. *Kinky Boots*, on the other hand, was met with cynical and dismissive, haterational praise. The critics, while not dismissing us fully, chose to focus on our show's message as being too "preachy." Like that's a problem? Sometimes folks need preaching. Sometimes the message of love, inclusion, and equality *needs* to be direct and clear.

Ben Brantley of the *New York Times* wrote, "The sticky, sermonizing side of Mr. Fierstein—evident in parts of his book for *La Cage* and even in his breakthrough play, *Torch Song Trilogy*—casts its holy glow, and it is not a flattering light. Let me give you one little taste of what to expect: a dejected Lola sings an anthem of love and respect in a nursing home to a man in a wheelchair, who turns out to be . . ."

Just so we're clear, this anthem Mr. Brantley was referring to is the musical's eleven o'clock number, "Hold Me in Your Heart," and in this moment of the show my character chooses forgiveness. I, Billy, through the surrogate of Lola, was blessed with performing the act of forgiveness to a father figure, to my stepfather and biological father specifically, eight shows a week for three years. It was transformative. It was a blessing. And it set me on a path to a deeper kind of healing than I've ever known. So when y'all cynical haters can stop a Broadway musical dead in its tracks, while preaching an urgent message of love simultaneously—call a bitch! Until then—have several seats!

This is a profound example of the misguided and complicit complacency of the white liberal. The ones who think we're beyond the need for direct messages of equality. The "very good" white people, who most likely voted for Obama and think racism and white supremacy are over. The people who truly believe that my Blackness, and my queerness, weren't a factor in the elevation of *Kinky Boots*. The white folks whose unconscious— or conscious, for that matter—*privilege* blinds them to the fact that the character/archetype of Lola in *Kinky Boots* is a revolutionary act simply because he/she's a Black person, and with my interpretation imbedded into the character's DNA, Lola is wholly, completely, and unapologetically queer. The world had never seen it before. And most folk didn't even know "it" was happening. But I sure as hell did!

My art is my calling, my purpose, dare I say my ministry, and I will proudly and unequivocally use my platform to "preach" the gospel of truth and love for as long as I have breath in my body. Because, truth be told, as we have seen the events of the last five-plus years unfold, there is still half of our country who doesn't get it. There are still factions of hate all over the world who believe in absolute, male, straight, white supremacy power, in perpetuity, at any cost. Our job as artists and storytellers is to teach and, when necessary, *preach* the gospel of true humanity in all its forms. Toni Morrison once said, "This is precisely the time when artists go to work. There is no time for despair, no place for self-pity, no need for silence, no room for fear. We speak, we write, we do language. That is how civilizations heal."

I had taken the first decade of the twenty-first century trying to get my house in order. Trying to rebuild what was left of my career. Rebuilding my voice, my superpower, from the claws of internalized shame and sickness. I had spent over a decade on the precipice of obscurity, but now I saw a light shimmering on the horizon. Telling me just to hold on a little while longer. *Kinky Boots* was that horizon, and everybody on the planet knew it. And the fact that there were haters tryin' to get in my head about it still to this day makes me wanna vomit.

I asked Jack O'Brien for some guidance at that Jerry Mitchell honoring, tribute thingy. I really needed some affirmation from an outside observer that the *shade* I thought was happening was actually happening. Jack affirmed me with his very Truman Capote–esque, drop-the-mic flair, "Honey, you know exactly what's happening. You just pulled a rabbit out of a hat. Everybody in this business had decided you had gone as far as you could go. Everybody was comfortable with your seeming plateau. Fuck them all! Next time somebody comes into your dressing room talking that smack, simply excuse them from your presence and move the fuck on!"

Or something like that . . .

Thank you, Jack O'Brien, for the fortification I needed in that moment to run on and live inside of the unlimited possibilities of the life that lay before me.

* * *

The Tony nominations came out on April 30, 2013, and both I and my costar Stark Sands were nominated for Outstanding Actor in a Musical. Annaleigh Ashford was also nominated, for Outstanding Feature Actress in a Musical. The musical itself received nine more nominations: Best Musical; Best Direction and Choreography of a Musical for Jerry Mitchell; Best Book of a Musical for Harvey Fierstein; Best Original Score for Cyndi Lauper; Best Scenic Design of a Musical for David Rockwell; Best Costume Design of a Musical for Gregg Barnes; Best Lighting Design of a Musical for Kenneth Posner; Best Sound Design of a Musical for John Shivers; Best Orchestrations for Stephen Oremus. And the horse race of Tony voting month began.

Awards seasons are like horse races. And everybody wants to act like the awards don't matter and they don't care. "It's just an honor to be nominated," is the party line across the board. I find this to be a bit disingenuous, and I've even frolicked in this particular trope to try to exude the attitude of gratitude. Awards are a necessary and potential evil of our business, and if one is not careful one can be swept up into the dark side of the process.

One of these dark sides can come in the form of award predictions. My suggestion for anyone entering this market is to *stay away* from reading anything, and I mean *anything*, during the voting period for any awards-season race. I made the mistake of reading a couple of articles. There's a lot of pitting productions and people against each other. I didn't like that feeling. Historically, Broadway is a community of artists who, for the most part, are very supportive of each other. The Tony nominations made me feel a bit disconnected from my colleagues, so I decided to do something about it. I decided to invite all the nominees in my category for a supper, fellowship, celebration situation. I believe it was after one of our Sunday matinee performances leading up to the Tony Awards ceremony. I was pleased that all of the other four nominees accepted my invitation to dine and imbibe.

We met at the very popular 44 & X, which is located just where the name denotes—on the corner of Forty-Fourth Street and Tenth Avenue—and is owned by my friends Scott and Bruce. The guests and nominees included my costar and little brother Stark Sands (*Kinky Boots*), Bertie Carvel (*Matilda*), Santino Fontana (*Cinderella*), and Rob McClure (*Chaplin*). Our dinner was one of celebration, fellowship, and support. One of the waiters took a photo of the five of us that sits in a frame in my office to this very day. I am proud, honored, and humbled to have been counted in that number with these incredible artists.

* * *

Sally Field and Matthew Broderick glided onto the stage at Radio City Music Hall to present both Best Actor and Best Actress in a musical. The men were first.

Uh-oh . . . must be time for my category. The cameraman just crouched down in front of me. All up in my mug. My mouth is dry. All of a sudden I'm trembling. It's okay, Billy, M&M is by your side. It's an honor to be nominated.

Sally: "It is our pleasure . . . both our pleasures . . ."

It's an honor to be nominated

". . . exemplary performers who gave their characters . . ."

It's an honor to be nominated

Matthew: "Five incredibly gifted artists . . ."

It's an honor to be nominated

". . . five diverse roles. Each one original, compelling, unrivaled . . ."

It'sanhonortobenominated

It'sanhonortobenominated

It'sanhonortobenominated

". . . the nominees for Best Actor in a Musical are . . ."

Sally and Matthew sound like gibberish. I can't make heads or tails of . . .

Sally: "Billy Porter: Kinky Boots."

Why, full-on terror. Smile, bitch

Matthew: "Stark Sands: Kinky Boots."

Make nice with the camera all up in your face

And smile

Matthew: "And the American Theatre Wing's Tony goes to . . ."

OMG! That's me, that's my name! Get up there quick. You got ninety seconds to get it all out. You forgot to kiss your sister . . . From the time your name gets called, you get ninety seconds to speak before the band starts playing you off. Why is everything blurry? Why is everything muted? Why am I out of breath? Why is everything in slow motion? Sally Field just hugged me. She handed me my TONY AWARD.

"Oh, my God! Oh, my GOD!!! Okay . . . Okay . . . So . . ."

Get to talkin', bitch! Time's a tickin'. Tempus fugit.

"Umm . . ."

Get out your notes. Shit! Now my hands aren't free, AND THEY'RE TREMBLING! Couldn't have planned for this . . .

"I'm gonna put this on the ground."

Thank you—very nice Black man with locks who just saved me from the faux pas of placing my lifelong-dream Tony Award on the fucking floor! Focus, focus, focus . . . on the notecards. The pink notecards that match the ascot!

"Okay, so Shakespeare said, 'To thine own self be true.' When I was eleven years old, my journey to truth began when I discovered the Tony Awards, washing dishes in my kitchen, and the performance of Jennifer Holliday and the cast of *Dreamgirls*, on the Tony Awards, took my breath away."

That got some applause—good!

"That moment changed my life. And I'm here before you today. I wanna thank my family, the best sister that a brother could ever have, MaryMartha Ford. My mother, Cloerinda Jean Johnson Porter-Ford, at home in Pittsburgh—you are the personification of true Christianity. Your willingness to embrace that which you don't understand with unconditional love is a template that the world could benefit from employing. Your courage gives me life and I love you."

Mommy gots some applause. Yay!

"To my *Kinky Boots* family. To my amazing cast and crew and everybody at the Al Hirschfeld Theatre. Our producers, Hal Luftig and Daryl Roth. To Harvey Fierstein and Cyndi Lauper, who created the template that allows for me to express the journey of forgiveness and acceptance and ultimately a necessary healing for my soul.

"To Jerry Mitchell: for reaching back, lifting up an old friend, and giving me a space to soar. To my costar Stark Sands: You are my rock, my sword, my shield. Your grace gives me presence. I . . . share this with you (I'ma keep it at my house, but I share it wit' chu.)"

And BOOM! The joke landed! WERK! FUCK! They're playin' that hook music already . . .

Werk it out, bitch!

"To my glam squad, who keeps Miss Lola fierce every day. I love you."

I'm talking as fast as I can! I hear you, orchestra! I'ma git dis last part out, though, so hold the fuck UP!

"Ah, to my patron Suzi Dietz, George C. Wolfe, Tracy Brigden at Cit—ah . . . Bill Butler, my manager of twenty-two years, and everybody . . .

"God Bless you!

"I love you!

"I love you!

"I love you!"

CHAPTER NINETEEN

DECEMBER 30, 2016

I proposed to Adam last night. He said yes! He was actually surprised. I was surprised that he was surprised, as we both agreed last year, when we got back together after our five-year break, on that Sunday afternoon in March 2015 where we took in a pre-Broadway performance of Hamilton *at the Public Theater for his birthday. Yes, we broke up but stayed together in so many ways. We loved each other from afar and kept a safe place in both of our hearts for the other. In Act 2 the* Hamilton *cast sings a song of forgiveness. Our hands touched. We held on. We got back together that afternoon and shortly thereafter declared that that if we were still together by the end of the following year—which would place us in the fourth quarter of 2016—we would get married.*

I always do what I say I'ma do! He's learning this fact. I asked all of my coupled friends for guidance for the proposal rollout. I was anxious about the thing not being romantic enough. I've come to discover that I'm not a very romantic person. I wanted to try to be romantic. I wanted to make it a thing. My friends all advised me that it should be a thing. So I called our friends Karsten and Michael, who we met on an Atlantis Cruise earlier in the summer, and we three planned the covert operation, dubbed Operation European En-GAG-ement! She was very grand; she was very romantic. A

European dreamscape. Our London buddies helped me arrange a table for the four of us at the Michelin-starred dining establishment City Social, sitting high on the twenty-fourth floor of Tower 42. Our secluded booth overlooked the majestic Foggy London Town. I got down on one knee, just before dessert arrived, and presented the love of my life the Cartier Love Band. He said yes!

Unfortunately, the following morning our blissed-out homosexual love was incinerated in a blink, with breaking-news headlines around the world about one of my favorite gospel singers going off on a homophobic rant while she was preaching at the church I believe she pastors. The artist and preacher in question was Kim Burrell. Her words were scathing, her hate on full display—in Jesus's name. In her sermon she called us perverted:

". . . but that homosexual spirit is a spirit of delusion and confusion, and has deceived many men and women . . . You as a man will open your mouth and take a man's penis in your face. You are perverted and you better not tell me—for thus sayeth the Lord, 'You are perverted!'"

And once again our gay love is only seen through the lens of sex; a private interaction between adults that ain't nobody's business but the grown folk engaging in the act.

This posture is nothing new from the gospel music world. I'd simply gotten very used to separating the message from the messenger. The morning of December 30, 2016, was the day all of that ended for me. No more separating. I had stood by and stayed silent on this issue for years, hoping that the church would evolve. But I saw that evolution is not what religious folk were in search of, so it was time to disengage from those who sought to destroy me. Kim's lashings felt personal this time. *And* disingenuous. Because, as many folk brought to light in the subsequent overall canceling of Ms. Burrell that came very swiftly and was very exacting, she was fine with the faggots when it served her bank account—note her duet with the out musician Frank Ocean. And while the cancel/consequence culture let that bitch fully have it—she lost her radio show; Ellen canceled an appearance that was to happen the following week, where she was supposed to sing a duet with Pharrell in support of the film *Hidden Figures*—her betrayal gutted my soul, because it was us, her mainly Black, LGBTQ+ fan base, who supported her. We didn't care that she had an obesity issue, which incidentally is directly connected to one of the Seven Deadly Sins. Gluttony! And yet, we loved her and supported her unconditionally. Fuck that! Many celebrities released statements condemning Ms. Burrell's hate speech. Pharrell wrote, "I condemn hate speech of any kind. There is no room in this world for any kind of prejudice. My greatest hope is for inclusion and love for all humanity in 2017 and beyond." *Good luck wit dat!*

All I have to say is thank you to the qween in Ms. Burrell's congregation who had clearly gotten tired of her hypocrisy and surreptitiously filmed what I know, from experience inside the church, to be the total erasure of an entire community's humanity. My old trauma was so activated that I penned an open letter to Ms. Burrell that ran on *Out* magazine's website on January 8, 2017. I wrote that "as a deeply spiritual, self-identified church sissy who grew up in the Pentecostal church, I cannot stay silent when church folk like you, however well intentioned, think that it's God's will to use the Bible to demean and erase the LGBTQ community."

"Words have power, and your words are murderous," I continued, and added that "I waited for 47 years for somebody to have the courage to speak our collective gay truth to your theoretical power. Now I realize it is I who must give voice to the voiceless."

They truly believe that their way is the only way and that everyone else is going to burn in the pits of hell. The Bible is the greatest artistic achievement in the history of the world. And I mean that with every fiber of my being. The fact that a book written by forty different men with forty different perspectives on faith can still be so omnipresent in controlling the masses is . . . I mean—every war ever fought has essentially been boiled down to "my God is better than yours." It's just not right.

JANUARY 5, 2017

I had to buy a new computer yesterday. My MacBook Pro of three years is on the fritz. It's not working. I got the blank screen with a question mark a few weeks back and got the hard drive replaced. Unfortunately, I got the same thing a couple of days ago. It's time to move on, and I'm gonna start with a blank slate. I'm leaving it totally empty and just going to add shit as I need it. Keep the hard drive clean and working better.

Adam and I decided it would be best to just get married before Trump takes office. He's trying to find his divorce decree. Which apparently is not such an easy task: The filing system is so antiquated. It's not computerized at all. Nobody knows where it is. Or how to find it in any way. It's fucking crazy.

JANUARY 10, 2017

We got our marriage license yesterday. That was an emotional experience I wasn't anticipating. It hearkens back to that idea that all this time we've lived with the painful reality that our love didn't matter. That our love was somehow less than theirs. That their straightness made their love superior to ours, and I believed them. I didn't know I was believing them, but my actions in past relationships reflected just that. Lack of belief in it. Nothing and no one around to support it. I tried to be strong and act like this was not the case, but what else could it be? My heart has been cracked open in a way I've never seen or ever felt. It's a beautiful feeling and I don't ever want it to go away. For the first time in my life, I feel safe. Truly safe to know that somebody is in my . . .

JANUARY 11, 2017

. . . corner for all things. And I for him. He is truly my best friend. The one I need to confide in. The first call I need to make when any type of news needs to be shared. The idea of till death do us part never entered my brain until Adam. Now, do I believe in happily ever after? Not so much. I want to create vows that are attainable. One day at a time. Wake up and choose to love. I choose to love him. And while I have no choice in the matter because the heart does what it wants, I am fully aware of what I need to do to make our love function. I'm becoming a better person because of this man. I am learning how to receive this kind of love. A love that is much bigger than me, or him for that matter. It found us and made sure that we stayed together. The idea that we could meet in 2009, date for a year, then break up, to five years later have him come back and not only forgive me, but profess his consistent love for me in spite of my mistakes. In spite of my imperfections. That's huge. We are huge. Our love is huge. And quiet. It's a quiet thing.

JANUARY 15, 2017

What a day! Yesterday was the greatest day of my life. Wedding days are exactly what people say they are. As we stood in front of our friends and chosen family, I was moved by the love in the room. The support for our union. Who we are and how we live is still a bit of a mystery to many. They don't see it, so they fear it. And then for some reason they feel like they should create dysfunction and punishment for us. Standing in front of people, in public, and sharing vows with the one you love . . . ? God, it's just so deep. I could feel the relationship go deeper . . . in minutes, seconds right before my very eyes. I saw all of my sweet Adam's insecurities melt away the day I proposed to him. I could see it on his face. I could feel it in his spirit. That's what he needed. It's what I needed. We needed to commit! Spiritually and legally to this union. To each other. We needed it more than I ever understood.

After all this time, I feel it. I feel it deeper than I've ever felt anything in my life. It's in my soul. It's deep, deep down inside of me. I totally feel safe. I feel loved. I don't know that I've ever allowed myself to feel it so deeply before. I don't know that it was ever given so deeply before. I don't even have the words to describe how it feels. What it feels like to be loved. To have support for your love. To receive it like never before. I've never felt it. I didn't know this is what it's like. I'm trying not to be mad that "they" got to withhold it from us for so long. And for what . . . ? 'Cause The Bible told them so. The Bible gave them permission to hate. To treat another group as less than. I hate hate. I really do. And it takes everything within me not to hate these people in return. But LOVE has to win. We have to be the change we want to see. We MUST. And now I get to do that with my soul mate. The love of my life like no other I've ever experienced. The Porter-Smiths are getting ready to change the world!

JANUARY 20, 2017

Less than a week after our wedding, Donald J. Trump, aka Orangina 45, was inaugurated. The void I felt in my soul was real. I didn't know where to go or how to get there anymore. I believed in democracy. I believed in our government. I'd shown up in every way possible to make this world a better place. We'd been there already. We'd done this before. But that day I had no idea what to expect. I just knew that whatever was comin' was gonna be pretty bad. *Fasten your seatbelts, children—it's gonna be a bumpy ride.*

Look at these muthafuckas! I thought. Smug in their whiteness on that dais, every single solitary one of them was—*wait . . . wait a fucking minute. Is that . . . FUCK ME! That's fucking Daryl Roth behind that orange bitch. On the dais?!?! I know that husband of hers is a Trump supporter, but Daryl?!? The producer of* Kinky Boots?!?! *The musical that dared to "preach" the gospel of authenticity, equality, and inclusion? 'Cause who needs to hear that? The producer? I . . . I . . . just . . . Really? I literally feel like I've been raped. In a back alley. With no lube! Oh my God! Oh! My! Fucking! God! We are not safe anywhere!*

In his letter from a Birmingham jail, the Reverend Dr. Martin Luther King, Jr., wrote:

> I have almost reached the regrettable conclusion that the Negro's great stumbling block in his stride toward freedom is not the White Citizen's Council-er or the Ku Klux Klanner, but the white moderate, who is more devoted to "order" than to justice; who prefers a negative peace which is the absence of tension to a positive peace which is the presence of justice; who constantly says: "I agree with you in the goal you seek, but I cannot agree with your methods of direct action"; who paternalistically believes he can set the timetable for another man's freedom; who lives by a mythical concept of time and who constantly advises the Negro to wait for a "more convenient season."

Dr. King's words had never rung more true to me than in that moment. I don't think I've ever felt that depth of betrayal of myself, of my multi-hyphenate marginalized truths and authenticities, but most specifically and most devastating, the betrayal of my beloved Broadway community, and what Ms. Roth believes is *her* community as well. The facts: Daryl Roth stood behind that monster, on the dais, at his inauguration, with a blowout for your nerves, Henny. The lewk was sitting, as per usual with Ms. Roth— but I digress. She stood beside her husband, Steven Roth, and in very close proximity behind Oragnina 45, knowing full well his sinister intentions to blow up American democracy. But as we know, *money* reigns supreme in this world, and the 1.5-trillion-dollar tax-break gift to the wealthy, banks, and large corporations was swift to come.

The Roth family are the epitome of the wealthy one percent in America—the one percent of the one percent. Their wealth is the kind that never goes away, the kind of wealth that can buy their queer son Jordan the Jujamcyn Theatre Organization (the third-largest theater owner on Broadway, behind the Shubert Organization and the Nederlander Organization). They have the kind of wealth that can simply be invested into artistic ventures for the love of it, or for write-offs, and never lose a dime.

Daryl loves the arts. She and her son are dedicated to the theater, which is evident from Ms. Roth's "singular distinction of producing seven Pulitzer Prize–winning plays." She was a lead producer of Nilo Cruz's *Anna in the Tropics*, Margaret Edson's *Wit*, Paula Vogel's *How I Learned to Drive*, and Edward Albee's *Three Tall Women*, and a co-producer of Bruce Norris's *Clybourne Park*, Tracy Letts's *August: Osage County*, and David Auburn's *Proof*. And pre-pandemic, her son Jordan was really breathing new life into the heart and soul of the Jujamcyn Organization, with fresh ideas and bona fide hits in all five of his theaters running concurrently at any given time. The Roth family's presence in and contribution to the New York arts community, particularly Broadway, are unparalleled, which is what made their disappearance when the American shit hit the fan all the more devastating.

According to the *New York Times*, Ms. Roth "attended the Trump inauguration with her husband and has avoided publicly taking sides on the administration." Let me be very clear to all of you readers trying to make heads or tails of why I'm ranting so publicly. This moment is not about a takedown of Ms. Roth or the Roth family. However, the betrayal and the hypocrisy *must* be addressed, and addressed publicly. I've waited—no, the entire community has waited—for four-plus years to hear from Ms. Roth and, even more troubling, her queer son Jordan and his husband, Richie. No one in our community has been brave enough or had enough conviction to call bullshit. So I will.

In the wake of all of the civil unrest of the last year, and COVID-19 ravaging our nation (as of the day I'm writing this, with 31.6 million cases and 566,000 deaths and counting), all the way to the Big Lie and the insurrection at our nation's capital, I've pondered in exasperated disbelief—where are you? The silence from you all in one of America's darkest moments of need is deafening. *Silence is violence. Silence = Death.* Maya Angelou said, "When people show you who they are, believe them, the first time."

As I sit in my brand-new home on Long Island, I can truly see life from both sides now. I, personally, am the personification of what it means to "pull yourself up by your own bootstraps." I know what it means to be dirt poor with nothing, and I now blessedly know what it feels like to finally break free from the systemic racist infrastructure of America that is set up to keep folks like me from succeeding at anything at any time! It's comfortable. It's easy. I want to hold myself up behind the gate of my perfectly manicured estate as well and act like everything is okay. But everything is *not* okay. The American democratic experiment is melting, and it's up to we the people to show up, use our platforms, and do something about it!

Some of us, no matter how successful or how wealthy we become, can never buy our way out of the trauma inflicted upon us daily, and for centuries, by our own government and its white, racist, xenophobic citizenry. Elie Weisel said, "We must take sides. Neutrality helps the oppressor, never the victim." And please believe me when I say that this is not a takedown or canceling of anyone. I don't love you all any less. But this is a call to arms for anyone who has a compassionate bone in their bodies. The Roths are not the only Broadway producers (and beyond) who I'm speaking to. They just happen to be the most public in this moment. I'm asking to build a bridge, a real one this time. I'm asking that our white so-called allies join the rest of us in this fight. The work is far from done and we need radical help, not agonizing silence. *I'll take that soapbox back now . . .*

* * *

I was still swirling from my first return to the American stage post–Tony and Grammy award wins for *Kinky Boots*, and I had spent the better part of 2015–2016 workshopping and rehearsing for *Shuffle Along, or, the Making of the Musical Sensation of 1921 and All That Followed*. We were slated to open on Broadway on April 21, 2016. That date got pushed early on to April 28—the last possible date of eligibility for the 2016 Tony Awards.

I, a Tony and Grammy Award winner, shared top billing with six-time Tony Award winner Audra McDonald. Tony winner Brian Stokes Mitchell. And Tony nominees Brandon Victor Dixon and Joshua Henry. The infamously toxic and abusive Scott Rudin was set to produce. George C. Wolfe wrote and directed, and Savion Glover was set to choreograph.

I'm not gonna spend a lot of time on this one. It's a pretty open-and-shut case, in my opinion. First and foremost, our leading lady was pregnant. Which is not to say that the demise of our production had anything to do with Audra's pregnancy; let me be clear. When the show was announced in the summer of 2015, Audra was contracted to leave our production a month after the Tony Award ceremony to go to London for three months to reprise her role of Billie Holliday in *Lady Day at Emerson's Bar & Grill*, for which she'd won her sixth Tony. The announcement was made, and there was no replacement of note announced at the time. We were almost a year out at this point. There was also the juggernaut of musical theater heaven that is *Hamilton*. I personally think had we waited a year and let *Hamilton* run its due course, we could have opened the following year and probably still be running today. Unfortunately, I believe that Scott Rudin's hubris thought he could just steamroll right over the *Hamilton* sensation, just as he has been known to do in every area of his career. How could Scott and George not see that the very story we were telling in *Shuffle Along*—that being the making of the first all-Black musical, introducing jazz music to Broadway audiences for the first time, was parallel to what Lin-Manuel and the artists up the street from us were doing? Lin-Manuel's magnum opus cemented hip-hop/rap as a viable form of music for the theater, a space that had largely rejected the genre. *Shuffle Along* was an amazing piece of work based on times gone by (we were the old guys). *Hamilton* was new. PERIOD! We were nominated for ten Tony Awards. We lost all ten to *Hamilton*. As well we should have. They deserved every last one of them!

We got our closing notice in early July 2016, a mere two months after officially opening. Scott Rudin didn't even have the decency to show up at the theater to tell us himself. He saddled one of his cronies with that dirty-work responsibility.

My time post–*Kinky Boots* was fraught with confusion for me. While I'm very grateful for the *Shuffle Along* of it all, my focus was set on the film and television glow-up. I still couldn't get no love. More of the same dismissive, "too flamboyant" feedback. I was asked to replace Andrew Rannells in *Hedwig and the Angry Inch* on Broadway. I turned that shit right on down. I had no delusion of my name-brand money-making, butts-in-seats power at that time. Neil Patrick Harris opened the show and won the Tony Award for his performance in 2014. NPH has been a star since he was a teenager starring in *Doogie Howser, MD*, a medical drama that ran for four seasons on ABC from 1989 to 1993. He then transitioned in adulthood to playing the role of Barney Stinson on *How I Met Your Mother*, for which he was nominated for four Emmy Awards. Neil sold that shit out for the entirety of his yearlong stint with *Hedwig*. When Andrew replaced him, most of the reviews focused not on Andrew's brilliant performance, but on how far the box office receipts had dropped as a result. I was not going to have these bitches close a show on my back. I knew it would be premature and presumptuous to think that any other outcome would be possible. So that opportunity was a hard pass. And let's not forget—fifteen years prior, when I was begging for an audition to replace John Cameron Mitchell in the original Off-Broadway run, the answer was an unequivocal NO! So . . . no love lost.

* * *

I couldn't stop sobbing. I pulled my car over at 132nd and Lenox. I was driving home from directing a production of *Topdog/Underdog* at the Huntington Theatre in Boston. I was downloading on my sister, complaining about still feeling disenfranchised and dismissed in the industry. Here I was, a Tony and Grammy Award winner, and I couldn't book the stupidest of television shows. I had just come off of the first pilot season in my whole career where I actually had a regular series of auditions. At least fifteen of them. In previous years I usually only had one or two, maybe five tops. So that was good news. The complicated news is that I still wasn't booking, and the fucking "he's too flamboyant" trope, after they were specifically *asking for* flamboyant, was literally making me lose it! I was losing roles meant to be "flamboyant" and "gay" to straight men. I wanted to scream! So, I pulled the car over and did just that. With my sister on the other end of my rant.

Television and film are the next step after Tony *and* Grammy, but it was not going that way for me. I was slipping back to the margins. I feared I would become one of those artists who wins major awards and then is never heard from again. No shade. Just facts. It happens all the time, and at no fault of the artist. Just this fucked-up industry.

Not even ten minutes after my breakdown, my phone rang. It was Bill Butler with an audition for me.

"Ryan Murphy is doing a new show on FX about the eighties house ball culture. Based on that documentary *Paris Is Burning*."

I cackled! "Are you for real? Is this a joke?"

"Yeah, it's real and it's major. The casting director, Alexa Fogel, wants to see you tomorrow. The role is for a dance teacher."

"A dance teacher? Is this 'dance teacher' in the ballroom culture of the show?" I quizzed him.

"I'm not sure. But that doesn't matter. Just go get in the room and let Ryan see you. I'm confident if nothing's there right now, he has the power to craft something specifically for you."

I prepared for my audition for the "dance teacher," knowing full well in my spirit that I wasn't gonna be nobody's dance teacher! When there are *balls* to be MC'd. I finished my first, in-person audition with Alexa, and then I went right in.

"So, Alexa—can I just say something? I'm not trying to overstep my bounds, but I have to say—I'm old enough to have lived through the AIDS crisis. The ball culture, the plague, all of it. I know this world intimately. It would be a waste of everyone's time to have me on this show, but not use me in the actual world. Isn't there anything for me as, like, a *mother of the house* or something?"

To which Alexa replied, "Ryan's idea is to have all the mothers be transgender actresses of color."

I teared up at the brilliance of this idea. This information let me know that these divas were gonna do this shit right! Centering actual transgender women of color to tell their own stories, our Black and Brown queer-people stories. I tried to hold it together, but I was bursting at the seams with excitement at the infinite possibilities.

I asked Alexa to see if Mr. Murphy could make some room for me over at the bawwwwlllls!

Alexa promised to bring this idea up with Ryan Murphy and that she would get back to me. Three weeks later we heard back.

"I spoke with Ryan. He wants you to come back in and meet the entire team and says if you can impersonate the spirit of the MC from *Paris Is Burning*, they will create something for you!"

Can I impersonate the MC from Paris Is Burning? *Am I Black? Bitch, the entire world has been impersonating the MC from* Paris Is Burning *since that shit came out over twenty-five years ago! So, yes, bitches! I'm 'bout to snatch some edges.*

I came in on the train from Fire Island that muggy Friday, July 28, 2017. I wore a tasteful forest green romper from Mr. Turk that I had purchased specifically for the audition. I served a bedazzled black loafer with a silver, red, and green skull encrusted on top. My fedora was cocked to the side over my right eye, which had become my trademark silhouette in the years of late.

I had been sent about seventeen pages of sides, which were not really scenes, but more *declarations*. Seventeen pages of the fiercest shade, reads, gathers, and edge snatching this Black church sissy could ever dream of. I believe Mr. Murphy also understood how to present us New York folk to the L.A. folk. Specifically for Mj Rodriguez and me—we both come from the theater. Putting myself on tape for film and TV roles, and then sending them off to have some Muppet-Baby assistant "screen" the work and then decide that my acting choices are too "flamboyant" to be afforded the respect I've earned in this industry to at least be given notes and the opportunity to try again, was never my experience. Being in a big room, with the entire creative team present, *in person*, in real time, was very familiar to me. This is how we do it on Broadway. Ryan set up our final callbacks/screen tests like the final callback for a Broadway show. He set me up for a win!

The room felt warm, an inviting embrace. It's hard to describe, but it felt like a loving space. A welcoming, inspiring space. I felt completely protected.

I stood in the center of the room and did what I do! I let the kids have it with all of my declaration. Everyone in the room erupted into side-splitting laughter, the likes of which almost felt fake to me. 'Cause I was serving full-on, Billy P realness with no filter. If there was gonna be any place for me as a series regular on mainstream television, it was gonna be *this* show, at *this* very moment, with *this* crew of creatives who were clearly pickin' up what I was puttin' down.

"Won't you have a seat for me, Billy?" Ryan asked after my slayage of the seventeen pages of declarations I had prepared. "I just wanna to talk to you for a minute."

Now, I can't remember the specific question Ryan asked, but all I remember is it was something about Orangina 45, politics, and the state of our union. *Child, you don't have to ask me twice.* I went off! I let those bitches know under no uncertain terms how filled with rage I was, and how it's up to *we the people* to get up off our asses to do something about the mess that America has found itself in, and how we've seen this all before, and nobody should be surprised about nuthin', and how I wish the press would just stop covering and covering up the lies, and that they are *all* lies, and how *eternal vigilance is the price of liberty*, and so on and so on and so on . . . About forty-five minutes later, when Ryan could finally get a word in edgewise, he spoke in language that sounded like a veiled offer in the room, but she was serving a bit of nebulous-realness. *Daddy don't do ambiguity no more, so I'll wait to get excited when that offer is a concrete one.*

I got right back on the LIRR to return to my Fire Island vacation. Adam and I were staying at Jerry Mitchell's house for the week. *Is this real? Is this really happening? Did I just book a series regular on a Ryan Murphy television show? The auteur of such hits as* Glee, Nip/Tuck, American Horror Story, *and* American Crime Story: O. J. Simpson *and* Versace?

Literally the moment I was ready to throw in the towel—again, is this happening? I know this is going to happen. Ryan Murphy has been on my vision board for over a decade. I scoured the landscape trying to find artists in positions of power in the film and television space who would understand me. Someone who would not be afraid of all that I embody. Ryan's work always made me feel seen. He has always had the unique ability to take the archetypes typically relegated to supporting characters and center them right in the middle of mainstream narratives. Even knowing this, I could not have predicted what would come next!

My iPhone rang just as I was arriving at the Sayville Ferry to cross back over to the Fire Island Pines.

"You got it!" Bill Butler squealed with glee. "Ryan fucking Murphy is creating a role specifically for you!"

The tears streamed down my cheeks as the late-afternoon sun warmed my face. The mist from the ferry slicing through the water felt healing. Like a baptism of grace. My heart skipped a beat of joy. My soul felt lifted. If just for a moment. *This* is the moment I'd been waiting for my entire life. I knew in the deepest parts of my being that *this* was my moment, the moment— and I was more than ready for it!

* * *

The mirror ball was mesmerizing. The hundreds of beams shot outward in all directions from the center, the core. The ballroom is the center of our show. The core value structure is centered around family. Chosen family, if you will. I know a little sumthin' sumthin' about that! The mastermind himself, Ryan Murphy, was directing the pilot and the second episode of the first season, so as to set the visual look and emotional tone of the show. We started with my MC of the ballroom coverage, because I was doing double-duty back starring in *Kinky Boots* for the last fifteen weeks of the year of our Lord 2017. I had agreed to the offer to revisit Lola prior to *Pose* even being an option. The contracts were already signed, so Bill Butler worked it out so that I could do both gigs! *Kerching. Ker-muthafucking-ching!!!*

"Action!" I heard Ryan declare from video village somewhere in a far-off-set land.

"Royalty! The category is—Royalty!" I launched into the toned-down, muted version of myself that I assumed was the requirement for my very first series-regular role. I didn't wanna fuck it up! God forbid I come off as too flamboyant.

"CUT!" Ryan roared from video village. The entire set came to a screeching halt. *We're filming our first ball scene ever, and I have already fucked it up! Here I am in front of a room filled with about two hundred people, and I'm about to get my ass handed to me by the boss man herself!* Ryan wafted through the throngs of eighties vintage ball realness, with his signature coat-draped-over-the-shoulder gaggeration, and met me at the podium.

"I need you to give me awwwlll of *you*! There is nothing you can do that will be too broad, too big, too much, or too flamboyant! Let us have it all!"

I stood in silent disbelief for a split second. "You sure? 'Cause once you unleash the Kraken, there ain't no going back!" I sassed.

"Well, unleash her, bitch! The world is waiting!"

And thus, Pray Tell was born!

* * *

"I'm gonna need you to lean into the joy!" Ryan Murphy said to me as soon as I was seated at his regular corner booth at Freds at Barneys New York on Wilshire Boulevard in Los Angeles. I was thrown by his exacting assessment of my state of mind. The swirl was real. I thought I was hiding it. My cautious optimism. My fear.

I shouldn't have been surprised that Ryan clocked the protective gauze of optimism that shrouded my entire being. We had shot the entire season and were gearing up for the premiere. That's why I was in Los Angeles to begin with. That lunch at Freds with boss man Murphy was transformative. Once again—angels.

"I'm gonna need you to lean into the joy!" he sacredly admonished. "I know how hard it's been. I know you don't trust this yet. But I'll tell you—I've just finished editing episodes four and six, and I can say for certain, after the world sees your astonishing work, no one will ever question anything you do again. Please know, no matter what—*I got chu.*"

I sat there quietly, perfectly still. Trying to feel it. Trying to believe. Trying to lean into the joy. "I'm speechless . . ."

"Don't be! You've earned this. Every bit of glorious stuff that's about to come flooding your world. It's gonna be intense because you're the first, and the firsts of anything carry a weight that not many understand. *And . . .* you're ready. It's time for you to sit on your throne!"

Well, you ain't gotta tell me twice!

"What's your biggest dream?" Ryan inquired. Leaning in closer to me, with an intense, nurturing gaze. I met Ryan's gaze with a parallel vulnerability. I was slightly hesitant to tell the whole truth. I was nervous . . . nervous it might turn. I locked eyes with Ryan so that I could see into his soul when I spoke my unmitigated truth.

"I want to be like you!" I pierced, directly and fully present for whatever was to come next.

His eyes grinned like the mouth of the Cheshire Cat. He leaned back in the booth and raised his right hand to his chin, rotating his hand ever so delicately.

"I see," he cooed with a wink. "So, you want an *empire!*"

"Yes, sir. I do!"

"Then let's go get you an *empire!*"

Ryan then proceeded to explain to me that I was the leading man of *Pose.* I thought I was the side man.

"I'm not the lead!" I begged.

"You're the lead!" he shot back.

"I'm not the lead. This show is about those ladies, not me—and it's an ensemble show. You can't submit me for awards in the Best Leading Actor in a Drama Series category! I'll be the laughingstock!"

Ryan explained that the reason why I felt like I wasn't the lead probably had to do with the fact that they created this character for me *after* the show was well into development. He continued to bolster my confidence.

"You'll have even more juicy material next season. And for this season, I will be submitting you for Best Lead Actor in a Drama Series for awwwlll the awards, dawling. You're the adult in the room. You're the artist with the most experience. You are a Black, gay leading man. The world needs to see what that looks like, and you're just the bitch to do it!"

I took a deep breath. I tried to lean in . . . to the joy. There was a spark in my heart, but ultimately the light of joy in my soul is dim. For decades I had no idea that my relationship to joy was so nebulous. And there weren't a lot of opportunities in my life to experience pure, unadulterated joy. I've been happy in my life. Happiness is good. But happiness and joy are two separate things, in my opinion. Happiness feels to me to be exterior. Happiness is reliant on exterior *things* to exist. On the other hand, *joy* comes from the inside. Joy just is. It's a state of simply being. Non-reliant on exterior or material things. We used to sing a song in church whose lyric proclaims, "This joy that I have, the world didn't give it to me. The world didn't give it, and the world can't take it away!" I never truly understood that song—until now.

Awards are a tricky part of show business. On the surface, they are about our artistic communities coming together to celebrate excellence. They exist to honor and illuminate our achievements and shine a light on the artists who create the art that heals our civilization.

The "campaign" process. This is a real thing. The artist must engage in the campaign process, which tends to feel more like a run for the presidency of the United States of America. I mean, fo' real, fo' real.

The process starts with campaigning for the nomination. Yes! You heard right. The artist's publicity team and studio create opportunities for said artist to be seen, get the buzz going. I had months of pre-nomination press for both the Golden Globes and the Emmy nominations. I have to say it's really weird to have full round-table conversations and press events centered around "potential" and "predictive" nominees. All I could think of during this awkward process was, *What happens if I don't get nominated—after alla this!*

Blessedly, my first Golden Globe nomination for Best Lead Actor in a Drama Series came for my performance as Pray Tell in *Pose.* It was the morning of December 6, 2018. I was on set filming one of my scenes from the Paramount comedy *Like a Boss*, starring Tiffany Haddish, Rose Byrne, Salma Hayek, and Jennifer Coolidge. My stomach was in knots. My palms were sweaty. My whole body was trembling. Everybody on set knew it was the day, and everybody was very kind in not speaking of the *nominations* at all. And then, in between takes at around 11:30 A.M. East Coast time, a producer stepped onto set.

"Excuse me, everyone, we need to pause for a moment, because congratulations are in order. We have a Golden Globe nominee in our midst. Give it up for Golden Globe nominee for Best Lead Actor in a Drama Series—Billy Porter!"

Everyone on the set erupted into applause and effusive, laudatory praise. Tears streaked my cheeks. I was happy and yet, not quite joyful. I hadn't learned yet that not being able to feel joy is a trauma response. I would come to learn this fact in my future targeted, immersive, COVID-19-epidemic-induced trauma therapy. All of my dreams seemed to be coming true in ways I could have never dreamed of, and yet, something was still blocking my joy.

* * *

I woke up on January 6, 2019, to a text from somebody I can't remember, with a snapshot of a headline from the Sunday *New York Times* Fashion section that read: "Golden Globes 2019: At the Parties, the Winner Is Billy Porter."

The Carpetbagger, Kyle Buchanan, wrote: "In a room full of stars, which one is the sun? The Hollywood parties this weekend, all held in advance of Sunday's Golden Globes, haven't lacked for big names like Bradley Cooper, Nicole Kidman and Viola Davis. Still, they were reduced to mere satellites whenever Billy Porter showed up, swanning through each crowd in a new wrap dress and cackling with evident pleasure."

The Golden Globes weekend of 2019 was my coming-out! I didn't know I was gonna come out. It just kinda happened. My fashion plan for awards day had been months in the making. My visionary stylist at the time, Sam

Ratelle, had secured the creation of a custom couture piece by New York fashion designer Randi Rahm. Ms. Rahm generally works in the highest of couture gown spaces, dressing celebrities ranging from Carrie Underwood and Beyoncé to Mariah Carey.

We had several creative concept sessions with Ms. Rahm to come up with a *lewk* that would alert the presses that *that bitch* has arrived! Online news outlet Refinery29 proclaimed, "Billy Porter made the Golden Globes his runway." *The Hollywood Reporter* reported, "Billy Porter peacocked onto the red carpet in a colorful, OTT ensemble that took six months to make. A creation of New York–based bridal and eveningwear designer Randi Rahm, who spoke exclusively to *The Hollywood Reporter*, the bold look included a lavishly hand-beaded and embroidered jacket with an attached, fuchsia-lined cape layered over a form-fitting beaded and embroidered tulle shirt with a silk collar."

I had to look up what *OTT* means: Over The Top. Two adjectives used in practically every article written describing my weekend of sartorial slayage were *OTT* and *flamboyant*. Although this time neither one of those adjectives seemed to be used as a pejorative. My bold fashion choices for the weekend of Golden Globes realness began to crack open a different kind of public conversation concerning what garments are and are not acceptable for men to wear at these cultural red carpet events.

The leap into my obscuring of gender norms in my fashion came organically: "Geek chic" was the *lewk* I landed on during my run in *Kinky Boots*. The voice of my aunt Dot, *Dress for the job you want, not the one you have*, has been ringing in my consciousness for my entire life. Therefore, the side-eyes and mockery I endured from shady factions in the Broadway community, who didn't understand my fashion takeover long game, didn't deter me one bit! I served the children English-Dandy-Fop-Realness with Black American faggoty flair on purpose and with pride. I was intentional. The result—an international Gap ad alongside Cyndi Lauper during the holiday season of 2013. My visage was splattered the world over in Gap store windows, billboards, buses, subways, construction sites, and all the rest. *WERK!*

Now, while my fit-out was set for the proper Golden Globes awards ceremony itself, I discovered a week out that there were "the parties." In a panic, on the day before my departure for Los Angeles, I feverishly went shopping on my own for potential party *lewks*. I stumbled into the Calvin Klein flagship store, then at 654 Madison Avenue, featuring creative director Raf Simons's designs. I was pulling boy clothes from various radiant canary-yellow scaffolding-inspired racks. A flowing, shimmering, iridescent gold floor-length dress caught my eye on the sale rack tucked in the back of artist Sterling Rudy's installation, displaying the high-end clothing within an under-construction environment. I snatched her up! I continued digging in the sale rack and found another sleek, shimmering, black-jersey floor-length number that I snapped right on up too! None of the boy clothes made the cut. And thank God! I followed my instincts, instincts that had been questioned, mocked, and shamed for decades. What came next surprised even me.

I lost the Golden Globe that night to Richard Madden for *Bodyguard*, but nevertheless, I walked away the winner. I was finally in the room where it all happens. Firmly planted in my authenticity and on my own terms.

An invitation to the Met Gala came to me by way of Ryan Murphy. Ryan had purchased a table for the annual fundraising gala for the benefit of the Metropolitan Museum of Art's Costume Institute in New York City. This yearly event marks the opening of the Costume Institute's annual fashion exhibit. Each year's event celebrates the theme of that year's Costume Institute exhibition, and the exhibition sets the tone for the formal dress of the night, since guests are expected to choose their fashion to match the theme of the exhibit. The theme for 2019 was—*CAMP!*

The *Vogue* headline was the first to appear online, reporting on my full-on *camp* entrance and *lewk*: "Billy Porter Just Made the Most Fabulous Entrance in Met Gala History!"

Christian Allaire went on to write, "Tonight, Billy Porter shut down the Met Gala red carpet when he arrived on a litter—carried by six shirtless men!—in a theatrical nod to Ancient Egypt. The *Pose* star's custom 'Sun God' ensemble, by the Blonds, included a bejeweled catsuit outfitted with 10-foot wings, a 24-karat gold headpiece, as well as custom gold-leaf Giuseppe Zanotti shoes and fine jewels by Andreoli, John Hardy, and Oscar Heyman. The mic-drop served as half fashion moment, half performance art—perfectly executed on an evening when stars were asked to unleash their utmost creativity."

Well . . . WERK!

Out of the blue, I got a call from the producers of the 2019 Academy Awards ceremony, to co-host the pre-Oscar red carpet situation on ABC. We were less than two weeks out, and I knew from experience that this would be a significant seize-the-day kind of moment for me. Back at the 86th Oscars ceremony, when John Travolta mispronounced my friend Idina Menzel's name, calling her Adele Dazeem in his introduction of her performance of "Let It Go," from *Frozen*.

The simmering Hollywood buzz surrounding me was bubbling up to a low boil. My personal and my professional authentic persona was beginning to connect with the multitudes, not just in the LGBTQ+ community, not just the Black community, not just in America. *Pose* was becoming an international phenomenon. And the blessing of embodying my character of Pray Tell exposed me to the masses in a surprising mainstream way. I mean, 'cause let's face it, on paper *Pose* isn't supposed to be a thing. Nobody wants to see a show about the Black and Brown, LGBTQ+ ballroom culture during the AIDS crisis of the eighties and nineties, starring five, yes count 'em, FIVE Black and Latinx transgender women of color! That shit wasn't a thing. Our creator, Steven Canals, had 166 meetings where the answer from Hollywood gatekeepers was a hard pass! And then enter . . . Ryan Murphy. Legend would have it that when producer Sherry Marsh read Steven's pilot, it became her mission to make the project happen. Ms. Marsh made the intro to Ryan Murphy and he snatched up the project on the spot! Ryan then proceeded to demand the proper production and marketing budget from the FX Network to make sure the show would be seen. This, my people, is what true allyship looks like—using one's powers for good to bless somebody else. Thank you all for seeing us!

* * *

It was New York Fashion Week and I had been tapped to be the ambassador for the Council of Fashion Designers of America (CFDA). The week was a whirlwind from dawn till dusk of five to six fashion shows per day, changing on-site into lewks provided by the fashion houses themselves, so as to snatch those front-row celebrity shots the world has become too obsessed with. The high-fashion fabulosity parties would soldier on well into the evening, leaving a bitch longing for a bit of rest. *Sleep when you're dead! This fashion thing you been banking on for decades is werkin' out!*

I had the idea. The definitive idea. But what designer would be brave enough to jump off the ledge with me? Sam Ratalle, my stylist, and I were getting enormous pushback from the more established fashion houses when we would ask to pull men's and women's wear. Word would come back to us in some form or another that they weren't down with exploding gender norms and having the different and complex conversation surrounding the "why" of separation of masculine vs. feminine silhouettes in fashion. Why is it strong for a woman to rock a business suit, but when a man wears a dress he's weak and perverted? I knew that now was the time to crack that shit wide open, and . . . the person to do it was me!

Lucky for me, I was front row at the Christian Siriano runway show when the inspiration sparked in my spirit. I was stunned as each model's reveal was a different type of woman. All shapes. All sizes. All ethnicities. And as each woman stomped-the-runway-down-boots, I was reminded of the spirit of inclusion in Christian's work from the beginning of his career. I remembered him winning the "make a dress for normal women" challenge on *Project Runway* with a stunning creation he made for his mother. The design was effortless. I knew from his focus and vision on that episode that he would take the whole thing, because his vision teemed with the spirit of inclusion even then: high fashion for all people, no matter the shape, no matter the size.

In 2018 Christian won that season—the fourth—of *Project Runway*, becoming the series's youngest winner. He launched his namesake Christian Siriano collection, and by 2010, it had brought in revenue of over $1.2 million. By 2012 revenue was estimated to have reached $5 million. And you wanna know why? Because he dared to create sickening lewks for celebrity women above a size 7. Yes, you heard right. Until Christian came along, I would hear of nightmare stories from some of my female celebrity friends who could not get any designers to dress them because being a size 8 was considered fat in the fashion industry, and nobody in fashion, for a long, long time, cared enough to address the particular body-shaming infrastructure that the fashion world was built upon. What those bitches didn't know was that their little snobbish, elitist, humiliating power structure, built on the foundation of exclusion and elitism, was about to be burned to the very ground it had constructed for itself.

In my opinion, Christian's fashion career popped off so quickly because he became the go-to designer for the forgotten woman. And let's face it, up until recently, in fashion, most women, and most men for that matter, were totally forgotten, invisible. Truly.

My idea: What if the top half of the fit-out was a traditional tuxedo, velvet black jacket, crisp formal white shirt, bow-tie and such, so that the initial camera shot would make it appear that I was just serving a regular, traditional masculine silhouette, only to gag the nation when the camera pulls out to reveal a full fantasy antebellum ballgown skirt.

I whispered my idea into Christian's ear on the dance floor at the fashion show after-party in celebration of his Fall 2019 ready-to-wear collection. He fainted with glee in my arms and vowed to create my vision in the very small window of ten days that we had before the Oscars.

We got a call from ABC about five days pre-Oscars to talk about the ball gown. I was nervous for the conference call, because I assumed that I would be encouraged not to wear the gown. But instead, I got a very supportive response. Turns out, what ABC was concerned about was not the man-in-a-ball-gown-ovah-ovahness at all. The concern was all about logistics. For you see, I was set to be stationed on the "B" stage, which was situated in between the front stage and the main stage, smack-dab in the middle of the red carpet journey. I would be required to move through large masses of folks to ping-pong to and from the other two stages that bookended mine. And I was also informed that the circumference of my ball skirt would probably be too big for sharing my assigned postage stamp–sized stage with cohost Elaine Welteroth—best known for being the youngest and Blackest editor in chief of *Teen Vogue*, receiving her promotion at age twenty-nine, making her the youngest editor in Condé Nast history at that time. We were 'bout to serve the children some full-time fancy Black Girl Magic for your nerves, Henny!

One of the ABC executives laid out the truth: ". . . and let's face it, you in a ball gown? Nobody will be able to pay attention to the nominees you'll be interviewing."

'Tis true, 'tis true. The gagosity is real, bitches! We all came to an expeditious compromise: I would arrive first on the red carpet, get the shot, then run to my trailer and change into a pair of black velvet, high-waisted, flared pants that Christian stitched together in a matter of hours. Whew, fashion tragedy averted!

I was the very first to arrive on the Oscars red carpet. The photographers went wild. We got singles, we got angles, we got doubles with my husband, and then I was whisked off to change into my party pants and get to work. It's wasn't until about an hour later when my stylist and husband came to my stage, from watching me in the hotel room, and revealed to me that I had broken the internet. Everyone, the world over, was fully gagged. The in-real-time headline from journalist Rachel Syme in the *New Yorker* read: "Billy Porter Won the Oscar Red Carpet Before It Even Began."

Lots of think pieces were written about the why and the wherefore of my sartorial splendor that dreamy Oscar night. The majority of the world's response was positive. There were, of course, lots of hateration attacks. Some particularly triggered, toxically masculine Black men spewed venous tropes on social media that by wearing my ball gown to the Oscars, I was the cause of the emasculation of the Black man. When asked by a journalist what my response was to this vitriol, I responded, "First of all, if your masculinity is that weak, it should be attacked. Secondly, I didn't know I had that much power, but now that I do know, you can expect I'll be wielding it every fucking chance I get! Every chance! My goal is to be a walking piece of political art every time I show up! It's a calling. It's my ministry. It's intentional. I know exactly what I'm here for. And that's power!" Guess that shit is werkin'! Git into it, bitches! Git into it! #I'mnottheone #IsaidwhatIsaid

* * *

The second Sunday in June 2019 brought with it another dramatic red-carpet shut-down with a custom creation by Celestino Couture: a gender-fluid evening suit, featuring a sweeping train and thirty thousand Swarovski crystals. The suit holds special meaning for me, because it was made of an upcycled curtain backdrop from the Broadway production of *Kinky Boots*. The show-stopping red velvet and pink tulle look also rocked an embroidered uterus motif that I selected to support women's reproductive rights amid the current political upheaval about the issue.

I was a presenter at the Tony Awards, so had been whisked backstage early in the ceremony, as the producers feared my uterus train might slow me down and I would miss my hit. Have we met? Clearly not!

Waiting backstage for over an hour meant I missed the whole James Corden pulling Broadway stars out of the audience to sing from a karaoke song list during commercial breaks situation. When James later made a beeline to me with his songbook and microphone in hand, I was happy to oblige. What I didn't understand at the top of our exchange were the rules that had already been established. Apparently, folks had been singing full songs accompanied by a piano player in the pit. "Everything's Coming Up Roses" was the only song title I could read in Corden's karaoke songbook. I wasn't wearing my progressive lenses, so reading text up close was futile. Once my aging eyesight focused on a title I knew, I launched into the chorus, full-out . . .

"*Curtain up, light the lights . . .*" James abruptly cut me off.

"Wait, wait for the piano!"

"I hope it's in the right key," I mused out loud. Knowing that shit was too high!

I sang the intro. Reaching and technically placing the highest note in, what we Broadway folk call, the mask, singing.

". . . *they think that we're through . . .*" I cleared that high note and then quipped, "I didn't come here to work tonight!"

To which, without skipping a muthafucking beat, James shot back, comically wrenching the mic from my hands, "No, you clearly wanted no one to look at you!"

The crowd went wild!

"... *but baby*," and then, the savior of my ass—the accompanist in the pit—struck a note on the piano, kindly and compassionately lowering the key.

"Oh ... you changin' the key?" The piano player struck the lower note again, locking us both into simpatico.

"Thank you, bitch!"

And that was all she wrote. I launched into full Mama Rose realness and had the audience in the palm of my hands. I was singing for so long that the director in me was concerned that the commercial break would be over before I would finish. I yelled back to James, as I was slowly creeping to center stage of the passarelle at Radio City Music Hall, "You gonna make me do the whole thing?!?!"

James nodded yes, and that's all the inspiration I needed.

Permission to slay! And the slayage was epic! I shut that shit down. During the commercial break. A complete standing ovation. It instantly became such an unexpected viral moment that James Corden spotlighted the entire performance on his wildly popular late-night talk show the following evening,

"Billy Porter must be the only man in history to get a standing ovation from six thousand people in the commercial break!"

WERK!

* * *

I was on vacation in Provincetown, Massachusetts, on July 19, 2019—the day of the Emmy nominations. I tried to not think about it. I tried to ignore my nerves. Compartmentalize. Disassociate. I'm really good at that. I couldn't sleep the night before. I tried numbing myself with party substances to mute my nerves at the dance party we went to the night before at the Crown & Anchor. It was "Bear Week" in P-Town (you know the gays love a theme). We were staying at a friend's residence, and I didn't sleep a wink!

I took a bike ride that morning to calm my nerves as I waited for Los Angeles to awaken and announce the nominees. It was around 11:30 A.M. when the call came in. My husband and our out-of-town guests were still sleeping. They didn't know it was the day. I hadn't wanted to reminded anyone, as we were in our vacation swirl the day before. The whole point was to try to relax. To try to decompresses from the rising-star mania of the previous two straight years that I had tried to navigate with grace, gratitude, and full, faggoty flair! The thing was happening. Dreams I didn't even know I had were coming true. On my own terms. The "you will never be blessed" rhetoric of my childhood years was in fear of obliteration, annihilation, if you will. The weight of what an Emmy nomination would mean for me took on deeper significance. And a win . . . well—can you even imagine?

My manager, Bill Butler, and his associate Michelle Kittrell were the first to call with congratulatory praise. Ryan Murphy was soon to follow, and then a mighty, rushing flood of love came pouring in from all the different chosen-family relationships in my life, and many friends past and present. My iPhone was a cornucopia of text messages and voice messages and emails and Instagram DMs, marking this historic day. The day when the first Black gay man was nominated for the Emmy for Best Lead Actor in a Drama Series.

Whew . . . baybee. All I can say is . . . well—WERK!

The campaign from July to September was steroidal. I referred back to my iCal to write this, and there wasn't a single day that I wasn't doing something, between New York and Los Angeles, with the backing of Ryan Murphy and FX Studios, to secure the win! It's a business, babies. And if you want it—ya' gotta go git it! The divas had my back. I felt so blessed after thirty-plus years in this business that these people in positions of power, the gatekeepers and power brokers of the show-biz machine, supported me. Stood with me. Held me up. Our allies. There are no words . . . other than, from the bottom of my heart and soul—thank you!

Michael Kors signed on to create a custom, disco-inspired lewk with a custom hat by British millinery designer Stephen Jones. My shimmery ensemble included a bejeweled black pinstripe suit, an extra-long scarf as a tie, and platform Ric Owens boots. The hat was the gag. There were many post-show memes comparing it to the Nike swish. She was very what the kids call "extra," which . . . well . . . *why are you all gagging so; you know she brings it to you every ball!*

I knew it was time for my category when a cameraman parked himself directly in front of me during the commercial break. My sister was my date for the evening, like at the Tonys. She grabbed my trembling hand and held it to her heart, thereby reminding me to breathe—*thank you, sis!*

Actress and activist Kerry Washington sashayed onto the Emmy stage, envelope in hand, to present my category. Looking stunning as per usual, she seemed to have gotten the *disco realness* memo, serving the kids a white Alexandre Vauthier tuxedo blouse with the collar popped up, black sequined pants, and peep-toe heels. She waxed poetic about the amazing uniqueness and originality of us nominees: "What they all share is their vast talent and their ability to create truly unforgettable characters. Here are the nominees for Lead Actor in a Drama Series: Milo Ventimiglia (*This Is Us*); Jason Bateman (*Ozark*); Bob Odenkirk (*Better Call Saul*); Kit Harington (*Game of Thrones*); Sterling K. Brown (*This Is Us*); Billy Porter (*Pose*).

Ms. Washington opened the envelope, peeped at the name, and took an emotional gasp. ". . . and once again we witness history unfold. The Emmy goes to . . . BILLY PORTER!"

I broke down. I remembered to kiss my sis this time. And then I arm-flailed and skipped (like a gurl) up the stairs to Kerry, who joined me in the celebration by mirroring me, arm-flailing and skipping (like a gurl), in place. The voice-over man, comedian Thomas Lennon, underscored my ascent: "They will be kicking up their Kinky Boots tonight for a hometown hero. And apologies to anyone sitting right behind him to the left!" Oh, I see—they got jokes! Kerry and I hugged like old sister-friend siblings, and I asked her to hold the Emmy while I spoke (no putting that shit on the floor this time!).

I turned to the audience with arms outstretched and took the whole room in.

"Ahhhhh . . . !"

Everyone in the building was on their feet. They cut to my *Pose* cast, who were cheering me on like they were at a Beyoncé concert or something.

"Oh my God, I gotta read! I gotta read!"

I slipped on my chunky black DITA (Creator) eyewear, the accessory seen the world over in my Gap ad with Cyndi Lauper.

"Oh my God! God bless you all!" Then I focused on my notecards that were at the ready. *I'm glad a bitch prepared a speech. It's only right, right? To honor the moment. To take the moment and say something good to the people!*

"The category is . . . Love, y'all—LOVE! I am so overwhelmed, and I am so overjoyed to have lived long enough to see this day. James Baldwin said, 'It took many years of vomiting up all the filth I'd been taught about myself, and half-believed, before I was able to walk on the earth like I had a right to be here.' I have the right! You have the right! We awwwlll have the right! There are so many people who helped me get here along the way, so I'ma just say thank you. Thank you first of all to the other exquisitely talented men in my category. I love you all so much. It is such an honor to be up here breathing the same air that y'all breathe. Thank you, thank you, thank you. My mama, Cloerinda—there's no stronger, more resilient woman who has graced this earth. I love you, Mommy. Much love to the Actors Fund nursing home. My sister, M&M, my husband, Adam Porter-Smith, Suzi Dietz and Lenny Beer, Bill Butler—my manager of twenty-nine years, twenty-nine years, you helped me believe in myself when I couldn't believe . . . ah—FX! All the people at FX. My SlatePR family. Alexa Fogel. My *Pose* cast. Everybody in my *Pose* cast. Ryan Murphy, Ryan Murphy, Ryan Murphy—you saw me. You believed in us. Thankyouthankyouthankyouthankyou. Oh my goodness, oh my goodness . . . We are the people, we as artists are the people that get to change the molecular structure of the hearts and minds of the people who live on this planet. Please don't ever stop doin' that! Please don't ever stop tellin' the truth, I love you all . . . they're tellin' me to please stop—God bless you! God bless you! If I forgot anybody, I'm sorry. I love you all!"

And in an instant, one's life can be changed for good. I floated backstage to the press room where I immediately had to read a ratchet journalist from

Essence magazine who tried to pit me against RuPaul (who won, I believe, his third Emmy that night for hosting *RuPaul's Drag Race*). Here we go already. Trying to pit the two Emmy-winning qweens against each other. I wasn't havin' it! I let her have it! I shut her down.

I forgot to thank Steven Canals. I forgot to thank Janet Mock, and Brad Falchuk, and Mj Rodriguez, Dominique Jackson, Indya Moore, Angelica Ross, Hailie Sahar, Sandra Bernhard, Ryan Jamaal Swain, Dyllón Burnside, Angel Bismark Curiel, Jason A. Rodriguez, Jeremy McClain. Charge it to my brain and not my heart. For my heart is full. Full of love. Enough love to stretch beyond eternity. I have so much left to do. I have so much left to give. For my whole life, everybody told me that my truth and authenticity would be my liability. And it was . . . for decades . . . until it wasn't.

I have learned a lot about livin' in my time on this earth, and the more I think I know, the less I can comprehend. But this I know for sure—when one's intention is shifted from the egoic state of man to the intention of service, all the rest will work itself out. Oprah Winfrey, Dr. Maya Angelou, and Iyanla Vanzant told me that! Over twenty years ago, when I heard these ladies speaking on the power of this radical truth, I peered at myself in the mirror and asked, "How can I truly be of service in an industry and, quite frankly, an entire planet that is inherently narcissistic? In a moment it hit me like a ton of bricks: *Your service is leaning into your truth, your queerness, your authenticity. Yeah, that thing you been told needed to be fixed. Yeah, the thing everyone told you would be your lifelong liability. You are enough, just as you are.*

I have always said, it's easy to be who you are when *what* you are is what's popular! I chose myself in the face of nothing. And after a time, a very long time, the world has begun to lean in with me. My prayer is that anyone who lives in fear of their truth being maligned by outside validating forces will find, through seeing the manifestation in my life quest, the ultimate peace that comes with living one's personal truth unapologetically. Always believe in yourself. Always choose *you* first, no matter the cost, for in due season the light and the joy of living a glorious life will be revealed— and I am living proof that when you dare to dream the impossible, impossible dreams *do* come true.

AFTERWORD

"They crucified Jesus, you'll be fine." That's what Mommy said to me. Now, I'm aware that on the surface, to many, that response would seem uncompassionate, especially coming from a mother to her hurting seven-year-old child. However, now in retrospect, I have a different understanding. Mommy was telling the truth. Mommy was simply trying to prepare me for life and all its violent disappointments. In recent years I've been searching to connect to a different kind of spiritual practice from the Christianity construct I was raised in. I've been exploring the various tenents of Buddhism. One of the first guideposts in the Buddhist doctrine states that "life is suffering." And when we say yes to the fact that life's suffering is a given, when we can be present in how uncomfortable this truth is, we as humans will all suffer less. My mother did not have the complex language or any understanding of how to create a context for this truth for her little boy. But what I know now is that she was simply trying to arm me with the tools to move through life with grace, compassion, forgiveness, and of course—style!

The entire world has found itself at a tipping point. One that requires collective reflection. One that requires compassion and respect and human decency, and the willingness to grow. The world only spins forward. We've been here before. We've lived through the worst/best of and the most hopeless of times. Hope is a choice. My ancestors laid down their lives so that I can be the human being I am today. It's time to remind the world who we are. So don't be scared. Don't be terrified. Don't wait till the battle is over; fight now. Because love always wins.

I discovered midway through the writing of this book that my story was not just about overcoming adversity—my life is a testimony to the power that art has to heal trauma.

We are all living in the strangest of times, a global reckoning if you will—and in moments like these, I have always relied on my art, my calling, my purpose, and dare I say my ministry to keep me grounded and present. I stand on the shoulders of the angels who came before me. We all do. So, my final offering in this tome is a song I recently wrote that I feel encapsulates this truth. We must keep the faith and continue to get in some good trouble along the way. Thank you all for spending some time with me. God bless you all. Peace.

"Stranger Things"
by Billy Porter, Andrea Martin, and Future Cut

Blue Rabbit crossin' the street
Red pills for me to eat
I'm down to my last treat
Losin' rubber to my soul
Hopin' I can let this go
But it's out of my control

You see me more than I see me
I can't do nuthin' but turn that energy
Into something I can be
So fear me

I'ma keep it together
Make it rain forever
'Cause stranger things have happened to me

I'ma make the world see
And be more than a memory
'Cause stranger things have happened to me

Red flares in the sky
Fueled by the big red lies
So I started a revolution
That I ain't never losin'

If you could see the things I've seen
Connect with all the unhuman beings
You'd get emotional

Cain't eat or sleep
Tryin' to find my peace
And I ain't movin' silently
No no no no no no no . . .

Friendship forever
We can't lose when we stick together
'Cause stranger things have happened to me

I'ma make the world see
And be more than a memory
'Cause stranger things have happened to me

Stranger things, stranger things
Have happened to me . . .

I'ma keep it together
Make it rain forever
'Cause stranger things have happened to me

I'ma make the world see
And be more than a memory
'Cause stranger things have happened to me

No weapon formed against me shall prosper
No no no no no no no . . .
I'm tired of being scared
I'm tired of being terrified, y'all
'Cause stranger
'Cause stranger things
Have happened to me, y'all
I got a testimony
'Cause stranger things have happened to me